STUDIA LATINA STOCKHOLMIENSIA

LXII

Ars Edendi

LECTURE SERIES

Volume IV

Edited by

Barbara Crostini, Gunilla Iversen, and Brian M. Jensen

2016

STOCKHOLM UNIVERSITY PRESS

Published by
Stockholm University Press
Stockholm University
SE-106 91 Stockholm
Sweden
www.stockholmuniversitypress.se

Supporting Agency (funding): Riksbankens Jubileumsfond

First published 2016
Cover Illustration: Miniature from Den Haag, Koninklijke Bibliotheek, ms 71 A 24, fol.2v, containing the legend of the monk Theophilus.
Cover image copyright: CC-BY-NC-ND
Cover design by SUP

Studia Latina Stockholmiensia (Online) ISSN: 2002-472X

ISBN (Paperback): 978-91-7635-039-3
ISBN (PDF): 978-91-7635-036-2
ISBN (EPUB): 978-91-7635-037-9
ISBN (Mobi/Kindle): 978-91-7635-038-6

DOI: http://dx.doi.org/10.16993/baj

Studia Latina Stockholmiensia

Studia Latina Stockholmiensia is a peer-reviewed series of scholarly editions of Latin texts as well as monographs and anthologies of Latin studies. While continuing Stockholm University's tradition of Medieval studies, the series is also open to Latin from the Ancient and the Modern periods.

The textual editions include an introduction, a critical apparatus and usually a translation. The literary, linguistic and other philological studies of Latin feature a range of methodological approaches, both modern and traditional.

SLS includes Ars Edendi Lectures as a sub-series.

Studia Latina Stockholmiensia was previously included in the series Acta Universitatis Stockholmiensis (ISSN 0491-2764).

Editorial board

Maria Plaza, PhD, Associate Professor of Latin, Dept. of Romance Studies and Classics, Stockholm University, Sweden.
ORCID: 0000-0003-1643-2660
Hans Aili, PhD, Professor emeritus of Latin, Dept. of Romance Studies and Classics, Stockholm University, Sweden.
Erika Kihlman, PhD, Associate Professor of Latin, Dept. of Romance Studies and Classics, Stockholm University, Sweden.
ORCID: 0000-0001-8081-1740

Titles in the series

62. Barbara Crostini, Gunilla Iversen, Brian M. Jensen, ed. 2016. *Ars Edendi Lecture Series, vol. IV*. Stockholm: Stockholm University Press.

Table of Contents

Introduction   vii
Barbara Crostini, Gunilla Iversen and Brian M. Jensen

Contributors   xii

Writing in the Blank Space of Manuscripts: Evidence from the Ninth Century   1
Mariken Teeuwen

Editing Errors   26
Giovanni Paolo Maggioni

The Ordinary Chants of the Roman Mass, with their Tropes: The Odyssey of an Edition   50
Charles M. Atkinson

Ars computistica ancilla artis editionum: Modern IT at the Service of Editors of (Greek) Texts   85
Charalambos Dendrinos and Philip Taylor

How to Read and Reconstruct a Herculaneum Papyrus   117
Richard Janko

What is a Critical Edition?   162
Glenn W. Most

The Digital Revolution in Scholarly Editing   181
Peter Robinson

Introduction

Barbara Crostini, Gunilla Iversen and Brian M. Jensen

The fourth volume of the by now established Ars Edendi Lectures Series is also the last to be published within the Riksbankens Jubileumsfond programme by the same name that ran at the University of Stockholm 2008-2015. As in the other volumes, the reader will find here gathered the lectures, printed in the same order in which they were chronologically delivered, which animated the main themes of that programme, but also echoed more closely the concerns of this or that researcher who contributed to the event. Fittingly, this volume is edited by Barbara Crostini, Gunilla Iversen, and Brian M. Jensen, who were responsible for organizing most of the events that see the light of publication in this volume.

The contributions to this volume are well balanced between Latin and Greek, the two languages at the centre of the programme, and reflect the range of approaches to editing and types of editions that well exemplify the activity of the group throughout these years. Both a reflection on the fundamentals (e.g. What is a critical edition?) and a closer look at the specifics (e.g. marginalia, errors, musical notation) of editing are explored by the topics addressed by our expert lecturers, whose participation in the Ars edendi programme we gratefully acknowledge here. Their contributions have broadened and enlivened our work on our own editions, and given us food for thought in the knowledge that we were confronted with state-of-the-art approaches in our respective fields. The oral tone of the presentations has not been entirely edited out from this book.

Mariken Teeuwen represented the distinguished Huygens Institute for Text-Critical Studies, and focused our attention on the margins of the manuscripts, and what the annotations there can offer us for a knowledge of their texts, history, and readership; in many ways, her research is at

How to cite this book chapter:
Crostini, B., Iversen, G. and Jensen, B. M. 2016. Introduction. In: Crostini, B., Iversen, G. and Jensen, B. M. (eds.) *Ars Edendi Lecture Series, vol. IV.* Pp. vii–xi. Stockholm: Stockholm University Press. DOI: http://dx.doi.org/10.16993/baj.a. License: CC-BY 4.0

the forefront of the new interest in 'paratexts', intended broadly, as an area so far neglected but which appears very fruitful for the textual and cultural scholar. Teeuwen suggests different editorial strategies to present the glosses and annotations to the reader: a digital edition, where it is possible to highlight with colours which parts came first, which later. She discusses questions of how to encode the interconnectedness of marginal texts to other texts. A marginal text is in fact a set of texts, and each individual annotation would need its own apparatus, but it would result in a rather confusing page when presented in the standard lay-out of a modern scholarly edition. Thus, she concludes, we need better means to visualize structure and movement, in order to gain a better understanding of these marginal texts.

The edition by Giovanni Maggioni of one of the major (if not *the* major) medieval collection of hagiographies, the *Legenda aurea*, puts him in a privileged position of the hands-on scholar with a vast experience of the world of borrowings, reworkings, and translations, the essential ingredients of such influential compilations. These formed the cultural (and cultual) perspective of generations of medieval and early modern Christians. The examples discussed are therefore taken mainly from Maggioni's own editions of the *Legenda aurea* and are compared to the primary source for Jacobus's work, Jean de Mailly's *Abbreviatio in gestis sanctorum*.

Maggioni's application of Lachmannian principles for the understanding of textual issues is a fascinating journey into the mechanics and dynamics of manuscript copying. 'Error' has been a significant term in philology from the very beginning of editorial practice and *the* central issue in the traditional editorial method named after Karl Lachmann. Maggioni defines error as "something (a term, a phrase, a chronological notation) that contradicts the culture of the author, as we know it, [...] and is incompatible with the author's actual work of composition and edition". How do we then recognize authorial errors in the textual complexity of sources, author, original, archetype, copies and readers? *Primum recensere!* was the lesson of Karl Lachmann, and Maggioni underlines the importance of *recensio*, the traditional distinction between original and archetype, an editor's knowledge of the sources the author used for his work and acquaintance with an author's method of composition as a means to recognize these errors.

The distinguished musicologist Charles Atkinson combines in a similar way the traditional principles of critical editing with a complex situation where texts are found together with music. The musicological knowledge and transmission of the texts sung in the medieval liturgy need to be translated for a modern public, in order that not only scholars, but musicians themselves can benefit from the result in a practical way. Beginning from the fact that the musical notation in the earliest manuscripts cannot be transcribed and discussing ways of making an edition that provides performable music, Atkinson says:

> since the texts were clearly sung in their role as parts of the liturgy, but lacking an oral tradition that extends back to the ninth or tenth centuries, we must present them in a type of musical notation that a modern singer can read, i.e., in ordinary staff notation [...].

He concludes that in order to answer to the needs of both performers and scholars the best way must be to present editions of texts with their melodies as they appear in specific manuscripts representing specific geographical areas and liturgical traditions. Thus he suggests an edition based on manuscript sources, not on genres of chant: even if such a musical edition cannot pretend to be a "complete critical edition," in the sense that the editions of the texts in *Corpus Troporum* are, it can at least provide a representative sample.

With Charalambos Dendrinos, author of a much appreciated electronic edition of a Greek manuscript from the British Library, we turn to a different approach towards modern concepts of editing. Dendrinos's contribution comes across as a pioneering work exploring some of the dynamic displays possible when editing in the digital age. The full potential of alternative visualizations has been exploited for this short text: diplomatic and critical editions and translations overlap; links to grammatical explanations for each word are available, a feature that revolutionizes the approach to ancient languages and their teaching. A substantial portion of his paper, written by his collaborator Philip Taylor, is essentially technical, setting out in detail the questions and the solutions found at each stage of the process of digitizing and building the web-site. The further plan of adding a vocal performance of the text to the visual alternatives made available to the user will in the future complete this ambitious project. Surely the enterprise has benefitted from the contributions of a dedicated team of collaborators, whose services are, however, not always very easy to come by.

With Richard Janko's detailed paper on how to study Herculaneum papyri we return to the 'old' techniques of pencil-and-paper *in situ* transcription, presenting their own problems, which reveal the patience and expertise with which Janko has produced much of his recent editions of the works by Philodemus. The editor is set in a tradition of recordings and evaluations of the primary evidence that forms layer after layer of precious information, any details of which, if lost or badly handled, may impinge on the final outcome. Thus knowledge of the circumstances of the finds and their subsequent storage is part of a precious piling up of knowledge that makes the editor an expert in his field of research. There is a distinct sense of dedication and quiet triumph in the making out of words from charred, broken letters in the extant scraps of papyrus rolls, adding up to broaden our knowledge of ancient civilizations literally bit by bit.

The last two papers, by Glenn Most and Peter Robinson respectively, unexpectedly —perhaps— fit together in providing broader perspectives on attitudes to texts and editorial work.

Most takes the long-term historical approach to lead us by the hand in the significance of textual scrutiny from the time of Ancient Greece, where reading and comparing texts was already a known practice. Most closely reviews the approach of three early editors of Homer, Antimachus, Zenodotus and Aristarchus, asking quite what each had to contribute to the methodology of editing the texts of the epics. The rationale behind these early editors' choices and their peculiar working practices are lost between their own inchoate methods and the portion of aurality contained in the explanations that were delivered by them only in the classroom. On firmer grounds, the pre-critical editions of the nineteenth-century German scholars, notably beginning with the exposition in Friedrich August Wolf's *Prolegomena ad Homerum* of 1795, bring us closer to modern theories of editing, if not precisely to the term "critical edition".

Most also surprisingly takes us on a detour to China, where the work of scribes was demonstrably set within the intellectual structures of a complex society: by analysing two pieces of visual evidence, Most highlights similarities and differences in how texts can be handled and shared. It is a fascinating journey into how confrontation with and through a text can be a place for interpersonal relationship, a strategy for communication. As he states, "Collation is [...] the transmission of certain values —attention, obedience, precision, collegiality— that are important not only for their embodiment in canonical texts but also for their instantiation in the acts by which those texts are copied and checked".

Peter Robinson looks forward to a different type of sharing texts, *en masse*, on the world-wide web. His question concerning the digital revolution is really one about the status of the editor, and how s/he is being transformed into a facilitator for collaborative work by the means of mass outreach that digital material and open web-sites can allow.

In itself access to manuscript images changes nothing fundamental in textual scholarship, other than that thousands of manuscripts and books online are immediately available as 'archives' or 'research collections'. Unless scholars combine this access with radically new digital tools and use them to make new editions, in a manner never seen before, we cannot yet talk about a digital revolution. For example, Stefan Hagel's Classical Text Editor software and Wilhelm Ott's TUSTEP system are only going part of the way as they are just tools to produce traditional editions. In Robinson's own words, "If in the digital world, we do not change what we do, we do not change what we make, we do not change who we are: there is no revolution".

Concluding the presentation of these three elements of change and their consequences in digital editing, Robinson states: "We all know the topos, that we are standing on the shoulders of the scholars who have preceded us. The digital age offers a variant on this. As well as stand on the shoulders of others, we should help others to stand on our shoulders. This will change who we are. Now, that would be revolutionary". While Robinson certainly represents one of the foremost authorities in this field, both in the experimental and in the theoretical sense, his reflexions provide a measure of the relative novelty that these means are offering, and the need to deepen the understanding of both the potential and the challenges they will pose.

In conclusion, we would like to thank all the speakers who have contributed to this volume, as well as the Bank of Sweden Tercentenary Foundation for funding the publication of this volume. We thank our colleagues in Ars edendi, Elisabet Göransson, Erika Kihlman, Eva Odelman and Denis Searby for their active participation at these events. Special thanks to our research assistant, Agnes Vendel, who took care of the practical arrangements for the lectures and helped copy-editing this volume. Thanks are also due to colleagues in our department, especially Professor Maria Plaza, editor in chief of Studia Latina Stockholmiensia, for supporting our work. It is our hope that the Ars Edendi Lecture Series will continue function as an important forum for textual philology at Stockholm University in the future, although the first funding period of the Ars edendi programme has ended.

Barbara Crostini, Gunilla Iversen, Brian M. Jensen

Contributors

Mariken Teeuwen is Professor at the Huygens Institute for the History of the Netherlands, Royal Netherlands Academy of Arts and Sciences. She directs the Research Project 'Marginal Scholarship: the Practice of Learning in the Early Middle Ages (c. 800–c. 1000)', sponsored by the Netherlands Organisation of Scientific Research (NWO). She has a background in Musicology and in Medieval Studies, with an emphasis on manuscript studies and medieval Latin. She is a member of the Board of the International Medieval Latin Committee.

Giovanni Paolo Maggioni has been Associate Professor at the Università degli Studi del Molise, Italy, since 2005. His main fields of research are medieval hagiography and sermon studies. In 2007, he published the critical edition of Jacobus de Voragine's *Legenda aurea*, with an Italian translation, followed in 2013 by the *editio princeps* of Jean de Mailly's *Abbreviatio in gestis sanctorum*. In addition he has published a great number of studies on saints' *vitae*, covering aspects of transmission, context and content. He is a member of the international scholarly network *Sermones*, directed by Nicole Bériou at Lyon (www.sermones. net). A critical edition of Jacobus de Voragine's *Sermones de sanctis* and *Sermones de tempore* is in preparation.

Charles M. Atkinson is University Distinguished Professor and Arts and Humanities Distinguished Professor of Music at The Ohio State University. He specializes in the music and music theory of Greek Antiquity and the Middle Ages. He has received numerous scholarly awards, including the Alfred Einstein and Otto Kinkeldey Awards of the American Musicological Society, the Van Courtlandt Elliot Prize and the Charles Homer Haskins Medal of the Medieval Academy of America, and The Ohio State University Distinguished Scholar and Distinguished Lecturer Awards. He served as president of the American Musicological Society, 2007–2008. He is the author of *The Critical Nexus: Tone-System, Mode, and Notation in Early Medieval Music* (Oxford University Press, 2009).

Charalambos Dendrinos is Senior Lecturer at the Department of History, Royal Holloway, University of London, and Director of the Hellenic Institute. His research interests focus on Byzantine literature and Greek palaeography, including Byzantine hagiography and the transmission of Greek texts in Byzantium and the West. His critical editions focus on texts of the Palaeologan period, in particular those by Emperor Manuel II Palaeologus (1391–1425) and members of his intellectual entourage. He is a member of the advisory group to the British Library Greek Manuscripts Digitization Project, and has accomplished one of the first online editions of a Greek manuscript from MS BL Royal 16 C X.

Richard Janko was Professor of Greek at University College London (1995–2002) and is currently Gerald F. Else Distinguished University Professor of Classical Studies at the University of Michigan, Ann Arbor. His studies on the Homeric question and his new reading of the Derveni Papyrus are well known, and he is also one of the foremost experts in the study of the papyri at Herculaneum, above all with his editions of the writings of Philodemus of Gadara (c. 40 BC), an Epicurean philosopher. He holds an impressive list of awards, but his untiring enthusiasm and intellectual liveliness are perhaps even more impressive.

Glenn W. Most is Professor on the Committee on Social Thought at the University of Chicago, and since 2001 he has been simultaneously Professor of Greek Philology at the Scuola Normale Superiore di Pisa. He has published books on Classics, on the history and methodology of Classical studies, on the Classical tradition and Comparative Literature, on literary theory, and on the history of art, as well as articles on modern philosophy and literature. Among his recent projects are a four-volume Greek and English Loeb edition of the Presocratics, and a bilingual edition of the complete corpus of ancient and mediaeval scholia and commentaries to Hesiod's *Theogony*.

Peter Robinson is Professor of English at the University of Saskatchewan, Canada (College of Arts and Science). He is one of the world's leading experts in the development of digital humanities. Investigating and exploring methods for digital editions and analysis of large manuscripts traditions like Geoffrey Chaucer's *Canterbury Tales* and Dante Alighieri's *Divina Commedia*, he has applied techniques from evolutionary biology, the so-called phylogenetic method, in his description of manuscript traditions. Among his many publications, his edition of Geoffrey

Chaucer, *The Wife of Bath's Prologue on CD-ROM* (The Canterbury Tales Project. Cambridge: Cambridge Univ. Press, 1996) earned him the English Association Beatrice White Prize 1998. More recently his edition of *The Miller's Tale on CD-ROM* (Leicester: Scholarly Digital Editions, 2004) can be mentioned here.

The Editors

Barbara Crostini has a D. Phil. In Byzantine Studies from Oxford University. She worked as a member of the Ars edendi project 2010-2015 on an electronic edition of a Byzantine illuminated psalter with catena commentary. She convened an international workshop about this manuscript in Rome now published as *A Book of Psalms from Eleventh-Century Byzantium: the Complex of Texts and Images in Psalter Vat. gr. 752: Proceedings of an Ars edendi Workshop, Rome, 11-13 June 2012*, co-edited with G. Peers, Studi e Testi (Vatican City, 2016). She is currently Assistant Professor in Greek at the Department of Linguistics and Philology, Uppsala University. ORCID: 0000-0001-9138-1766

Gunilla Iversen is Professor and former Chair of Latin at Stockholm University, leader of the Ars edendi Research Programme. Editor of the Corpus Troporum volumes of Ordinary tropes to the *Sanctus, Agnus Dei*, and *Gloria*, and co-editor of the Proper tropes to the feasts in the Easter cycle. She has published innumerable scholarly articles on medieval liturgical poetry as well as articles and translations dealing with the texts of Hildegard of Bingen and Catullus. With Marie-Noël Colette she is the author of *La parole chantée. Invention poétique et musicale dans le Haut Moyen Âge occidentale* (Turnhout 2014). ORCID: 0000-0002-2556-5740

Brian M. Jensen is Associate Professor in Latin at Stockholm University and member of the Ars edendi research programme. Editor of *Lectionarium Placentinum. Edition of a Twelfth Century Lectionary for the Divine Office* I-IV (Firenze: SISMEL – Edizioni del Galluzo, 2016-2017). He has published numerous studies on medieval liturgical poetry, Mariology and hagiography, especially in Piacentinian sources, e.g. the commentary to the facsimile edition of the Liber Magistri from 1142 and an anlysis of its selection of tropes and sequences. Moreover, he has published the first complete Danish translation of *Regula Benedicti* and studies on Cicero's *pro Caelio* and the fables of Phaedrus. ORCID: 0000-0003-3446-0016

Writing in the Blank Space of Manuscripts: Evidence from the Ninth Century

Mariken Teeuwen

Huygens Institute, The Hague, The Netherlands

In medieval manuscripts the main text is only one aspect of what these books reveal to us about the past. The vast majority of manuscripts that survive also contain annotations and additions, which reflect how these manuscripts were read, used, extended, summarized or criticized by their circles of copyists and readers. In the project 'Marginal Scholarship: the Practice of Learning in the Early Middle Ages (c. 800–c. 1000)', it is our aim to map these textual practices, in order to gain a better understanding of the intellectual world they reflect.[1] We make an inventory of phenomena we encounter in the margin, such as marginal keywords or indices, organizing or structuring strategies, commentaries and signs. Scribal activity in the margin is characterized by its own set of specific characteristics and practices. It displays, for example, the tendency to be built up in layers and to accumulate over time. It has, furthermore, a typical commonness of various sets of signs, such as Tironian notes, signs for textual criticism and reader guidance, or signs linking annotations to words or phrases in the main text. These practices may be individual or shared; they may be either characteristic for certain individuals, or for certain scribal communities or even certain periods. Their developments, consequently, illustrate not only how schools or communities developed their own 'scribal identity', but also how practices were shared between monasteries or scholars through travel and intellectual contact. Thus an analysis of these features may give us valuable tools for comparison, distinction, dating and localization, just as the palaeographical and codicological analyses of manuscripts do. The mapping of such features is one of the goals of the project as a whole.

This lecture was given on 22 October 2012 at Stockholm University.

How to cite this book chapter:
Teeuwen, M. 2016. Writing in the Blank Space of Manuscripts: Evidence from the Ninth Century. In: Crostini, B., Iversen, G. and Jensen, B. M. (eds.) *Ars Edendi Lecture Series, vol. IV.* Pp. 1–25. Stockholm: Stockholm University Press. DOI: http://dx.doi.org/10.16993/baj.b. License: CC-BY 4.0

Let me state this, however, in advance: the main focus of our project is *not* on the *edition* of marginal texts. This subject is problematic and, in my view, has greatly suffered under the traditional philological approach, where the text in the centre of the page was generally cast as the protagonist, and marginal text ignored. In the traditional philological approach, furthermore, it is generally assumed that the text has a stable, optimal form which can be reconstructed by the comparison of variants. Marginal texts are among those, which do not always adhere to this dogma; in many cases they are fundamentally different in nature.[2] Thus, even if we do not intend to make scholarly editions of marginal texts part of our project, it seems important to discuss the matter with an audience of textual scholars, in order to establish how marginal texts *should* be treated by editors (and cataloguers) in such a way that they give access to the information they contain in the best possible way.

Before I start with observations on the phenomenon of writing in the margin in the Carolingian period, I would like to make clear that the phenomenon was not new in this period. On the contrary: in all ages and regions and from our earliest written witnesses on, we can see that the space around a text attracted new text. 'Marginalia' are inscribed on the sides of Babylonian clay tablets, and we have annotations on first century papyri.[3] If we zoom in on the history of writing practices in the western European world and leaf through the invaluable *Codices Latini Antiquiores*, close to sixty manuscripts which are described in Lowe's volumes are observed to contain some form of annotation. Moreover, in about two-thirds of these cases, the annotations are contemporary or near contemporary.[4]

Already in the late-antique material, these annotating practices can be observed to come in many different shapes and sizes. Often they took the form of occasional reflections on the text, such as the insertion of corrections, variant readings or the presence of lacunae. A large scale annotation with scholiae or settled commentary traditions is also found, already in Late Antiquity, and so is the insertion of extra, not necessarily related texts into marginal space.[5] Commentary traditions, however, could also be transmitted in separate, free-standing manuscripts, where the connection to the main text to which the commentary is linked is only present in the form of *lemmata*.[6]

Carolingian scribes thus encountered the practice of annotating a text in the margin in the codices they inherited from Late Antiquity. They were not inventing a new technique when they filled the margins and interlinear spaces of their own manuscripts. Still, it is obvious that the practice of writing in the margin underwent a significant change in the Carolingian period.[7] The new approach of Carolingian culture to manuscripts, teaching and learning boosted a practice which amplified the practice of writing in the blank space of manuscripts, and which would lead up to the complex biblical *glossa ordinaria* lay-outs that we know from the twelfth and thirteenth centuries.[8] The features of Caroline minuscule, and the Carolingian concern with developing a new book lay-out suited a practice of writing text in the margin: in this period, books were created with wide margins, extra columns, relatively wide spacing in between the lines.[9] These changes in layout and script support the hypothesis that textual practices changed, and that writing annotations around a text gained in frequency and importance in the period.

A numerical comparison of the manuscript evidence from the Carolingian period and the period before is also telling, although we have to take into account a degree of uncertainty here because of the scarcity of material that survived from before the ninth century. Nevertheless, a rough guess of the percentage of manuscripts with annotations in the margins in the period before the ninth century, counting from papyri collections and the descriptions in *Codices Latini Antiquiores*, would give us a figure of less than 10%. From the ninth century onwards, on the other hand, we would guess that figure is closer to 80% or 90%. It is hard to be precise here, because a systematic evaluation of scribal activity in all Carolingian manuscripts has not been conducted, and is perhaps unfeasible considering their high number. But an inventory of manuscripts from the Bavarian region (digitized by the Bayerische Staatsbibliothek) gave us this percentage, even when the Bavarian region is not particularly known for its high-end intellectual culture in the period.[10]

Indeed, this observation is confirmed by a more general survey of marginal activity in early medieval manuscripts. In a database in which we are collecting our observations on marginal activity, annotated manuscripts are the rule, and manuscripts with blank margins and empty interlinear spaces are the exception. They are found in the category of *Prachthandschriften*, manuscripts that are beautifully written, richly decorated, prepared to be given to a king, such as, for example, the Vivien Bible, made in Tours in the middle of the ninth century for Charles the Bald.[11] This makes sense: no scribe would write in the margins of such a beautiful and costly book. Perhaps there are more categories to be found of 'empty books', that is, books with empty margins.

The extent of annotation in non-empty books varies widely, of course. The scale goes from just a few words in the margin —sometimes not even words but simply some signs or numbers—, to a fully filled space around the main text. In order to understand and be able to describe the practices of annotating in the early middle ages, questions of quantity were among the first we asked ourselves: How many annotations make a manuscript 'densely annotated'? Are different categories of texts to be accompanied by different expectation patterns? The proverbial schoolbook, for example, is certainly more prone to acquire layers of dense annotation over time than a liturgical book, or even the work of a Church Father. In order to measure the amount of annotation, we devised a three-fold method. Given the time-span of the project and the complexity of the *mise-en-page* of commentary texts, it is just not feasible to count single annotations on pages. Instead, we chose to count the number of pages that have annotations out of the first 40 pages. Second, we count the total number of 'blank' pages (that is 'with pristine margins and interlinear spaces') in a manuscript, and third, we measure the percentage of the margin filled with writing on the most densely annotated page. Next to these data with measurements, we also store information about the kind of text that is in a manuscript (poetry, liturgy, liberal arts, etcetera), so that we are able to establish the relation between textual genres and density of annotation. Thus, we will be able to filter out the norm and the exception: a schoolbook with only a 5% filled margin on the most densely annotated page will pop up as an exceptionally empty book, whereas a copy of Augustine's *De civitate dei* with the same percentage in the same observation field will be closer to the norm.

Next to these data on the quantity of annotations, we store information about dates, places of origin, places of provenance and persons and locations involved in the history of a manuscript. We hope to be able to detect patterns here as well: who were the agents involved in writing marginal annotations, and where is the evidence for certain annotating practices stronger than elsewhere? Which specific writing practices could be linked to specific writing centres, to certain scholars or their circles, or to a certain period? Once our database will be filled with a wide-enough sample of data, we will be able to see the answers to these and similar questions.[12] For the moment, however, my observations on the nature of marginal scholarship will be more haphazard and intuitive, based on examples gathered from my earlier research on Martianus Capella commentary traditions and enriched by leafing through manuscripts, digital facsimiles, articles and editions.

Purpose and function of annotated books

In his article *Talking Back to the Text* Christopher Baswell wrote: 'medieval edges (especially codicological) are the places that make space for new and characteristic ideas, communities, and voices in the period'.[13] He argues that the practice of annotating manuscripts with commentary and authoritative explanations, which were meant for the classroom, had the perhaps unwanted side-effect of creating a space for differences of opinion, for doubting the authorities and for rebellion. He illustrates this with late medieval examples in Latin and Middle English, but according to me he raises a crucial point for our approach to marginal text, which previous scholarship has failed to uncover. Yes, the margin was a space in which the authorities were given their authorial weight, by explaining them and elaborating upon their arguments. But it was also a space where multiple authorities were gathered, where their contradictions, weaknesses and errors were openly displayed, and where discussion took place. Moreover, when we assess the annotated book solely as a book meant for the classroom, we do not do full justice to the manuscript material that we have, and we do not see the whole picture of how medieval scribes, scholars and readers dealt with their texts. Outside the narrow view of the schoolbook, annotating practices also took place, for example in the shape of personal markings which redacted, summarized and reorganized texts in order to make them ready for a transport to new contexts. And even within the traditional schoolbook context, a new approach which includes these other kinds of annotating practices makes the margin much more interesting than the traditional view, in which the schoolteacher's glosses are to be categorized into prosodical glosses, lexical glosses, morphological glosses, syntactical glosses, etcetera.[14] Of course, patiently educating voices of grammar teachers are *also* present in the margin, and to analyse how text is explained in the classroom is valuable research, but there is more to discover. The following examples support this claim.

Collecting authorities and related material

In Martianus Capella's *De nuptiis* the seven liberal arts are treated in a nutshell, embedded in the story of how Mercury seeks a suitable bride, and finds her in the earthly maiden Philology. With the consent of the gods, it is decided that Philology will be allowed to make a journey into heaven, being deified in the process, and that the newly-weds will receive the gift of the Seven Liberal Arts at the wedding banquet.[15]

Martianus is an embellisher: he likes to dress up his dreary knowledge with rich clothes, to give them mysterious epithets and to use wit and even a bit of sex in the frame story. The Carolingian scholars engaging with the text loved him for it. They ate his book like heavily honeyed porridge, spilling none of it. That at least is the impression one gets when looking at the margins of Martianus manuscripts, which tend to be filled to the brim with annotations. Let me give you an illustration of Martianus's literary world with a passage from the first book:

> [174] There came also a girl of beauty and extreme modesty, the guardian and protectress of the Cyllenian's home, by name Themis or Astraea or Erigone; she carried in her hand stalks of grain and an ebony tablet engraved with this image: [175] In the middle of it was that bird of Egypt which the Egyptians call an ibis. [176] It was wearing a broad-brimmed hat, and it had a most beautiful head and mouth, which was being caressed by a pair of serpents entwined; under them was a gleaming staff, gold-headed, gray in the middle and black at the foot; under the ibis' right foot was a tortoise and a threatening scorpion, and on its left a goat. [177] The goat was driving a rooster into a contest to find out which of the birds of divination was the gentler. [178] The ibis wore on its front the name of a Memphitic month.[16]

The passage is an apt illustration of the abstruse, mystifying world of Martianus.[17] Erigone comes in carrying an ivory image: on it, an ibis is depicted, wearing a 'sombrero' style hat, the name of a Memphitic month on its chest; snakes curling around its beak; it stands on a tortoise, a scorpion and a goat kicking a rooster into action —the meaning of all this must have been completely beyond any reader who did not have the same cultural and educational background as Martianus Capella himself. Why, then, did Carolingian scholars read this, and how did they interpret its bewildering imagery? The passage, as found in one of the oldest and fullest annotated manuscripts that has survived, Leiden, UB, VLF 48, fol. 17r, is transcribed in the digital edition which I created in collaboration with Sinead O'Sullivan, Mary Garrison, Natalia Lozovsky, Jean-Yves Guillaumin and Bruce Eastwood. It is attached to this paper in an appendix.[18]

As we can see there, our Carolingian readers and interpreters certainly did not give up easily: no less than 27 annotations are attached to this passage, interacting with the text at different levels: explaining, paraphrasing, widening the scope of the reader's understanding by presenting him/her material from different sources on the same subject: material that is found in Isidore's *Etymologies*, in Hyginus' *Fabulae*, in Bede's *De temporum ratione*, and in the late antique glossary tradition.[19] By assembling a collection of references to other materials, the annotations create a context for Martianus' fleeting allusions to a world that was no longer part of the background of the average reader.

This method is definitely not peculiar to annotations on Martianus Capella. I have argued elsewhere that the oldest layers of commentary added to Boethius' *De institutione musica* reflect the same approach to the text as those added to Martianus.[20] The two traditions frequently refer to each other's central texts (especially on the subjects of arithmetic and music, because Boethius wrote two handbooks on these arts); they compare the claims of Boethius with those of Martianus and vice versa. In other words: the voices in the margins of Martianus's text connect his learning with that of Boethius, and the other way around.

The nature of Carolingian glosses added to Priscian was analyzed by Franck Cinato, and he found the same principles of creating in the margin a network of authorities in his sources.[21] And in the Carolingian commentary traditions on Virgil, currently under research by Silvia Ottaviano and Sinead O'Sullivan, exactly the same kind of processes are observed.[22] The margin is a place suited for a *collection* of related material —a place where one can bring together all the material one has on a certain subject, be it some piece of geographical learning which can be found in Pliny, or a piece of mythological learning which could be gained from Servius' commentary to Virgil, or a piece of technical learning on the liberal arts, to be gained from Martianus or Boethius.

Sorting, selecting and criticizing

Apart from *collecting* extra material, *organizing* material is one of the most common phenomena used in the margins: very often, annotations organize the text for the reader, to make it easier to follow, to find, to remember. Examples of such organizing strategies are marginal indexing —the repeat of a key term in a passage in the margin, often in capitals—; numbers in the margin; the indication of names in the margin in a text which is a collection of material from others. The purpose of these marginalia is to help or facilitate the process of knowledge management.[23] The scholarly content of the book was stored, sorted, selected, and summarized with the help of a set of shared practices, involving the visualisation of textual structure with a shared set of signs and marks: nota signs, numbers, s or ss for quotes, capital letters for indexing glosses, critical signs such as asterisk and obelus.

The latter category of signs is an intriguing element of the writing practices of the time. Evina Steinová is at present preparing a study on the practice of using these signs to mark passages in the margin: dots, lines, crosses, circles, diple, obelus, asteriscus, chrisimon, achriston, fietro, theta, etcetera.[24] Their history can be traced back to Antiquity: in the time of the great library of Alexandria, they were used for textual criticism, to mark variants and suspicious textual passages. In the books of the Church fathers they are deployed not only for textual critique, but also for content critique, to mark passages where dogmatic differences may be detected. This already happened before the Carolingian period, and Carolingian writers in turn adopted signs, created new ones and used them according to their own new systems of meaning. When we study the late antique and medieval testimonies that reflect upon the theory of using the signs and about their meaning, it becomes clear that there is no uniformity here, but rather a range of different traditions. The practice of using the signs in medieval manuscripts, moreover, shows a similar widely varying plethora of shapes and meanings.

For example, the Greek theta is used in Antiquity to mark the fallen in the list of soldiers who entered in a battle, or in law the names of those sentenced to death, theta being short for 'thanatos', death, as is described in Isidore's *Etymologies* I.3.8, in the section on *De litteris communibus*. But an anonymous Irishman working in Milan in the second half of the ninth century (once thought to be Sedulius Scottus) uses the theta to give structure to his translation work: he compares the Greek, Hebrew and Latin versions of the Psalter, and flags in his translation passages which are superfluous in the Latin version with a theta. Here the theta means: this passage is only present in the Latin version, and it is neither present in the Greek version nor in the Hebrew one.[25] Prudentius of Troyes uses it in yet a different manner: he marks the words of John the Scot with a theta in his treatise against John in the Predestination debate. With the use of the theta, he flags his unease and disagreement with John the Scot's words, against whose opinions he strongly argued in this particular, heated debate.[26] Thus Prudentius seems to blend practices here and give them a new layer of meaning: not only does he organize the main text, indicating to the reader where the words of John are used in the text, but he also voices his criticism, by indicating with the theta signs that these words are to be mistrusted, to be dismissed, or even: declared dead.

Open criticism

The use of signs may perhaps be interpreted as a silent way of voicing critique: passages to be treated with suspicion were flagged, but not removed or openly doubted or attacked. One could argue that these practices were meant just for insiders or the scholar in question himself and his close circle. We also have, however, more eloquent examples of 'talking back to the text'. The most famous of these is perhaps the attack on Amalarius of Metz by Florus of Lyon or people from his circle as apparent in Paris, BnF, NAL 329.[27] Florus was deacon in Lyon in a troubled time, when Amalarius was appointed there by Louis the Pious as interim archbishop —to the chagrin of the monastic community, for he replaced Agobard, who was much preferred by them. Florus was also the person in charge of the scriptorium of Lyon, where he ruled the activities of his scribes in a most meticulous fashion.[28] In a manuscript of Amalarius' treatise on the liturgy, *the Liber officialis*, copied in Lyon at the time of Florus, the margins are filled with denigrating remarks about the main text: 'rara insania', 'exiguissimi sensus verba', 'mira vanitas', 'rabida locutio', 'stultissimum mendacium' and 'insanissima falsitas'. On several instances, the annotations directly address Amalarius in second person. The sarcastic tone is abundantly clear from an annotation responding to Amalarius' explanation of the symbolic meaning of a shaved head (namely to get rid of superfluous thoughts from the upper part of the mind):[29]

> Si capilli superflui superfluas cogitationes significant et ideo tonderi aut radi debent, multum tibi necesse erat ut non solum caput corporis sed etiam mentem raderes unde tanta superflua prodeunt.[30]

> If superfluous hairs signify superfluous thoughts and therefore are to be tonsured or shaved, then it is very necessary for you that you should not only shave the head of your body, but also your brain, since so many superfluous things come from it.

The 'talking back to the text' can thus take various shapes: from bringing structure to widening the scope of a text, embedding it into a context, to the addition of other authorities, differing authorities, criticism, or even biting off each other's heads. Baswell remarks that the margin was seen as a 'safe arena', a space where 'ignored or suppressed voices or preoccupations (and the textual communities implicit behind them) ... are able to enter into conflict with it'.[31] One of his examples is William of Conches, who allowed himself to speculate on the Platonic World-Soul as the Holy Spirit, even though this sets off alarm bells ringing in his head, screaming 'heresy'.[32] Within the *Marginal Scholarship* project we are finding our own examples of these processes in the ninth century: for example, predestination being explored even after the synod that explicitly stated that this subject should be put to rest, at least for the time being.[33]

In this case, moreover, an 'empty' book may be a telling example of annotating practices and their importance in the ninth century: Paris, Bibliothèque de l'Arsenal, ms. 663, a copy of the *Libri Carolini*, made in Rheims in 869 or 870 and containing Theodulf of Orléans' contribution to the debate about the use of images in church. It is remarkable that this book has empty margins except for a few numbers marking sections. The debate was one of the larger debates in the Carolingian empire, in which king Charles the Bald involved the greatest minds of his intellectual circle. In the *Libri Carolini* statements must have been included to which others would have wanted to raise objections. We could speculate that the blank margins are, in this case, a statement rather than a coincidence. Perhaps these empty margins display the king's wish to end the debate with this book, even when no consensus had been reached.[34]

Quotations and associative connections to different authorities

So, the interaction with the text and the 'vocal' quality of it, as described by Baswell, is a phenomenon that an editor should be sensitive to, and try to take into account when preparing an edition of marginal text. The other major aspect that makes marginal texts hard to deal with from an editorial point of view, is their intertextuality: in the margins we can see how scholars were cutting up their texts into digestible pieces, 'nuggets of knowledge' so to speak, that could be comprehended and stored in the memory. For example: the margins of *De nuptiis* are full of repeats of definitions, or pointers to places where definitions occur in Martianus' text. These definitions ended up in other places: for example, the definition of 'tonus' a tone, namely a 'spatium cum legitima quantitate', a space with a legitimate quantity, is found in *De nuptiis*, quoted in the oldest commentary traditions to Boethius *De institutione musica*, and found again in the later ninth- and tenth-century music treatises by writers such as Aurelian, Regino of Prüm, or Hucbald.[35] The chopping up of the text into easy to store chunks and moving those around to other places happens on a wide scale. The margins could be likened to a magpie's stash, containing shining items of hard-won learning from other authorities.[36]

The phenomenon of explicit referral to other authorities or texts is frequent, but implicit quotation is even more frequent. For example, a long annotation is added on the subject of the myth of Orpheus and Eurydice in the margins of Martianus Capella-manuscript Leiden, BPL 88, fol. 170v, written in an Irish hand which has been identified as I[2], a hand belonging to someone from the close circle of John the Scot.[37]

> Eyridice: id est profunda intentio. ipsa ars musica in suis profundissimis rationibus eyridice dicitur. Cuius quasi maritus orpheus dicitur hoc est OPIOC ΦONOY id est pulcra vox. qui maritus si aliqua neglegentia artis virtutem perdiderit. veluti in quendam infernum profundae disciplinae descendit. de qua iterum artis regulas iuxta quas musicae voces disponuntur reducit. sed dum voces corporeas et transitorias profundae artis intentioni comparat. fugit iterum in profunditatem dicipline ipsa intentio. quoniam in vocibus apperere non potest. ac per hoc tristis remanet orpheus vocem musicam sine ratione retinens.

> Eurydice: this is profound (intellectual) effort. The art of music itself is said to be Eurydice, in its deepest principles. And as her husband Orpheus is mentioned, that is 'orios fonou' that is beautiful voice. And this husband had lost the virtue of this art through some kind of negligence, as if he descends into a certain hell of profound discipline. And out of this he brings back again the rules of the art, according to which musical voices are ordered. But when he compares corporeal and transient voices of the profound intellectual effort of his art, this intellectual effort itself flees again in the depth of discipline, for it cannot appear in (human) voices. And for that reason Orpheus remains sad, having a musical voice without reason.

Orpheus, the magical singer from ancient myth, is here interpreted with a silent reference to Fulgentius' *Mythologies*: he is the source for the etymology of 'orea phone', or 'optima vox'.[38] In Fulgentius, Eurydice is explained with *profunda diiudicatio* (profound judgement), but *profunda intentio* is frequent, for example, in the oldest gloss tradition to Martianus Capella, which precedes that of John the Scot. The myth of Orpheus and Eurydice is here presented as an allegory of the difficult and perhaps even impossible path of learning: the beautiful voice (that is, the scholar with his eloquence and hard earned learning) strives to capture and keep profound understanding of the pure knowledge of the liberal arts. He even descends to Hell to recapture it after having lost it for the first time. But his strivings are in vain: he will never be able to fully understand, it is out of his reach. So the Fulgentian setting was taken as a starting point to go somewhere else, to a line of thinking and reasoning that is, in fact, very recognizable in other writings by John the Scot, but not part of the immediate context of the annotation.[39]

One wonders how the Carolingian scholars actually went about to accomplish their work in the margin: were they using the books they had in their library? Were they relying on their memory? Were they using intermediary collections, such as glossaries or compendia? Were they using intermediate materials, such as wax tablets or scraps of parchment to organize their material before starting to work? Probably all of the above, but how, then, can we trace their working methods? In order to answer these questions, more research is needed: too few texts of the above described kind have been edited with an eye for their intertextual relationships, and their connections to other texts that were part of the web of texts deployed for reading, understanding and studying the ancient learned tradition. It will be a challenge for the future to map the relations between marginal annotations and other genres of knowledge texts, such as glossaries, encyclopaedic collections and personal notebooks, and develop a more firm grip on the shared strategies for the management of knowledge in the early Middle Ages in the process.

How to make editions of marginal texts? Some observations

Let us now return to the core business of this group: how could we or should we make editions of marginal texts? I have tried to sketch the aspects of marginal text that make them interesting research material, but also difficult from the viewpoint of the editor. As Rita Copeland observed: 'a manuscript containing marginal commentary was a personal item, specific to the teaching and interests of its owner, and unlikely to be copied in exactly the same way'.[40] This results in a fluidity, an essential quality of variance with which traditional philology is not comfortable. Another essential quality of marginal text seems to be that it attracts new text: new layers of marginal text entered by contemporary or later scribes, creating a process of text accumulation rather than a static single text.

I also talked about marginal features, which are not always textual in nature —the marginal symbols that bring structure and attach new meaning or interpretational levels to a text— pointing the reader in a certain direction, cautioning him or her, or even attacking the author.

An editor will perhaps be inclined to dismiss these as 'not in his job description', since they are not always 'text'. Still, they may contain important information that reveal the voices talking back to the text.

Further, I talked about marginalia as nodes in intertextual webs of texts: they use other texts, cut them up, transform them in the process, deploy them in new settings, and embed texts in new contexts. What kinds of information would an edition ideally offer to get a grip on these phenomena?

First, in order to gain an understanding of the content and meaning of marginal texts, we need to know about their 'centre', so to speak: we need to know the content and gist of the main text to which they respond. I would therefore demand from every edition of a commentary tradition that it includes enough of the main text to get an idea, and plead for an edition in which larger portions of the main text are first presented, and then the individual lemmata to which annotations are attached are listed.

Second, to get an understanding of the fluidity of the texts, it would be necessary to have (if possible) multiple manuscripts in the comparison. Only when several exemplars of an annotated text are compared to each other it becomes possible to assess which part of the commentary tradition is more fixed, belongs to the 'core' of the tradition, so to speak, and which part is unique to a particular manuscript or set of manuscripts. Only then can we distinguish individual *ad hoc* annotations from set commentary traditions —by which I mean marginal text which is transmitted as a set text that adheres (to a certain degree) to the rules of standard text transmission: a certain striving for stability and consistency. But, as I have indicated earlier, in the case of marginal text this is always a matter of a certain scale of fluidity versus stability, a gliding scale between the two extremes.

To gain an understanding of the layers of marginal text, it would be necessary to apply some kind of genetic criticism, to encode the growth or development of a particular marginal unit, a marginal set of texts so that at some point, the user can see what was added when, and possibly also where. Where in traditional scholarship editors experimented with adding a 1 and 2 to correcting hands, to mark which one wrote first, and which one second, we could perhaps find new ways to visualize these layers of change to a text in a clearer way. In a digital edition, we could perhaps design a moving map of a certain manuscript, highlighting with colours which parts came first, which later, and which in a third stage of study or use of the text. We could make them layers on a white canvas, which can be shown to the user in the combination or order he or she chooses. If available, we could perhaps even relate those stages to certain dates or persons. However, I am well aware that the visualization of the layers of a certain marginal text is difficult to combine with my earlier point about the fluidity of texts: whereas the fluidity of texts can only be shown in relation to other copies of it, the layers are bound to be unique for each manuscript.

The encoding of the interconnectedness of marginal texts to other texts is, to my mind, the trickiest aspect. The standard way to encode this is to set up an apparatus of 'sources' in the widest sense of the word,[41] but a marginal text is in fact a set of texts, and each individual annotation would need its own apparatus, creating a rather confusing page when presented in the standard layout of a modern scholarly edition.[42] But if we could visualize in some way how many and which other authorities marginal texts connect to the main texts, this would indeed improve our understanding of the basic set of texts available to our commentators. We could, for example, encode references to Isidore, Bede etcetera in different colours —yellow for Isidore, green for Bede— so that the elements from which the Carolingian scholar assembled his commentary will be visible as a coded wall built from colourful pieces.

I am well aware that the colour coding of each building block will be problematic: even if a piece of knowledge is retraceable to Bede, it will not necessarily have been taken from Bede, but can also come from intermediary sources. Yet it may advance our understanding of marginal text greatly if we stop seeing it as a set, solid text, and start seeing it as a web of texts, each annotation connected to other texts, forming nodes in the web. We may then, in the end, be able to see patterns: the preference of certain authorities in certain literary communities, the hierarchy of authorities on certain subjects, the deliberate spread of a certain text from a certain centre to other parts of the empire.

All these wishes and requirements for the edition of commentaries are, of course, entirely impractical. How on earth would we be able to build such an edition, and how many years would it take us to complete such a task? Still, I am convinced that marginal texts force us to think outside the box when it comes to making editions. The current paper format just does not suffice; we need more layers and better means to visualize structure and movement, in order to gain a better understanding of these marginal texts. I am challenging you to think about new strategies that could, perhaps, work, even if it is for only one facet of the complexities of marginal texts.

Appendix

Martianus Capella, De nuptiis II.174–178, as in Leiden, UB, VLF 48, fol. 17r: Diplomatic transcription (with abbreviations silently expanded) of text and annotations; the digital edition is freely accessible at http://martianus.huygens.knaw.nl.

§174§Venit etiam quaedam decens 31

a pudicissima 32 puellarum quae praesul 33 domus. custosque cylleniae. Verum themis 34 aut

astrea 35 aut aerigonae 36 dicebatur. spicas in manu caelatumque 37 ex hebeneo pinacem 38 39

argumentis talibus afferebat. §175§erat in medio 40 avis aegyptia quae ibis memoratur

ab incolis. §176§sed cum petaso 41 vertex atque os pulcherrimum videbatur. quod quidem serpen-

tis gemini lambebat implexio 42. subter quaedam praenitens 43 virga cuius caput auratum 44

media 45 glauca 46. piceus 47 finis extabat. sed dextro 48 textudo minitansque 49 nepa 50 a

leva 51 caprea. §177§sedilofon alitem quae sit oscinum mitior 52 in certaminis temptamenta 53

pulsabat 54. §178§Ipsa vero ibis praenotatum 55 gerit 56 nomen mensis 57 cuiusdam memphytici.

31 DECENS honesta

32 PUDICISSIMA castissima

33 PRAESUL deus qui inferorum potestatem et superiorum habet quasi ostiarius

34 THEMIS obscuritas

35 ASTREA stellata

36 AERIGONAE virgo

37 CAELATUMQUE scultam

38 PINACEM tabulam

39 EX HEBENEO PINACEM haec tabula sub figura artis negotiatoriae describitur. Mercurius itaque quasi mercatorum chirrius id est dominus. Erigone autem custos domus Cilleniae ipsam artem negotiatoria signat quae habet formam et imaginem petasi quia omnis negotiator velocissime omnes terras et regiones amore pecuniae motu quasi quoddam volatile lustrat. Habet serpentes quia institorum lingua venenosa est ad fallent habet virgam quasi ipsam artem quae primo introitu quasi pulcherrima

videtur in processu vero vilescit quod significatur per glaucum colorem
in fine ad mortem ducit. Per capream velocitas mercatorum significatur
40 IN MEDIO pinnacis
41 PETASO talaribus sumitas illius tabulae
42 LAMBEBAT implexio attingebat circumdatio
43 PRAENITENS pinnacem
44 AURATUM erat
45 MEDIA in medio
46 GLAUCA id est viridis
47 PICEUS nigerrimus
48 SED DEXTRO pinnacis indumento
49 MINITANSQUE illa virgo
50 NEPA nepa a nepais declinatur
51 LEVA ubi iste dicit quod a leva fuisset caprea dilofon dicit quod
fuisset ales cum serpentibus
52 OSCINUM MITIOR quasi mitissima omnium avium ore canentium
53 TEMPTAMENTA per inpedimenta
54 PULSABAT percutiebat
55 PRAENOTATUM praescriptum
56 GERIT portat
57 NOMEN MENSIS gerpeios et signum et mensis vocatur apud
Aegiptios mensis November et signum scorpios

Notes

1. This is a five-year VIDI project, sponsored by the Netherlands Organisation
of Scientific Research (NWO) and housed at the Huygens Institute for the
History of the Netherlands, Royal Netherlands Academy of Arts and Sciences.
It runs from May 2011 to April 2016, and it involves, besides myself as principal
investigator, Irene van Renswoude (PostDoc researcher) and Evina Steinova
(PhD researcher). See https://www.huygens.knaw.nl/marginal-scholarship-
vidi/.

2. Other contributions in this series make the same point for different textual
genres, e.g. E. Jeffreys, 'Tapestries of Quotation: The Challenges of Editing
Byzantine Texts', and D. d'Avray, 'Contamination, Stemmatics and the Editing
of Medieval Latin Texts', *Ars Edendi Lecture Series*, ed. by A. Bucossi and E.
Kihlman, Vol. II (Stockholm: Stockholm University Press, 2012), pp. 35–61
and 63–82. J.E.G. Zetzel makes the point for commentary texts: *Marginal
Scholarship and Textual Deviance: The 'Commentum Cornuti' and the Early
Scholia on Persius*, Bulletin of the Institute of Classical Studies Supplement 84
(London: Institute of Classical Studies, 2005), esp. Chapter 7, pp. 144–161.

3. K. McNamee, *Annotations in Greek and Latin texts from Egypt*, American Studies in Papyrology 45 (Oakville, Conn.: American Society of Papyrologists, 2007).

4. This information was given to me by David Ganz, who shared with me a list of annotated manuscripts in *CLA* and his observations on them; I am very grateful for his generosity.

5. L. Holtz, 'Le rôle des commentaires d'auteurs classiques dans l'émergence d'une mise en page associant texte et commentaire (Moyen Âge occidental)', in *Le commentaire entre tradition et innovation*, ed. by Tiziano Dorandi and Marie-Odile Goulet-Cazé (Paris: Vrin, 2000), pp. 101–117; R. Copeland, 'Gloss and Commentary', in *The Oxford Handbook of Medieval Latin Literature*, ed. by Ralph Hexter and David Townsend (Oxford: Oxford University Press, 2012), pp. 171–191.

6. Note that at least in Carolingian times, the relationship between the two forms is fluid: one can spill over into the other. Lemmatic commentary could be inserted in the margins, and marginal material could be stored in new, separate collections. Zetzel, *Marginal Scholarship*, esp. Chapter 5, pp. 86–126.

7. J.J. Contreni, 'The Carolingian Renaissance: Education and Literary Culture', and D. Ganz, 'Book Production in the Carolingian Empire and the Spread of Caroline Minuscule', in *The New Cambridge Medieval History Vol. II: c. 700 – c. 900*, *The New Cambridge Medieval History*, II: *c.700–c.900*, ed. by Rosamond McKitterick (Cambridge: Cambridge University Press, 2015), pp. 709–757 and 786–808.

8. Holtz, 'Le rôle des commentaires', pp. 111–116.

9. Ganz, 'Book Production', 789–805; R. McKitterick, 'Glossaries and Other Innovations in Carolingian Book Production', in *Turning Over a New Leaf: Change and Development in the Medieval Book*, ed. by E. Kwakkel *et al.* (Leiden: Leiden University Press, 2012), pp. 21–76 (esp. pp. 21–31).

10. Evina Steinová researched a set of about 150 manuscripts primarily from Freising and Regensburg which were produced from the second half of the eighth century to the late ninth century. A very high percentage of them contained some form of annotation.

11. Paris, BnF, Lat. 1, available on the Gallica-website of the Bibliothèque Nationale de France: http://gallica.bnf.fr/ark:/12148/btv1b8455903b [last consulted November 2014].

12. At this point (November 2014), the database contains about 350 files with descriptions of ninth- and tenth-century codicological units. The database is freely accessible online: http://marginalia.huygens.knaw.nl/view/codices [last consulted 28 Nov. 2014], but is emphatically a work in progress. It still contains

many inconsistencies and errors. The data that we collected in the database so far are: a good sample of Carolingian manuscripts from the Leiden University Library collection, manuscripts made in eighth-century Lorsch (accessible via the Bibliotheca Laureshamensis website), a sample of manuscripts from ninth-century Corbie [described in D. Ganz, *Corbie in the Carolingian Renaissance* (Sigmaringen: Thorbecke Verlag, 1990), and accessible (partly) via the Gallica website] and a large sample of manuscripts from the Bavarian region (accessible, mostly, via the website of the Bayerische Staatsbibliothek in München). We wish to collect more observations on manuscripts from Reims, Auxerre and Fleury, and on manuscripts which are connected to certain scholars, such as Lupus of Ferrières, Heiric of Auxerres and John Scottus Eriugena.

13. C. Baswell, 'Talking Back to the Text: Marginal Voices in Medieval Secular Literature', in *The Uses of Manuscripts in Literary Studies. Essays in Memory of Judson Boyce Allen*, ed. by Charlotte C. Morse, Penelope R. Doob and Marjorie C. Woods, Studies in Medieval Culture 31 (Michigan: Michigan University Press, 1992), pp. 121–160 (p. 121).

14. Gernot Wieland showed a very convincing case of a book glossed for the purpose of treatment in the classroom: *The Latin Glosses on Arator and Prudentius in Cambridge University Library Ms. Gg. 5. 35*, Studies and Texts 61 (Toronto: Pontifical Institute of Mediaeval Studies, 1983), but in the wake of his study every annotated book tended to be interpreted in the same manner. A good attempt to give the schoolbook model more complexity and depth is found in A. Tura, 'Essai sur les marginalia en tant que pratique et documents', in *Scientia in margine. Études sur les marginalia dans les manuscrits scientifiques du Moyen Âge à la Renaissance*, ed. by Danielle Jacquart and Charles Burnett (Genève: Droz, 2005), pp. 261–387.

15. On Martianus, see W.H. Stahl and R. Johnson, *Martianus Capella and the Seven Liberal Arts*, 2 vols (New York: Columbia University Press, 1971, repr. 1977); S. Grebe, *Martianus Capella 'De nuptiis Philologiae et Mercurii'. Darstellungen der sieben Freien Künste und ihrer Beziehungen zueinander*, Beiträge zur Altertumskunde 119 (Stuttgart, Leipzig: Teubner, 1999); I. Ramelli, *Marziano Capella, Le nozze di Filologia e Mercurio* (Milan: Bompiani, 2001).

16. Ed. J. Willis, *Martianus Capella* (Leipzig: Teubner, 1983), pp. 50–51; transl. Stahl & Johnson, *Martianus Capella*, Vol. 2, pp. 56–57.

17. I owe this example to a paper given by Padraíc Moran at the International Medieval Congress at Kalamazoo in May 2009.

18. The digital edition is online at http://martianus.huygens.knaw.nl/path [last consulted 28 Nov. 2014]; for a critical edition of the annotations to books I and II of *De nuptiis* comparing twenty manuscripts, we now also have Sinéad O'Sullivan's edition: *Glossae Aevi Carolini in libros I–II Martiani Capellae*

de nuptiis Philologiae et Mercurii, Corpus Christianorum Continuatio Mediaevalis 237 (Turnhout: Brepols, 2010).

19. O'Sullivan, *Glossae Carolini Aevi*, pp. 396–400.

20. M. Teeuwen, *Harmony and the Music of the Spheres. The Ars Musica in Ninth-Century Commentaries on Martianus Capella*, Mittellateinische Studien und Texte 30 (Leiden, Boston, Köln: Brill, 2002), pp. 162–183.

21. F. Cinato, 'Les gloses carolingiennes à l'*Ars Prisciani*: méthode d'analyse', in *Priscien. Transmission et refondation de la grammaire de l'Antiquité aux Modernes*, ed. by Marc Baratin, Bernard Colombat, and Louis Holtz, Studia Artistarum 21 (Turnhout: Brepols, 2009), pp. 429–444.

22. S. Ottaviano, 'Il Reg. Lat. 1669: un'edizione di Virgilio d'età carolingia', *Miscellanea Bibliothecae Apostolicae Vaticanae*, 16 (2009), 259–324 (esp. pp. 266–267; 293–296); S. Ottaviano, 'Scholia non Serviana nei manoscritti carolingi di Virgilio: prime notizie degli scavi', *Exemplaria Classica*, 17 (2013), 223–246 (esp. pp. 237–242).

23. Even though Ann Blair's book, *Too Much to Know: Managing Scholarly Information before the Modern Age* (New Haven, London: Yale University Press, 2010), focuses on a different period of history, her general ideas about information management are very apt here.

24. Evina Steinová, *Notam superponere studui: The Use of Technical Signs in the Early Middle Ages*, available online via the portal Narcis: http://www.narcis.nl/search/Language/NL/coll/publication/uquery/. For a first sketch, see Evina Steinová, '*Psalmos, notas, cantus*: the Meanings of *Nota* in the Carolingian Period', *Speculum*, 90:2 (2015), 424–457.

25. Example taken from Evina Steinová's work: Münich, Bayerische Staatsbibliothek, Clm 343, p. 6.

26. This example is treated in I. van Renswoude and E. Steinová, 'The Annotated Gottschalk: Symbolic Annotation and Control of Heterodoxy in the Carolingian Age', in *La controverse carolingienne sur la prédestination. Histoire, texte, manuscrits*, ed. by P. Chambert-Protat, J. Delmulle, W. Pezé and J. C. Thompson, Collection des Études Augustiniennes (Paris, forthcoming).

27. This case has been studied by Hanssens, Wilmart, Zechiel Eckes and Van Renswoude: J.-M. Hanssens, ed., *Amalarii episcopi opera liturgica omnia*, Vol. 2, *Liber officialis* (Città del Vaticano: Biblioteca Apostolica Vaticana, 1949); A. Wilmart, 'Un lecteur ennemi d'Amalaire', *Revue Bénédictine*, 36 (1924), 317–329; K. Zechiel-Eckes, *Florus von Lyon als Kirchenpolitiker und Publizist. Studien zur Persönlichkeit eines karolingischen "Intellektuellen" am Beispiel der Auseinandersetzung mit Amalarius (835–838) und des Prädestinationsstreits (851–855)*, Quellen und Forschungen zum Recht im Mittelalter, 8

(Stuttgart: Thorbecke Verlag, 1999), pp. 72–76; I. van Renswoude, 'The Art of Disputation: Dialogue, Dialectic and Debate in Late Antiquity and the Early Medieval West', forthcoming in a special issue of *Early Medieval Europe: Cultures of Dialogue and Debate in Late Antiquity and the Early Medieval West*, ed. by M. B. de Jong and I. van Renswoude (winter issue 2016). A digital facsimile of the manuscript is online available on the Gallica website: http:// gallica.bnf.fr/ark:/12148/btv1b10315686s [last visited 28 Nov. 2014].

28. C. Charlier, 'Les manuscrits personnels de Florus de Lyon et son activité littéraire', in *Mélanges E. Podechard. Études de sciences religieuses offertes pour son éméritat* (Lyon: Facultés Catholiques, 1945), pp. 71–84; repr. in *Revue Bénédictine*, 119 (2009), 252–267; L. Holtz, 'Le ms. Lyon, B.M. 484 (414) et la méthode de travail de Florus', *Revue Bénédictine*, 119 (2009), 270–315.

29. Amalarius, *Liber officialis*, II.5.5: "Superiorem partem capitis rasorio saepe renovamus, cum forti sollicitudine superfluas temporariasque cogitationes de superiore parte animi resecamus.": ed. Hanssens, Vol. II, p. 211, ll. 23–25.

30. Paris, BnF, NAL 329, fol. 82r; ed. Hanssens, Vol. II, p. 573.

31. Baswell, 'Talking Back to the Text', p. 122.

32. *Ibid.*, p. 135.

33. Renswoude and Steinová, 'The Annotated Gottschalk'.

34. There is also an annotated copy of the *Libri Carolini*, to wit Vatican City, BAV, Vat. lat. 7207. It has been suggested that this annotated copy was deliberately secured to *prevent* further transmission in the Vatican archives. See A. Freeman and P. Meyvaert, 'Further Studies in the "Libri carolini" III: the Marginal Notes in "Vaticanus latinus" 7207', in *Theodulf of Orleans: Charlemagne's Spokesman against the Second Council of Nicaea*, ed. by Ann Freeman and Paul Meyvaert (Aldershot: Variorum, 2003), pp. 597–612; I. van Renswoude and M. Teeuwen, 'Voorpublicatie, censuur en zelfcensuur in Oudheid en Middeleeuwen. Hoe een auteur zich kan wapenen tegen openbare kritiek en straf', in in *In vriendschap en vertrouwen. Cultuurhistorische essays over confidentialiteit*, ed. by Jos Gabriëls, Ineke Huysman *et al.* (Hilversum: Verloren, 2014), pp. 241–256 (p. 249).

35. Teeuwen, *Harmony*, pp. 162–183; M. Teeuwen, 'Writing between the Lines: Reflections of Scholarly Debate in a Carolingian Commentary Tradition', in *Carolingian Scholarship and Martianus Capella: Ninth-Century Commentary Traditions on 'De nuptiis' in Context*, ed. by M. Teeuwen and S. O'Sullivan, CELAMA 12 (Turnhout: Brepols, 2011), pp. 11–34 (pp. 28–31).

36. The metaphor was suggested by M. Garrison, 'Questions and Observations Based on Transcribing the Commentary on Books IV and V, Dialectic and Rhetoric', in *Marginal Scholarship and Martianus Capella*, ed. by Teeuwen

and O'Sullivan, pp. 153–174 (p. 174): "These preliminary soundings of the glosses to Books IV and V have not found a large role for either systematically arranged handbooks … nor for alphabetical compendia…. Rather, wide reading, sometimes imperfectly recalled, and perhaps expounded in discussion, seems to underlie the glosses…. And thus, though the topics chosen, and even the manner of elucidation, may sometimes seem whimsical rather than systematic, far from deserving comparison to intellectual fly-paper or a magpie's stash, the glosses were a truly precious repository of hard-won learning, worth saving even when later proven incorrect."

37. The page is available in the digital photograph collection of Leiden University Library: go to https://socrates.leidenuniv.nl/, and search for BPL 88 [last consulted in Nov. 2014]. For a thorough analysis of I¹ and I², see É. Jeauneau and P.E. Dutton, *The Autograph of Eriugena*, Corpus Christianorum Autographa Medii Aevi 3 (Turnhout: Brepols, 1996).

38. Fulgentius Mythographus, *Mythologiarum libri tres*, 3.10, ed. R. Helm [Leipzig 1898], 77.

39. See also S. Boynton, 'Sources and Significance of the Orpheus Myth', *Early Music History*, 18 (1999), 47–74.

40. Copeland, 'Gloss and Commentary', p. 174.

41. That is: including references to works which are not direct sources, but rather parallels in an indirect way, for example via a shared intermediary source.

42. This method was chosen by M. Bernhard and C.M. Bower, for their edition of the *Glossa maior in institutionem musicam Boethii*, 4 vols, Bayerische Akademie der Wissenschaften, Veröffentlichungen der Musichistorischen Kommission Band 9–12 (München: Verlag der Bayerischen Akademie der Wissenschaften, 1993, 1994, 1996, 2011). To my mind, it works rather well here, but a more complex commentary tradition will be difficult to capture.

Bibliography

Baswell, C., 'Talking Back to the Text: Marginal Voices in Medieval Secular Literature', in *The Uses of Manuscripts in Literary Studies. Essays in Memory of Judson Boyce Allen*, ed. by Charlotte C. Morse, Penelope R. Doob and Marjorie C. Woods, Studies in Medieval Culture 31 (Michigan: Michigan University Press, 1992), pp. 121–160

Bernhard, Mikael and Bower, C.M., eds, *Glossa maior in institutionem musicam Boethii*, 4 vols, Bayerische Akademie der Wissenschaften, Veröffentlichungen der Musichistorischen Kommission Band 9–12 (München: Verlag der Bayerischen Akademie der Wissenschaften, 1993, 1994, 1996, 2011)

Blair, Ann, *Too Much to Know: Managing Scholarly Information before the Modern Age* (New Haven, London: Yale University Press, 2010)

Boynton, Susan, 'Sources and Significance of the Orpheus Myth', *Early Music History*, 18 (1999), 47–74

Charlier, Célestin, 'Les manuscrits personnels de Florus de Lyon et son activité littéraire', in *Mélanges E. Podechard. Études de sciences religieuses offertes pour son éméritat* (Lyon: Facultés Catholiques, 1945), pp. 71–84; repr. in *Revue Bénédictine*, 119 (2009), 252–267

Cinato, Franc, 'Les gloses carolingiennes à l'*Ars Prisciani*: méthode d'analyse', in *Priscien. Transmission et refondation de la grammaire de l'Antiquité aux Modernes*, ed. by Marc Baratin, Bernard Colombat, and Louis Holtz, Studia Artistarum 21 (Turnhout: Brepols, 2009), pp. 429–444

Contreni, John J., 'The Carolingian Renaissance: Education and Literary Culture', in *The New Cambridge Medieval History, II: c.700–c.900*, ed. by Rosamond McKitterick (Cambridge: Cambridge University Press, 2015), pp. 709–757

Copeland, Rita, 'Gloss and Commentary', in *The Oxford Handbook of Medieval Latin Literature*, ed. by Ralph Hexter and David Townsend (Oxford: Oxford University Press, 2012), pp. 171–191

d'Avray, David, 'Contamination, Stemmatics and the Editing of Medieval Latin Texts', in *Ars Edendi Lecture Series*, ed. by A. Bucossi and E. Kihlman, Vol. II (Stockholm: Stockholm University Press, 2012), pp. 63–82

Freeman, Ann and Meyvaert, Paul, 'Further Studies in the "Libri carolini" III: the Marginal Notes in "Vaticanus latinus" 7207', in *Theodulf of Orleans: Charlemagne's Spokesman against the Second Council of Nicaea*, ed. by Ann Freeman and Paul Meyvaert (Aldershot: Variorum, 2003), pp. 597–612

Ganz, David, 'Book Production in the Carolingian Empire and the Spread of Caroline Minuscule', in *The New Cambridge Medieval History Vol. II: c. 700– c. 900*, *The New Cambridge Medieval History, II: c.700–c.900*, ed. by Rosamond McKitterick (Cambridge: Cambridge University Press, 2015), pp. 786–808

Ganz, David, *Corbie in the Carolingian Renaissance* (Sigmaringen: Thorbecke Verlag, 1990)

Garrison, Mary, 'Questions and Observations Based on Transcribing the Commentary on Books IV and V, Dialectic and Rhetoric', in *Carolingian Scholarship and Martianus Capella: Ninth-Century Commentary Traditions on 'De nuptiis' in Context*, ed. by Mariken Teeuwen and Sinéad O'Sullivan, CELAMA 12 (Turnhout: Brepols, 2011), pp. 147–176

Grebe, Sabine, *Martianus Capella 'De nuptiis Philologiae et Mercurii'. Darstellungen der sieben Freien Künste und ihrer Beziehungen zueinander*, Beiträge zur Altertumskunde 119 (Stuttgart, Leipzig: Teubner, 1999)

Hanssens, Jean-Michel, André Wilmart, Klaus Zechiel-Eckes, and Irene Van Renswoude, eds, *Amalarii episcopi opera liturgica omnia*, Vol. 2, *Liber officialis* (Città del Vaticano: Biblioteca Apostolica Vaticana, 1949)

Helm, Rudolf, ed., Fulgentius Mythographus, *Mythologiarum libri tres*, 3.10 [Leipzig 1898]

Holtz, Louis, 'Le ms. Lyon, B.M. 484 (414) et la méthode de travail de Florus', *Revue Bénédictine*, 119 (2009), 270–315

Holtz, Louis, 'Le rôle des commentaires d'auteurs classiques dans l'émergence d'une mise en page associant texte et commentaire (Moyen Âge occidental)', in *Le commentaire entre tradition et innovation*, ed. by Tiziano Dorandi and Marie-Odile Goulet-Cazé (Paris: Vrin, 2000), pp. 101–117

Jeauneau, Éduard, and Paul Edward Dutton, *The Autograph of Eriugena*, Corpus Christianorum Autographa Medii Aevi 3 (Turnhout: Brepols, 1996)

Jeffreys, Elisabeth M., 'Tapestries of Quotation: the Challenges of Editing Byzantine Texts', in *Ars Edendi Lecture Series*, Vol. II, ed. by Alessandra Bucossi and Erika Kihlman (Stockholm: Stockholm University Press, 2012), pp. 35–61

McKitterick, Rosamond, 'Glossaries and Other Innovations in Carolingian Book Production', in *Turning Over a New Leaf: Change and Development in the Medieval Book*, ed. by E. Kwakkel *et al.* (Leiden: Leiden University Press, 2012), pp. 21–76

McNamee, Kathleen, *Annotations in Greek and Latin Texts from Egypt*, American Studies in Papyrology 45 (Oakville, Conn.: American Society of Papyrologists, 2007)

O'Sullivan, Sinéad, ed., *Glossae Aevi Carolini in libros I-II Martiani Capellae de nuptiis Philologiae et Mercurii*, Corpus Christianorum Continuatio Mediaevalis 237 (Turnhout: Brepols, 2010)

Ottaviano, Silvia, 'Scholia non Serviana nei manoscritti carolingi di Virgilio: prime notizie degli scavi', *Exemplaria Classica*, 17 (2013), 223–246

Ottaviano, Silvia, 'Il Reg. Lat. 1669: un'edizione di Virgilio d'età carolingia', *Miscellanea Bibliothecae Apostolicae Vaticanae*, 16 (2009), 259–324

Ramelli, Ilaria, *Marziano Capella, Le nozze di Filologia e Mercurio* (Milan: Bompiani, 2001)

Renswoude, Irene van, and Evina Steinová, 'The Annotated Gottschalk:

Symbolic Annotation and Control of Heterodoxy in the Carolingian Age', *Collection des Études Augustiniennes* (forthcoming)

Renswoude, Irene van, and Mariken Teeuwen, 'Voorpublicatie, censuur en zelfcensuur in Oudheid en Middeleeuwen. Hoe een auteur zich kan wapenen tegen openbare kritiek en straf', in *In vriendschap en vertrouwen. Cultuurhistorische essays over confidentialiteit*, ed. by Jos Gabriëls, Ineke Huysman *et al.* (Hilversum: Verloren, 2014), pp. 241–256

Renswoude, Irene van, 'Dissent, Dialectic and Control of Christian Discourse in the Carolingian Period', paper for the International conference *Ethnicity and Christian Discourse in the Early Middle Ages*, Vienna 18–19 June 2012 (forthcoming)

Stahl, William Harris, and Richard Johnson, *Martianus Capella and the Seven Liberal Arts*, Vol. 1–2 (New York: Columbia University Press, 1971, repr. 1977)

Steinová, Evina, *Notam superponere studui: The Use of Technical Signs in the Early Middle Ages*, doctoral dissertation, University of Utrecht, 2016

Steinová, Evina, '*Psalmos, notas, cantus*: the Meanings of *Nota* in the Carolingian Period', *Speculum*, 90:2 (2015), 424–457

Teeuwen, Mariken, 'Writing between the Lines: Reflections of Scholarly Debate in a Carolingian Commentary Tradition', in *Carolingian Scholarship and Martianus Capella: Ninth-Century Commentary Traditions on 'De nuptiis' in Context*, ed. by Mariken Teeuwen and Sinéad O'Sullivan, CELAMA 12 (Turnhout: Brepols, 2011), 11–34

Teeuwen, Mariken, *Harmony and the Music of the Spheres. The Ars Musica in Ninth-Century Commentaries on Martianus Capella*, Mittellateinische Studien und Texte 30 (Leiden, Boston, Köln: Brill, 2002)

Tura, Adolfo, 'Essai sur les marginalia en tant que pratique et documents', in *Scientia in margine. Études sur les marginalia dans les manuscrits scientifiques du Moyen Âge à la Renaissance*, ed. by Danielle Jacquart and Charles Burnett (Genève: Droz, 2005), pp. 261–387

Wieland, Gernot, *The Latin Glosses on Arator and Prudentius in Cambridge University Library Ms. Gg. 5. 35*, Studies and Texts 61 (Toronto: Pontifical Institute of Mediaeval Studies, 1983)

Willis, James, ed., *Martianus Capella* (Leipzig: Teubner, 1983)

Wilmart, André, 'Un lecteur ennemi d'Amalaire', *Revue Bénédictine*, 36 (1924), 317–329

Zechiel-Eckes, Klaus, *Florus von Lyon als Kirchenpolitiker und Publizist. Studien zur Persönlichkeit eines karolingischen "Intellektuellen" am*

Beispiel der Auseinandersetzung mit Amalarius (835–838) und des Prädestinationsstreits (851–855), Quellen und Forschungen zum Recht im Mittelalter 8 (Stuttgart: Thorbecke Verlag, 1999)

Zetzel, James E.G., *Marginal Scholarship and Textual Deviance: the 'Commentum Cornuti' and the Early Scholia on Persius*, Bulletin of the Institute of Classical Studies Supplement 84 (London: Institute of Classical Studies, 2005)

Manuscripts

Münich, Bayerische Staatsbibliothek, Clm 343
Paris, BnF, Paris. lat. 1, available on the Gallica-website of the Bibliothèque Nationale de France: http://gallica.bnf.fr/ark:/12148/btv1b8455903b
http://marginalia.huygens.knaw.nl/view/codices
http://gallica.bnf.fr/ark:/12148/btv1b10315686s
Paris, BnF, NAL 329
Vatican City, BAV, Vat. lat. 7207

Editing Errors

Giovanni Paolo Maggioni
Università di studi del Molise, Italy

In mediaeval Latin literature, the presence of editorial mistakes in the original text is not rare. These errors can spread in the whole manuscript tradition, not descending from the existence of a common archetype, but directly from the original exemplar. Some of them are not the result of the bad work of a single scribe, but the blame for them seems to be on the author. But this abnormal presence causes some troubles in the philologist's work. How can we recognize them? How can we distinguish them from scribal mistakes? And is it possible to assume that a reputed medieval author made veritable blunders and keep these oddities in a modern critical edition? This paper wants to show how a comparison between the sources and the *recensio* are irreplaceable tools for the analysis of the variants in the manuscript tradition of medieval Latin texts.

Reliability of a Text

Across the centuries, in the history of literature, philologists, scholars and simple readers have been faced with some fundamental questions facing a written text. Is this text reliable? Is it a perfect copy of the original work of the author?

The question was particularly crucial before the invention of print, when every manuscript was different from the others, but even today it is rather important: for instance, in 1990, in the first Italian edition of Ken Follett's *The Pillars of the Earth*, I found a certain saint mentioned as Symeon the 'Stylist',[1] a strange holy figure that evidently was more plausible for a Milanese publisher than the ancient saint, Symeon Stylites. In this case the correction is rather simple for a philologist, even if I can

---

This lecture was given on 20 November 2012 at Stockholm University.

How to cite this book chapter:
Maggioni, G. P. 2016. Editing Errors. In: Crostini, B., Iversen, G. and Jensen, B. M. (eds.) *Ars Edendi Lecture Series, vol. IV.* Pp. 26–49. Stockholm: Stockholm University Press. DOI: http://dx.doi.org/10.16993/baj.c. License: CC-BY 4.0

not exclude that some Italian readers today believe in the existence of a strange early saint patron of Versace or Prada. Fortunately, a case of this kind is rather rare, but it highlights some of the most important skills required for a philologist, that include knowledge of the language, knowledge of the subject and, last but not least, knowledge of the editorial context that produced the actual printed text (in this case, the lack of a qualified copy-editor).

Thanks to the work of many philologists, we all know how many advantages critical editions can offer to modern scholars, by removing errors that were produced through innumerable copies over the centuries. But sometimes even a critical text can surprise us, proposing a reconstruction that does not seem to correspond to our consideration of the author. For example, in the critical edition of the *Golden Legend*, we read, absurdly, that the Saracens sacked the Isle of Lipari in the fourth century: 'Anno domini cccxxxi Saraceni Siciliam inuadentes…'.[2] But Iacobus de Voragine, as well as being a hagiographer and a preacher, was also a historian who, besides the *Golden Legend* and the sermon collections, also wrote a historical *Chronicle of Genoa*. Nevertheless, the critical editor decided to print in the text the date '331' instead of the correct '831', even though this *emendatio* would have been an easy correction, since in the text the word that immediately precedes the year is '*Domini*' of *Anno Domini*, usually shortened in 'D', which is also the Latin number for 500: the origin of the mistake is thus clarified, and the correct century could have thus been easily restored with good reason. Similarly, we can read in the edition of the *Life of Theodora*, a ninth-century hagiographical text, that the saint found a man eating a beast, *hominem comedentem a bestia* (or, even more literally, 'a man eating from a beast'), where the beast is a crocodile.[3] I will get back to these 'errors' later.

Philology and errors[4]

Of course, philologists can make, and actually make, errors in their work, a fact that we experience every day, but in these pages I wish to deal with the particular case of faulty originals. My hypothesis is that an author can produce an original text with some unwanted errors in it. These mistakes force philologists, in a manner of speaking, to blemish the reputation of the author, fixing a number of 'errors' on a printed page of a modern edition. Here I want to discusss some particular cases in which an imperfect, but authorial, text was written and given to a scriptorium to be copied when its form was still in need of corrections.

An apparent contradiction: definition of error in philology and Lachmann's method

Let us start with a definition of error in philology: an error is something (a term, a phrase, a chronological notation) that contradicts the culture of the author, as we know it.[5] So, when we read in a manuscript some error of this kind, we suppose that the text has been modified by somebody else. Beside this term with this rather negative connotation, I will use here also the positive term 'innovation' and the more neutral term 'perturbation', to mean something that is not to be ascribed to the author, but to the conscious will or the unwanted carelessness of a copyist.[6]

If we admit that such an error can be in the original text itself, so the method with the name of Karl Lachmann,[7] as formulated by Paul Maas,[8] seems to collapse, since we do not have, apparently, any reliable reference points to reconstruct the lines of the manuscript tradition. If a perturbation could be caused by the author himself, then the notion of authorial error poses a difficult problem for the Lachmannian method. The question can be solved if we add another requirement to the definition of error: an error is not only what contradicts the culture of the author, but also what is incompatible with the author's actual work of composition and edition. We can spot occasions for this kind of error before, during and after what we usually define as the process of composition.

Instances of 'authorial' errors

A. Before composition

Medieval texts have a particularly strong relationship with their sources and with the canons of their peculiar literary tradition. These sources were often copied more or less literally from existing manuscripts, which naturally had their own errors and their textual perturbations. In facing these errors the author, or his collaborators, could behave as a philologist would, correcting *ex ingenio* the source, but it is possible, especially if a (tired or careless) collaborator copied the source, that the errors accidentally spread from the sources to the new text. This contamination, wherein the scribe switches from the exemplar to the source for a quotation, gives us important clues about the relationship between the text, its sources and the manuscripts actually used, but also muddles the reconstruction of the tradition and the definition of the critical text.[9]

B. During composition

During composition, most of the authorial errors are due to a sort of doubling, or even a multiplication, of the key elements in the process of composition: the writer and what we call his original text.

1. The author

Sometimes during the composition of the text the author was not alone, but he was helped by more or less skilled secretaries who could do a more or less good job. Normally, the author himself did the veritable editorial work and took care of revising and inserting the parts formerly transcribed by his secretaries. But sometimes it could happen that his review has been careless or superficial and that some error made by the secretary sneaked into the text. These errors could be simple copying mistakes, which could be made by anyone and could often be corrected by everyone, but they could also be more serious ones: for instance, the confusion between emperors or popes with almost the same name or other chronological mistakes. If, on behalf of the author, the secretary attached some additional notes, adding them in a piece of parchment inserted between the pages or transcribed in the margins of the page, every misunderstanding of the insertion marks could produce perturbations that could forever affect the text, its history and its tradition.

Translations from Greek to Latin or from Latin to vernacular languages are another example of perturbations to the original text, mainly when more than one person took part in the process of defining the text. The translator could share the same mother tongue as that of the original text, but he could be not so skilled in the target language of the translation and could thus need the help of another person with complementary skills. The communication and the division of work between them could be different: the translator could write a first version in the space between the lines, and the reviewer could correct it and eventually copy it; or one person could read the original text, while a second one was actually translating and writing it. Here textual perturbations could be caused by a bad handwriting or by a mishearing, mixed again with weariness or inattention.

2. The original text

But the largest number of authorial perturbations is caused by the instability of the original. The most common case is when there is more than one version of the text. Some time after the first draft the author could have reedited it without completely rewriting the text, but using an existing manuscript. Normally the author corrects the errors of this copy and adds some parts, with additional notes in the margins or on a piece of parchment, eliminates other parts by deleting them and occasionally transcribing alternative parts in the margins or on additional pages. But once more, the author or his secretary could be tired or occasionally careless. Copyists' errors in the manuscript of the first version could slip unnoticed in the new text and become authorial, because the author himself used them, inserting them in the second version of the text and giving them an authorial worth. In the same way, once again, extensive additions, transcribed on one or more additional pages could be copied in the wrong position, misunderstanding the insertion point. And again it is possible that the author did not notice these errors, causing their diffusion in the original text.

C. After composition

After composition, in most cases, text perturbations are caused by copyists.[10] Bad copyists can add their errors to the text, and good copyists can reproduce it faithfully. But for what concerns the authorial errors, we can note that good copyists can perturb the original text correcting it, while dumb ones can preserve what they found in their model.

Once again, even in this case, it is possible for the author to cause perturbations. For example, he could chase existing copies, trying to eliminate some authorial error.[11] He can correct some errors, but not others, perturbing the lines of the textual tradition and confusing the philological *recensio*.

There is, if possible, something even worse: the author can himself transcribe a copy of his work, as a gift for a friend, for example. And, it is the case of Boccaccio, he can be a good editor but a terrible copyist,[12] making more errors than a professional copyist and producing an autograph worse than other witnesses for the number of mistakes, despite a good *mise en page*. One can easily understand how many troubles such an autograph can cause to the philologists and to their efforts in reconstructing the original text.

The Text-Complex: Sources/Author/Original/ Archetype /Copies /Readers

At this point, a couple of questions can be raised: how can Lachmann's method be useful for a reconstruction of the lines of the textual tradition? Can a hypothetical reconstruction be any better than a real extant manuscript? Without doubt, the answers depend on our idea of text.

It is clear that the first Italian edition of *Pillars of the Earth* is a text, a solid existing book. But its literary worth is limited. It witnesses only to the sad decay of a glorious Italian publisher. The translation is of limited value in reconstructing Ken Follett's original work and reveals little concerning the translator's qualifications, since the error we pointed out above is an evident hyper-correctionism, i.e. a *lectio facilior* made by somebody in the publishing house. The first Italian edition is surely useful to the reconstruction of the history of the text, since the Italian translation is certainly one part of the history of Ken Follett's text. But without the knowledge of the original text, its worth is limited. The knowledge of the original form for a correct evaluation of the history of the text is especially necessary in medieval literature, in which there are very often no secure boundaries to define an author, distinguishing him and his work from other authors and their works, and to recognize a text distinguishing it from its sources. For the Middle Ages it is possible to talk of a communication system where sources, authors, copyists, readers, preachers, audiences have a part. For example, this system is particularly evident for hagiographic traditions in preaching (see Figure 1). In such cases, for a philogical study of the texts, of their history, of their transmission, of their tradition and of their reception, the idea of original/originary text has an extreme importance, allowing us to link and to anchor the communication system to a form that permits a critical evaluation of all the other forms and a correct reconstruction of the text's history. Surely we could not define the author's text without examining every copied witness, but neither could we understand the importance of the copy as it was actually read, without a (at least hypothetical) reconstruction of the original. Besides this, we have also to consider that every existing manuscript is a carrier of its own variants as *homoteleuta*. For this reason, a critical examination of the text is needed for any actually existing manuscript.

Nowadays we are often facing the theories of the so-called New Philology, some of which seem to privilegiate existing witnesses (the manuscripts) rather than a critically reconstructed text, considered as an abstract and theoretical entity. But it seems obvious to me that to evaluate correctly any variant we need to know the original starting point of the textual history, i.e. the authorial text. Beside this, we point out that any witness needs corrections and text formatting (interpreting abbreviations, uniforming graphies and so on), and also this slight and indispensable human intervention creates something that never existed before. This preference for what is immediately visible (and the consequent devaluation of the critical work of the intellect) is a trend that we can

Original hagiographic text (s. II – XIII)

Iohannes de Mailliaco, *Abbreviatio* A1   Bartolomeus Tridentinus, *Liber epil.*

Model sermons   Iacobus de Voragine, *Legenda* LA1

Preacher

Audience (s. XIII – XVI)

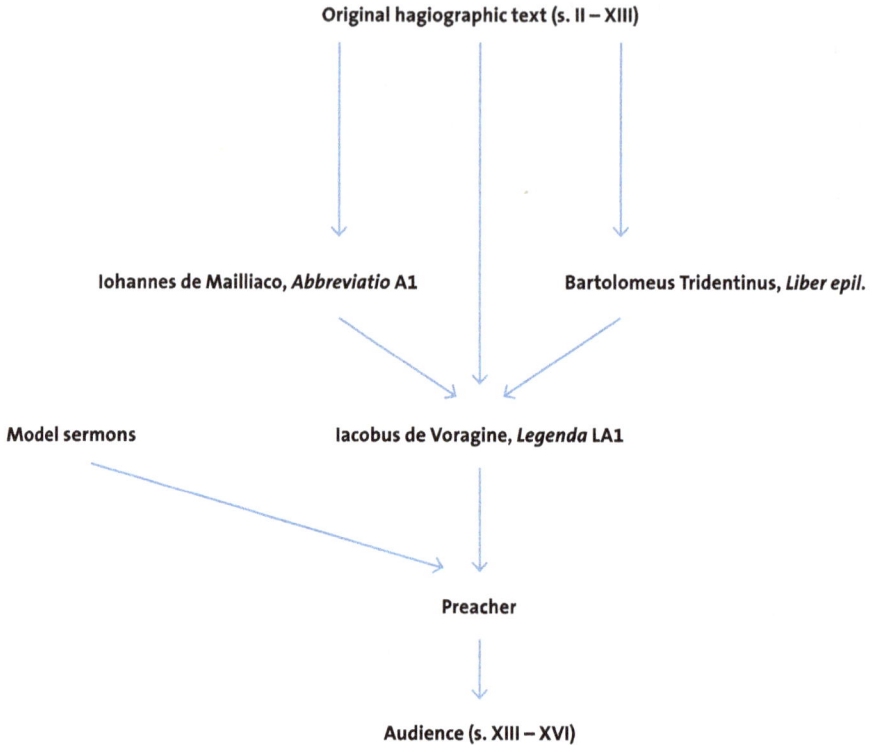

Figure 1. Hagiographical Texts in the Dominican Communication System.

recognize in contemporary society and in its global connection, where it is easier to find the digital reproduction of a manuscript than a critical edition, and where, in general, any assessment is seen as something unnatural and therefore considered with suspicion.

Importance of the *recensio* and of a Critical Evaluation of the Tradition

For these reasons we cannot forget the lesson of Karl Lachmann: *primum recensere!*[13] It is necessary to draw the lines of the manuscript tradition and evaluate the text and its history, starting from the sources and following the developments of the text and the work of the copyists in the *scriptoria*. We need as complete a reconstruction as possible to discriminate between the work of the author and the unintentional perturbations and the intentional corrections due to copyists' activity, since we need to recognize every variant that not only can not be ascribed to the culture of the author, but also can not have been generated by that author's techniques of composition, by his/her approach to the tradition and by his/her use of the sources.

How to recognize authorial errors

1. Recensio

To recognize mistakes and imperfections due to an author's work, we need to have a clear idea of the lines of the manuscript tradition and we need the best possible *recensio*. The authorial errors are generally present in all the branches of the tradition, since in most cases they spread from the original, unless the author generated them with a later direct intervention on an exemplar in a particular branch of the tradition. We have to keep in mind that authorial errors are very often errors that can be corrected, and that any copyist could eliminate. A *recensio* that is as complete as possible allows us a better judgment about the presence of an error in the original or in the archetype.

2. Original *versus* archetype

It is also necessary to consider the existence in the manuscript tradition of a common archetype from which all the existing witnesses could depend. A hypothesis of authorial errors could be contradicted by the existence of a model, placed/occurring just at the roots of the manuscript tradition, affected by at least one error spread in all the descending branches. If there is no such archetype and the manuscript tradition descends from the original itself, it is more probable that some mistakes are authorial errors due to the method of composition of the text, if they spread without clear reasons in different branches of the tradition.

3. Knowledge of the sources

A third condition that could help us to recognize authorial errors is the study of the tradition of the sources: if a textual error is present also in the former tradition of its source, it is probable that the same error passed in the authorial text, mainly if the text was composed with the help of secretaries who could be more or less qualified or interested to correct the source.

4. Knowledge of the method of composition

Last, but not least, as we have already said, we must try to reconstruct the method of composition of the text: for instance, if the author has worked alone or with one or more secretaries; if the text is a translation, and in that case if there was more than one translator, when the competences were split between several qualified persons with particular skills in Greek, Latin or vernacular languages.

How to Manage Errors: by Keeping or Eliminating Them?

When the textual critic encounters authorial errors, the 'author's will' (i.e. his original intention) cannot be the only reference point for the definition of the text. In my opinion the reconstruction must propose a sort of photography of the original just before the copy. If the author did not notice the error in the sources, or the imperfect work of his secretaries, we must keep that error in our edition. For instance, going back to the *Vita Theodorae* just quoted, in the case of the expression *invenit hominem comedentem a bestia*, I chose to keep the active participle against the witness of some manuscripts that attested the grammatically correct form *hominem comestum*. Since this text was translated from Greek, we may explain the error by the fact that the translation was made by a Greek who did not know how translate the aorist active participle in Latin, a language where the past participle is normally passive. The original form in the Greek text read: τρωφόμενον ὑπὸ τοῦ θηρίου. Similarly I kept the expression *inuidie ferentes* for 'carried by envy', whereas the Greek source read φθόνῳ φερόμενοι and at the same time I kept specular forms as *cognita que passa est*, for 'knowing what she suffered', where the perfect participle, passive, corresponds to the Greek active participle γνοῦσα. Here is the entire passage in parallel columns:

Vita Theodorae, Greek Text, BHG 1727–9[14]

Καὶ δραμοῦσα εὗρε τὸν ἄνθρωπον τρωγόμενον ὑπὸ τοῦ θηρίου καὶ κρατήσασα τὸ θηρίον ἀπὸ τοῦ φάριγγοι αὐτοῦ ἀπέστασε τὸν ἄνθρωπον καὶ εἶπεν πρὸς τὸν θηρίον· Χηρὸς ὁ βλαστὸς σου ὅτι τὴν εἰκόνα τοῦ θεοῦ ἐσθίεις.
ἐξ αὐτῶν φθόνῳ φερόμενοι
ἡ δὲ Θεοδώρα γνοῦσα τὸ τί ἔπαθεν.

Vita Theodorae, Latin Text, BHL 8070[15]

Et accurrens inuenit hominem comedentem a bestia et apprehendens bestiam a faucibus eius detulit hominem et dixit bestie: «Exsiccetur guttur tuum, quoniam imago dei comedisti».[16]

quidam ex illis inuidie ferentes[17]
Theodora uero cognita que sibi passa est.[18]

In the first passage we can also note that *imago* is used as accusative form: probably the Greek model for the translation had the variant εἴδωλον, neuter, and we can suppose that the translator used the correspondent term *imago* as neuter as well. Another possibility, suggested by Barbara Crostini, is that the phrase '*imago Dei*' was considered a kind of standard expression, and the translator did not think of inflecting the noun to fit the grammatical structure of his particular sentence. In the second example we find a perfect correspondence between φθόνῳ and *inuidie*. By the way, all these three examples show that the final result was a language that can not exactly be called Ciceronian Latin.

Examples from Thirteenth-Century Legendaries

To illustrate what I said before, I wish to take into consideration some authorial errors in the original text of the *Golden Legend* and in other hagiographic collections of the thirteenth century. These errors concern hagiographical traditions and affect names, dates, and historical circumstances; they are errors that are spread in the whole manuscript tradition and that do not descend from the existence of a common archetype, but directly from the original: consequently these errors are not the result of the bad work of a single scribe, but the blame for them seems to be on the author, even if for us it is hard to believe so. For example, we can hardly allow that Iacobus de Voragine, a Dominican friar who became archbishop of Genoa, could confuse Egypt with Ethiopia for St Matthew's apostolate, or assume that Saracens sacked a Mediterranean isle in 331.

I wish to show how some misunderstandings and some mistakes that have entered in the text and in its main tradition were produced in the special circumstances of a collective editorial work that, nevertheless, made it possible to achieve encyclopedic works like the *Golden Legend* or the other thirteenth-century Dominican collections. It was an enormous, difficult task that, even if done by qualified persons, needed effective editorial control. But evidently sometimes this supervision seems to have been imperfect or even lacking.

David D'Avray defined the Dominican cultural production in the thirteenth century as an attempt at mass communication.[19] This massive production of instruments for a better preaching was the product of a complex work in which many persons were involved. First, there were no real borderlines between the different Dominican hagiographers: the chapters of Iohannes de Mailliaco's *Abbreviatio in gestis sanctorum* are used in the *Speculum Historiale* of Vincent of Beauvais, and both the *Speculum* and the *Abbreviatio* are literally copied in Iacobus de Voragine's *Golden Legend,* without quoting the names of either Iohannes or of Vincent. Both these texts passed from one work to the other, quite physically, through pieces of parchment of various dimensions that could be inserted between the pages or added at the end of some copy or pecia. The outline in Figure 2 illustrates the complexity of such relationships between these legendaries and their sources, taking as an example the chapter *De Sancto Bartholomeo* in the *Golden Legend* and its sources.

Secondly, all these collections are themselves collective works. All these authors (Iohannes of Mailliaco, Vincent de Beauvais, Iacobus de Voragine), directed veritable teams of secretaries, to whom they entrusted tasks such as finding sources and copying them in the new text versions. This collective editorial work was a cause of errors that we find in the original texts of these collections. And we can incidentally observe how much human errors can interfere in the composition and in the assembling of a text.[20]

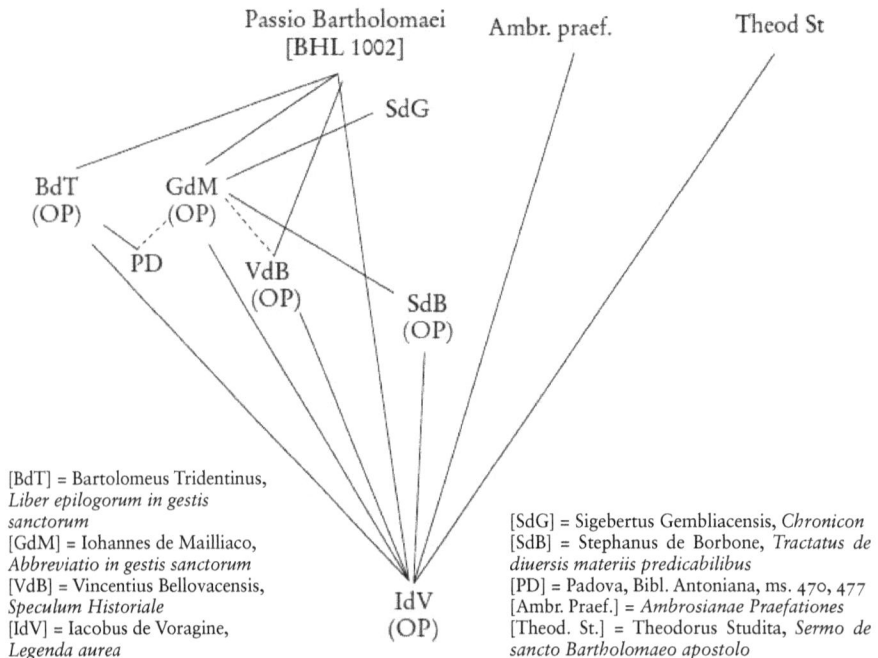

[BdT] = Bartolomeus Tridentinus, *Liber epilogorum in gestis sanctorum*
[GdM] = Iohannes de Mailliaco, *Abbreviatio in gestis sanctorum*
[VdB] = Vincentius Bellovacensis, *Speculum Historiale*
[IdV] = Iacobus de Voragine, *Legenda aurea*

[SdG] = Sigebertus Gembliacensis, *Chronicon*
[SdB] = Stephanus de Borbone, *Tractatus de diuersis materiis predicabilibus*
[PD] = Padova, Bibl. Antoniana, ms. 470, 477
[Ambr. Praef.] = *Ambrosianae Praefationes*
[Theod. St.] = Theodorus Studita, *Sermo de sancto Bartholomaeo apostolo*

Figure 2. The Sources of the Chapter *De sancto Bartholomeo* of the *Golden Legend*

How did these secretaries or compilers work? The direction was naturally in the hands of the author. He decided which saints and which texts were to be included in his book; he decided also the plan and the structure of each chapter. Then he assigned individual tasks to his secretaries. After that, he collected and assembled the material, inserted interlinear or marginal notes, corrected mistakes, interpolated or cut out passages that might be very different in length (a single word or a whole chapter or an entire series of chapters). Finally, he could copy this rough draft, or give it to a scribe to produce what now, after many centuries, we can call the 'original' text.

Any passage of this complex collective editorial work can be an occasion of errors that we can detect in the manuscript tradition. First, we can recognize some errors that were present in the manuscript tradition of the sources and that were merely copied later on: for example, in the chapter *De septem Dormientibus* in the *Golden Legend* we read of the proconsul Antipater, a recent arrival in the city.[21] But no proconsul with this name is quoted in Gregory of Tours' narration of the legend,[22] nor even in the original Greek text where the word ὁ ἀντύπατος is a common noun for the governor of the city.[23] The proper name *Antipater* in the *Golden Legend* and in its sources is an error caused by what can be described as a kind of dittography, probably derived from an interlinear note, formed from the translation (*proconsul*) and the transliteration (*Antipatus*)[24] of the same Greek term. This error is also present in the *Passio septem dormientium* edited in the *Biblioteca Casinensis*.[25]

Similarly, in the Golden Legend, in the chapter *De sancto Matheo*, we read that a magnet can attract rings but also straws (*festucas* in Latin).[26] Here the words *et sucinis* (transl.: 'and in amber objects') were omitted in the manuscript copy of the source (i.e. St Jerome's *Commentarii in euangelium Matthei*)[27] that was actually used for the compilation of the chapter of the *Golden Legend* and this error too remained unnoticed. Again in the same chapter the apostle Matthew, converting the king of Ethiopia Egyppus, leads to the true faith *totam Egyptum*.[28] And, as we have seen before, in the chapter *De sancto Bartholomeo*,[29] the Saracens invaded Sicily in AD 331: the Roman numeral for 831 begins with D, as the standard abbreviation for *Domini*, and this coincidence caused the disappearance of five centuries. Also in this case the mistake remained unnoticed by the secretary and by the author and/or corrector. However, we can point to the origin of these errors, since we know the source (Iohannes de Mailliaco or Jerome or the original text of the Seven Sleepers) and we know that those errors have been produced before the original, in the manuscript tradition of the source.[30] Consequently we can conclude that in the original text of the *Golden Legend* these 'errors' were present, since it is extremely improbable that all these textual perturbations have been produced independently in the source and in the manuscript tradition of the *Golden Legend*. These errors, like those that a secretary made in copying the source and which eluded the control of the author/corrector, are common to all the most ancient manuscripts and the editor chose to keep them in the text of the critical edition. And the critical text of Iohannes de Mailliaco's *Abbreviatio in gestis sanctorum*, the main source of the *Golden Legend*, confirms the presence of imperfections in the original text: here we can find notes like '*Require de hoc...*',[31] or blank spaces left for a dating that was never inserted,[32] or errors like a confusion between Emperor Constantine and Emperor Constans (who lived three centuries later),[33] a mistake that Iohannes de Mailliaco, who wrote a universal chronicle,[34] could not commit, but that his secretaries made.

In the examples shown above, the errors affect single words. But the special features of the editing work for the Dominican hagiographic collections of the thirteenth century have produced perturbations in the history of the text that are more evident in magnitude. In particular we have to consider the fact that all these works had different authorial versions. In other words, Iacobus de Voragine, as Jean de Mailly and Vincent de Beauvais before him, repeatedly revised his text, for example when he became aware of other sources or when he was elected archbishop and above all as his readers changed: there are more *Golden Legends* and the latest is not a collection written just for preachers, but it is a work that can be appreciated also by lay readers that could be looking for stories not only edifying, but also interesting and inspiring. I have drawn the outlines of the evolution of the history of the author and of his text in Figure 3.

To prepare a new and more complete *Golden Legend*, Iacobus de Voragine took an existing manuscript of the older version and, once again, he integrated it with marginal or interlinear notes and he (or his secretaries) inserted bigger parchment pieces and quires for longer passages and chapters. Once again, copying this rough draft was an occasion for errors. First, since the existing manuscript used to make the new edition had its own errors that, once again, remained unnoticed; secondly, since the copy of the added texts produced other errors; and in the third place, since this new rough draft formed by a sort of bundle of manuscript *folia* with marginal

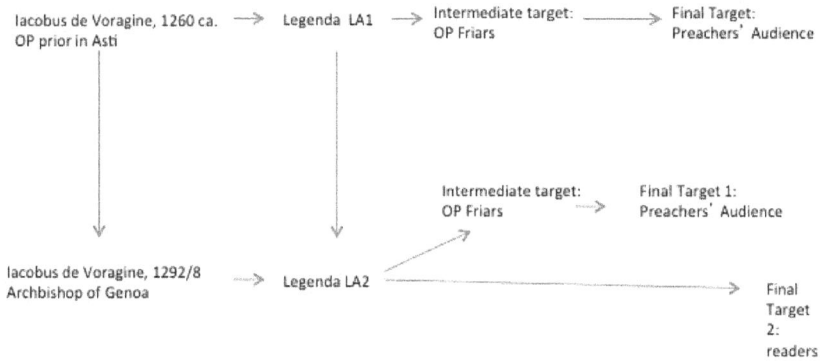

Iacobus de Voragine, 1260 ca. ⟶ Legenda LA1 ⟶ Intermediate target: ⟶ Final Target:
OP prior in Asti   OP Friars   Preachers' Audience

Intermediate target: Final Target 1:
OP Friars ⟶   Preachers' Audience

Iacobus de Voragine, 1292/8 ⟶ Legenda LA2 ⟶ Final Target 2: readers
Archbishop of Genoa

Differences:

Insertion of new chapters, Insertion of narrative parts, insertion of chronological data, insertion / removal of docrinal parts, insertion of explanatory notes for geografical terms and rare words.

Figure 3. Iacobus de Voragine and the Evolution of the *Golden Legend*

notes and pieces of parchment inserted between the pages or at the end. This material form was the cause of bigger errors that concerned the wrong position of big text parts or the wrong position of whole chapters. Since the *Golden Legend* follows the ecclesiastical year, these displacements are without doubt evident anomalies. For example, an evident displacement of a note is visible in Graesse's edition (the most important nineteenth-century edition) in the chapter on Saint Pelagius, where the history of King Theodericus and the philosopher Boethius is placed in the seventh century, between King Dagobert and Bede:[35] a copying mistake that forced Ryan, the English translator, to interpret the Latin expression *per idem tempus*, with the more probable, but much less faithful, *Earlier than all this.*[36]

To show even more macroscopic examples, in the *Golden Legend*, as we know it, in all the most ancient manuscripts and in the critical edition, the chapter of Saint Mamertinus is between Saint Lupus and the Birth of the Virgin.[37] But Saint Mamertinus is honored on 20 April, while the *dies natalis* of Saint Lupus is the first of September and the Feast of the Birth of the Virgin is the eighth of September. In the English translation (made on the nineteenth-century uncritical text of Theodore Graesse), the list of the chapters is not better, since Saint Mamertinus is between Saint Lupus and Saint Giles,[38] who are both honored the first of September.

This incongruence is easy to explain:[39] in the first version of the *Golden Legend* all the chapters between Saint Giles and the Birth of the Virgin were still missing. For the new version, Iacobus de Voragine asked a secretary to copy some new chapters from the *Abbreviatio in gestis sanctorum*: these new chapters were Saint Savinianus (29th of August), Saint Lupus (1st September) and, last, Saint Mamertinus (20th April). Probably the secretary copied these three chapters on a single quire and this quire was inserted whole in the rough exemplar in a place corresponding to the 1st of September. Maybe an insertion sign or an advisory note was written at the beginning of Saint Mamertinus, to indicate the right place were the chapter was to be inserted, but for some reason the entire quire and all the three chapters were copied in succession, while Mamertinus remained there, in September, five months after his *dies natalis*.

The strange position in the *Golden Legend* of the chapters of Saint Basil and Saint John the Almsgiver seems to have a similar origin.[40] Both chapters are between Saint Vincent (22nd January) and the Conversion of Saint Paul (25th January), a period that has nothing to do with the date of their cult (14th of June and 11th of November respectively). Their position on the other hand is near to the feast of another saint, a hierarch of the Byzantine Church: Saint John Chrysostom, who is honored on the 27th of January. The three saints (Basil, John the Almsgiver and John Chrysostom) are absent in the main source of Jacobus, Iohannes de Mailliaco's *Abbreviatio*, but are present in the second main source, the *Liber Epilogorum* of Bartholomaeus Tridentinus.[41] So it is possible that here, once again, the cause of the displacement may be a single quire with three different chapters, whose marks for insertion were neglected by the final scribe.

The case of Saint Fursa is similar: usually Fursa is honored on the 16th of January, his *dies natalis*, or sometimes on the 9th of February, the day of his translation. His position in the *Golden Legend* is between Saints Cosmas and Damian (27th September) and Saint Michael (29th of September).[42] There is no hagiographic reason for this, but there is an editorial one. This chapter is actually a sort of *exemplum* to illustrate a paragraph of the following chapter, on Saint Michael. In this chapter Iacobus, after the usual compendium about the cult traditions, deals with the reasons we should honor the angels: they are our guardians, our servants, our brothers and fellow citizens and, as in the case of Saint Fursa, they carry our souls to heaven. What we read as an independent chapter dedicated to Saint Fursa is actually a short abstract of the original *Vita Fursei*,[43] from which only the passage concerning the struggle between the angels was extrapolated. These angels want to carry Fursa's soul into Heaven, against the devils, who on the contrary want to carry it to Hell. Once again, the text has probably been transcribed on a piece of parchment and put together with the quire dedicated to Saint Michael and the angels, probably with a sign of insertion on it. But, for some reason, this fragment, probably a single parchment *folium*, was copied before, as an independent chapter, by a careless copyist.

In the *Golden Legend* a chapter dedicated to Saint Margaret, also called Pelagius or Pelagia (or Marina with an evident synonymic transposition between *pelagus* and *maris*), is inserted after Saint Pelagia, with the name *De sancta Margarita dicta Pelagius* in a position corresponding to the 8th of October.[44] However, there is no tradition of a cult that can justify this collocation, since Saint Margaret (or Saint Marina) is honored on 18 June, according to some manuscripts of the Roman Martyrology attributed to Jerome.[45] In the *Golden Legend* we actually find a chapter dedicated to Saint Margaret on the 18th of June as well.[46] The reason of this doubling is that two versions of the same legend have been transcribed into the *Golden Legend*. The first is the legend of Saint Marina that comes from Bartholomaeus Tridentinus' *Liber epilogorum* where we find it on the 18th of June;[47] the second one is the same legend, but under the name of Saint Margaret called Pelagia in October and comes from Iohannes de Mailliaco's *Abbreviatio in gestis sanctorum*.[48] But Iohannes inserted it in his legendary as a simple appendix of his chapter concerning Saint Pelagia, that is correctly on the 8th of October, with an introductory note where he explained that in this appendix he recorded the life of a virgin not less noteworthy for habits and very similar as to the name.[49] In the *Golden Legend*, a reworking of the whole chapter was copied, but, since the introductory note was omitted, the second part was considered as an independent one, worthy of a title, particular heading and illumination.

Other traditions in the *Golden Legend* have been created through the confluence of the two main sources of the legendary —the *Abbreviatio in gestis sanctorum* and the *Liber epilogorum*— and this has been the cause of other —sometimes surprising— doublings. A good example is the number of John the Baptist's fingers honoured in Saint-Jean-de-Maurienne, in

France, on the Alps near the Italian border. For Bartholomaeus Tridentinus, the finger is one and it is the forefinger with which he pointed at the Saviour,[50] according to John Beleth's *Summa de ecclesiasticis officiis*.[51] Also for Iohannes de Mailliaco, who follows Gregory of Tours[52] and Sigebert of Gembloux,[53] the finger is one, but it is the thumb that a Savoy matron miraculously obtained after many prayers: for him the index finger is in some church in Rome.[54] In the *Golden Legend*, the fingers in the church of Saint-Jean-de-Maurienne are two: the forefinger and the thumb, since the two passages are copied in succession.[55]

In these pages I have presented some mistakes that affect the original text of the *Golden Legend*. Some of them are very little and some more evident, but they have a common origin: an imperfect supervision of the author who did not remedy the incidents caused by the rough complexity of the original and its difficult copy process, not correcting, for example, the misunderstandings of insertion signs for different saints in the same quire or for interlinear and marginal notes.

Of course, all these errors are unintentional and do not suit the culture of Iacobus de Voragine, preacher and historian. Nevertheless these errors have entered into the Western hagiographic tradition. For example, Cardinal Baronius in the sixteenth century put the feast of Saint John the Almsgiver on the 23rd of January in the Roman Martyrology, presumably following the authority of the *Golden Legend*.[56] In other words, the *Golden Legend* was deemed to be authoritative for Saint John the Almsgiver and therefore created a new tradition. That same authority transformed a minor tradition, the apocryphal narration of Seth and the sprout of the tree of knowledge, in the main European tradition about the Holy Cross, through the preaching of the mendicant orders.

The above are some examples of authorial mistakes. They have been recognized through a former study of manuscript tradition and text history, which allowed to see how the author actually worked and to understand in which way the sources were actually used. In this way, mistakes that did not seem to be ascribed to the author's culture become compatible with that author's working methods. They were indeed present in the original, authorial text and they are not subsequent copyists' modifications of that text, wanted or unwanted.

A final remark: since these errors have been produced by an immediate and accidental cause that has deformed the text forever, in a manner of speaking we can see here an example of the influence of randomness in the human creative process.

Notes

1. Ken Follett, *I pilastri della terra* (Milano: Mondadori 1990), at p. 149: 'Il capitolo incominciò con la lettura di un brano su san Simeone lo Stilista, del quale ricorreva la festa'.

2. Iacopo da Varazze, *Legenda aurea*, ed. G.P. Maggioni (Firenze: SISMEL-Edizioni del Galluzzo/Milano: Biblioteca Ambrosiana 2007), at p. 926.

3. Giovanni Paolo Maggioni, 'La *Vita sanctae Theodorae* (BHL 8070). La revisione imperfetta di una traduzione perfettibile', *Hagiographica*, 7 (2000), 201–268. See p. 252: 'Et accurrens inuenit hominem comedentem a bestia et apprehendens bestiam a faucibus eius detulit hominem…'.

4. A recent article by Giovanni Orlandi is now an indispensable contribution on this topic: Giovanni Orlandi, 'Errore, corruttela, innovazione', *Filologia Mediolatina*, 15 (2008), 1–18, repr. in *Scritti di filologia mediolatina* (Firenze: SISMEL, 2008), pp. 233–347. In the article, Orlandi distinguishes between error, corruption and innovation in the textual history.

5. In other words, *lectiones* constrasting with the linguistic norms and the general knowledge of author's cultural environment.

6. Cf. Orlandi, 'Errore corruttela, innovazione', p. 234: "In realtà la distinzione tra errore e innovazione attiene fondamentalmente al punto di vista da cui si pone l'osservatore: errore è un dato negativo che però dovrebbe permettere di risalire, stadio per stadio, all'archetipo ed eventualmente all'originale; innovazione è un dato positivo per chi si interessi alla storia del testo e ai suoi sviluppi. Accanto al termine errore qui si è inserito anche il termine 'corruttela', il quale, pur nella prospettiva ricostruttiva dell'edizione critica tradizionale, appare più neutro e quindi, a mio gusto, preferibile all'altro. Per errore difatti può intendersi qualcosa che vada oltre e contro gli intenti stessi del copista e del tipografo, un lapsus, una disattenzione, un fraintendimento del proprio modello".

7. Paul Maas, *Textkritik* (Leipzig: B. G. Teubner, 1957). See also Elio Montanari, *La critica del testo secondo Paul Maas. Testo e commento* (Firenze: SISMEL, 2003).

8. See Sebastiano Timpanaro, *La genesi del metodo del Lachmann* (Padova: Liviana 1985²); Giovanni Fiesoli, *La genesi del lachmannismo* (Firenze: SISMEL–Edizioni del Galluzzo, 2000); Giorgio Pasquali, *Storia della tradizione e critica del testo* (Milano: Mondadori, 1974²).

9. I have dealt with this kind of errors in 'Autori distratti e redattori imprecisi. Microvarianti e capitoli fuori posto nel testo originale della Legenda aurea', *Filologia Mediolatina*, 15 (2008), 75–94, and in the introduction of Jean de

Mailly, *Abbreviatio in gestis sanctorum. Editio princeps* (Firenze: Sismel – Edizioni del Galluzzo, 2013), pp. CXCVIII – 588. Giovanni Orlandi and M. Herren have dealt with knowledge, skills and work of authors and scribes in pre-Carolingian period: Giovanni Orlandi, 'Un dilemma editoriale: ortografia e morfologia nelle *Historiae* di Gregorio di Tours', *Filologia Mediolatina*, 3 (1996), 35–71, Michael Herren, 'Is the Author Really Better than his Scribes?: Problems of Editing Pre-Carolingian Latin Texts', *Ars Edendi Lecture Series*, vol. II (Stockholm 2012), pp. 83–105.

10. On this topic see for example Leighton Durham Reynolds and Nigel Guy Wilson, *Scribes and Scholars. A Guide to the Transmission of Greek and Latin Literature*, 2nd edition (Oxford: Oxford University Press, 1974).

11. See, for example, the declared interventions of Marcus Tullius Cicero, as quoted by Pasquali, *Storia della tradizione*, pp. 397–400.

12. Such is the case of the famous MS Hamilton, see Vittore Branca and Pier Giorgio Ricci, *Un autografo del Decameron. (Codice Hamiltoniano 90)*, Opuscoli accademici 8 (Padova: C.E.D.A.M., 1962).

13. See Timpanaro, *La genesi del metodo del Lachmann*, p. 80.

14. Edited in Karl Wessely, 'Zu den griechischen papyri des Louvre und der Bibliothèque nationale. II. Die *Vita s. Theodorae*', in *Fünfzehnter Jahresbericht des K. K. Staatsgymnasiums in Hernals* (Wien, 1889).

15. Edited in G.P. Maggioni, 'La *Vita sanctae Theodorae* (BHL 8070)', pp. 242–268.

16. *Ibid.,* par. 149.

17. *Ibid.,* par.140.

18. *Ibid.,* par. 26.

19. On this topic, see for example David d'Avray, *Medieval Marriage Sermons: Mass Communication in a Culture without Print* (Oxford: Oxford University Press, 2001).

20. About secretaries and their work, see Edmund Colledge, 'James de Voragine's *Legenda sancti Augustini* and its Sources', *Augustiniana*, 35 (1985), 281–314; Antoine Dondaine, *Secrétaires de saint Thomas*, Rome (*Publications de la Commission Leonine pour l'édition des oeuvres de saint Thomas d'Aquin 4*).

21. Iacopo da Varazze, *Legenda aurea*, XCVII, 45, p. 750: 'Quod cum audissent sanctus Martinus episcopus et Antipater proconsul...'.

22. Gregorius Turonensis, *De gloria martyrum, Passio septem dormientium*, ed. Bruno Krusch, MGH *Script. rer. Mer.* I, 2 (Hannover, 1885) pp. 397–403, at p. 401: 'Viri autem apprehensum Malchum ducunt ad episcopum Marinum et ad praefectum urbis'.

23. See the *Passio* [BHG 1594] of Symeon Metaphrastes in PG 115, col. 428–448.

24. Iacopo da Varazze, *Legenda aurea*, XCVII, 45, p. 750: 'Quod cum audissent sanctus Martinus episcopus et Antipater proconsul...'.

25. *Passio Septem Dormientium* [BHL 2315], *Biblioteca Casinensis* (Monte Cassino, 1877), p. 257: 'et Antipatum proconsulem'.

26. Iacopo da Varazze, *Legenda aurea*, CXXXVI, 55, p. 1074: 'Si enim in magnete lapide hec esse uirtus dicitur ut annulos et festucas sibi copulet...'.

27. Hieronymus Stridonius, *Commentarii in evangelium Matthaei*, ed. David Hurst and Marc Adriaen (Turnhout: Brepols 1969), I, 9, 9.

28. Iacopo da Varazze, *Legenda aurea*, CXXXVI, 31, p. 1072: 'In qua (*scil.* ecclesia magna) apostolus triginata annis et tribus sedit et totam Egyptum ad deum conuertit'.

29. Iacopo da Varazze, *Legenda aurea*, CXIX, 89, p. 926: 'Anno autem domini CCCXXXI Saraceni Siciliam inuadentes Liparitanam insulam ubi corpus sancti Bartholomei quiescebat uastauerunt...'.

30. See for example Giovanni Paolo Maggioni, 'Il codice novarese di Jean de Mailly e la " Legenda aurea"', *Novarien*, 17 (1987), pp. 173–184.

31. Jean de Mailly, *Abbreviatio*, 10, 2–4: 'Nam cum esset sterilis miraculose habuit de Ioachim unam filiam Mariam matrem domini que fuit uxor Ioseph – Require de hoc in natiuutate beate Marie –. Mortuo autem pimo marito...'.

32. Jean de Mailly, *Abbreviatio*, 144, 23: 'Post longus tempus scilicet anno domini cum sancti sua corpora Theodoro Augustodunensi episcopo reuelassent...'.

33. Jean de Mailly, *Abbreviatio*, 169, 1: 'Martinus papa propter fidem Christi anno domini CCCL Ab imperatore Constantino de ecclesia raptus et perductus Constantinopolim relegatus apud Cersonam Lycie prouincie ibidem uitam finiuit, multis in eodem loco uirtutis signis usque hodie refulgens'.

34. We have two autographs of this chronicle in the MS Paris, BnF, *Paris. lat.* 14593. A partial edition is edited by George Waitz in MGH *Script.* XXIV (Hannover 1879), pp. 502–526.

35. Jacobi a Voragine, *Legenda aurea vulgo Historia Longobardica dicta*, ed. Theodore Graesse (Leipzig, 1850), p. 832.

36. Jacobus de Voragine, *The Golden Legend: Readings of the Saints*, trans. by William Granger Ryan, 2 vols (Princeton: Princeton University Press 1993), vol. 2, p. 374.

37. Iacopo da Varazze, *Legenda aurea*, pp. 1000–1003.

38. *Ibid.*, vol. 2, pp. 145–147.

39. See Giovanni Paolo Maggioni, *Ricerche sulla composizione e sulla trasmissione della «Legenda aurea»*, Biblioteca di Medioevo latino, 8 (Spoleto: Centro Italiano di Studi sull'Alto Medioevo 1995), pp. 137–139.

40. Iacopo da Varazze, *Legenda aurea*, pp. 214–231.

41. Bartolomeo da Trento, *Liber epilogorum in gesta sanctorum*, ed. Emore Paoli (Firenze: SISMEL – Edizioni del Galluzzo, 2001), pp. 141–142.

42. Iacopo da Varazze, *Legenda aurea*, pp. 1100–1103.

43. '*Vita sancti Fursei*', ed. Maria Pia Ciccarese, *Romano Barbarica*, 8 (1984–1985), pp. 279–303.

44. Iacopo da Varazze, *Legenda aurea*, pp. 1164–1165.

45. About Saint Marina, see Evelyne Patlagean, 'L'Histoire de la femme deguisée en moine et la evolution de la sainteté feminine à Byzance', *Studi Medievali*, 17 (IIIs.) (1976), pp. 1595–1623; *Vie et office de Sainte Marine*, ed. Léon Clugnet *et al.* (Paris: Picard et fils, 1905); Alfons Hilka, 'Une vie inédite de Sainte Marine', *Analecta Bollandiana*, 46 (1928), 67–68; *Bibliotheca Sanctorum* VIII (Roma: Istituto Giovanni XXIII della Pontificia Università lateranense, 1965), cols 1165–1170.

46. Iacopo da Varazze, *Legenda aurea*, pp. 690–695.

47. Bartolomeo da Trento, *Liber epilogorum*, pp. 183–184.

48. Jean de Mailly, *Abbreviatio*, pp. 421–425.

49. *Ibid.*, 154, 64, p. 424: 'Vitam cuiusdam uirginis non minus dignam miraculo legimus quam propter morum et nominum similitudinem breuiter hic notamus'.

50. Bartolomeo da Trento, *Liber epilogorum*, p. 266: 'Digitus vero cum quo Dominum ad se venientem demonstravit illuc inter cetera fuir translatus; quem sancta Tecla inter Alpes attulit et dicitur esse in ecclesia Mauriana'.

51. Iohannes Beleth, *Summa de ecclesiasticis officiis*, ed. Henri Douteil, Corpus Christianorum CM 41–41A (Turnhout: Brepols 1976), p. 147.

52. Gregorius Turonensis, *De gloria martyrum*, I, 14.

53. Sigebertus Gemblacensis, *Chronicon*, MGH *Script.* VI, ed. Ludwig Conrad Bethmann (Hannover 1844), p. 321.

54. Jean de Mailly, *Abbreviatio*, pp. 355–356: 'Anno domini DCXI sub Eraclio anno primi imperii eius uirtus et nomen sancti Iohannis baptiste miraculis declaratur apud urbem Galliem Mauriennam de reliquiis corporis ipsius hoc modo diuinitus illustratam. In ea olim mulier sancto baptiste nimis deuota expetebat a deo donari

sibi aliquid de membris eius; et in hac orando instantia per triennium existens cum alter quiuis desperare iam posset ipsa spem in deo ponens iurauit se non manducaturam donec quod peteret acciperet. Et sic septem diebus ieiunans septima tandem die desuper altari pollicem miri candoris apparere uidens letam donum dei accepit'.

55. Iacopo da Varazze, *Legenda aurea*, 121, pp. 153–159 and 160–163, p. 982.

56. *Bibliotheca Sanctorum* VI, col. 754.

Bibliography

Primary Sources

Bartholomaeus Tridentinus (Bartolomeo da Trento), *Liber epilogorum in gesta sanctorum*, ed. Emore Paoli (Firenze: SISMEL – Edizioni del Galluzzo, 2001)

Bibliotheca Sanctorum I–XII (Roma: Istituto Giovanni XXIII della Pontificia Università Lateranense. Città nuova, 1961–1970)

Follett, Ken, *I pilastri della terra* (Milano: Mondadori, 1990)

Iacobus de Voragine (Iacopo da Varazze), *Legenda aurea*, ed. G.P. Maggioni (Firenze: SISMEL-Edizioni del Galluzzo/Milano: Biblioteca Ambrosiana, 2007)

Iacobus de Voragine, *Legenda aurea vulgo Historia Longobardica dicta*, ed. Theodore Graesse (Leipzig, 1850)

Iacobus de Voragine (James de Voragine), *The Golden Legend: Readings of the Saints*, trans. by William Granger Ryan (Princeton: Princeton University Press, 1993)

Gregorius Turonensis, *De gloria martyrum*, ed. Bruno Krusch, MGH *Script. rer. Mer.* I.2 (Hannover, 1885)

Hieronymus Stridonius, *Commentarii in evangelium Matthaei*, ed. David Hurst and Marc Adriaen, Corpus Christianorum SL 77 (Turnhout: Brepols, 1969)

Iohannes Beleth, *Summa de ecclesiasticis officiis*, ed. Henri Douteil, Corpus Christianorum CM 41–41A (Turnhout: Brepols, 1976)

Iohannes de Mailliaco (Jean de Mailly), *Abbreviatio in gestis sanctorum. Editio princeps*, ed. Giovanni Paolo Maggioni (Firenze: SISMEL – Edizioni del Galluzzo, 2013)

Iohannes de Mailliaco, *Chronica Universalis Metensis*, Paris, BnF, ms. lat. 14593: exc. ed. George Waitz in MGH *Script.* XXIV (Hannover, 1879)

Passio Septem Dormientium [BHL 2315], *Biblioteca Casinensis* (Monte Cassino, 1877), pp. 252–256

Sigebertus Gemblacensis, *Chronicon* MGH *Script.* VI, ed. Ludwig Conrad Bethmann (Hannover 1844)

Symeon Metaphrastes, *Passio Septem Dormientium* (BHG 1594), PG 115, cols 428–448

Vie et office de Sainte Marine, ed. in Clugnet, Léon *et al.* (Paris: Picard et fils, 1905)

Vita Theodorae (BHL 8070), ed. G.P. Maggioni, 'La *Vita sanctae Theodorae* (BHL 8070). La revisione imperfetta di una traduzione perfettibile', *Hagiographica*, 7 (2000), pp. 201–268

Secondary Literature

Branca, Vittore and Ricci, Pier Giorgio, *Un autografo del Decameron. (Codice Hamiltoniano 90)*, Opuscoli accademici 8 (Padova: C.E.D.A.M., 1962)

Colledge, Edmund, 'James de Voragine's *Legenda sancti Augustini* and its Sources', *Augustiniana*, 35 (1985), 281–314

d'Avray, David, *Medieval Marriage Sermons: Mass Communication in a Culture without Print* (Oxford: Oxford University Press, 2001)

Dondaine, Antoine, *Secrétaires de saint Thomas*, Publications de la Commission Leonine pour l'édition des oeuvres de saint Thomas d'Aquin, 4 (Rome, 1956)

Fiesoli, Giovanni, *La genesi del lachmannismo* (Firenze: SISMEL, 2000)

Herren, Michael, 'Is the Author Really Better than his Scribes? Problems of Editing Pre-Carolingian Latin Texts', *Ars Edendi Lecture Series,* vol. 2, ed. by Alessandra Bucossi and Erika Kihlman (Stockholm, 2012), 83–105

Hilka, Alfons, 'Une Vie inédite de Sainte Marine', *Analecta Bollandiana*, 46 (1928), 68–77

Maas, Paul, *Textkritik* (Leipzig: B. G. Teubner, 1957)

Maggioni, Giovanni Paolo, 'Il codice novarese di Jean de Mailly e la "Legenda aurea"', *Novarien*, 17 (1987), 173–184

Maggioni, Giovanni Paolo, *Ricerche sulla composizione e sulla trasmissione della «Legenda aurea»*, Biblioteca di Medioevo latino 8 (Spoleto: Centro Italiano di Studi sull'Alto Medioevo, 1995)

Maggioni, Giovanni Paolo, 'La *Vita sanctae Theodorae* (BHL 8070). La revisione imperfetta di una traduzione perfettibile', *Hagiographica*, 7 (2000), 127–194

Maggioni, Giovanni Paolo, 'Autori distratti e redattori imprecisi. Microvarianti e capitoli fuori posto nel testo originale della Legenda aurea', *Filologia Mediolatina*, 15 (2008), 75–94

Montanari, Elio, *La critica del testo secondo Paul Maas. Testo e commento* (Firenze: SISMEL, 2003)

Orlandi, Giovanni, 'Un dilemma editoriale: ortografia e morfologia nelle *Historiae* di Gregorio di Tours', *Filologia Mediolatina*, 3 (1996), 35–71

Orlandi, Giovanni, 'Errore, corruttela, innovazione', *Filologia Mediolatina*, 15 (2008), 1–18

Orlandi, Giovanni, *Scritti di filologia mediolatina* (Firenze: SISMEL, 2008)

Giorgio Pasquali, *Storia della tradizione e critica del testo* (Milano: Mondadori 1974^2)

Patlagean, Evelyne, 'L'Histoire de la femme deguisée en moine et l'évolution de la sainteté feminine à Byzance', *Studi Medievali*, 17 (IIIs.) (1976), 1595–1623

Reynolds, Leighton D. and Nigel G. Wilson, *Scribes and Scholars. A Guide to the Transmission of Greek and Latin Literature*, 2nd edition (Oxford: Oxford University Press, 1974)

Sebastiano Timpanaro, *La genesi del metodo del Lachmann* (Padova: Liviana 1985^2)

Karl Wessely, 'Zu den griechischen papyri des Louvre und der Bibliothèque nationale. II. Die *Vita s. Theodorae*', in *Fünfzenter Jahresbericht des K. K. Staatsgymnasiums in Hernals* (Wien, 1889)

The Ordinary Chants of the Roman Mass, with their Tropes
The Odyssey of an Edition*

Charles M. Atkinson
The Ohio State University, USA

When, in the summer of 1976, Bruno Stäblein invited me to prepare an edition of the melodies for the Sanctus and Agnus Dei of the Roman mass, together with their tropes, for the series *Monumenta Monodica Medii Aevi*,[1] I had to say that I would be happy to do so, but would not be able to work on the project right away because of other commitments. Little did I know that it would be over thirty years, and that the world would go through at least two great recessions, the United States would elect six different presidents and engage in two different wars before I could finish even one part of the project, and that the edition would appear in a completely different series and in a completely different format from that for which it was originally conceived.[2] Rather than being an edition of the Sanctus and Agnus Dei and their tropes, the edition will now comprise the Kyrie and Gloria of the Roman mass and their prosulas and tropes as well.[3] The fact that I am writing this article (and gave the lecture upon which it is based) is one positive sign that work on the edition is well under way. But much water has flowed under the bridge between the inception of the project and its present state.

Granted, there are a number of things that kept me from completing this edition any sooner. One was a series of articles and then a book

---

This lecture was given 4 April 2013 at Stockholm University.

* I am grateful to Gunilla Iversen for the invitation to present the present article as a paper on the lecture series *Ars edendi*. I especially appreciated her comment in the publicity for the lecture: "In his lecture he will talk about thrilling challenges and solutions in editing text and music from medieval manuscripts". The present article preserves much of the content and form of the original paper.

How to cite this book chapter:
Atkinson, C. M. 2016. The Ordinary Chants of the Roman Mass, with their Tropes: The Odyssey of an Edition. In: Crostini, B., Iversen, G. and Jensen, B. M. (eds.) *Ars Edendi Lecture Series, vol. IV*. Pp. 50–84. Stockholm: Stockholm University Press. DOI: http://dx.doi.org/10.16993/baj.d. License: CC-BY 4.0

on a completely different subject, namely the nexus of tone-system, mode, and notation in early medieval music. When the book of that title appeared in 2009,[4] I could finally return to the editorial project in earnest. But I would have to admit that even greater obstacles were presented by the task of editing a large body of texts with music. Those will be the main focus of this article. But I shall discuss them within the broader framework that marks the history of this edition.[5]

As mentioned above, I am preparing an edition that includes the melodies for the Ordinary chants of the Roman mass *and* their tropes. This edition will indeed comprise both texts and music. But while the texts of the Ordinary chants themselves are relatively stable, the texts of the tropes for these chants are characterized more by their diversity than by their consistency. In her seminal article 'Problems in the Editing of Tropes', which appeared in the first issue of the journal *Text* in 1984,[6] Gunilla Iversen points out that with regard to the items that make up the Latin mass during the period between the ninth and the twelfth centuries, "the multiplicity, the great variety, is in fact more striking than the uniformity."[7] In that same article, she goes on to discuss editorial problems pertinent to various types of tropes, ranging from the prosulae added to melismas in various types of chant, to tropes for both the Proper and Ordinary of the mass. Since her remarks pertain as much to my edition as to hers, I should like to reiterate some of her points here.

Regarding the character of the Latin texts, she states that the Latinity of the tropes can vary considerably according to type of chant, the provenance of a manuscript, and even across chants within the same manuscript.[8] The language of prosulae, for example, as found in the Sanctus repertoire, can often be "very peculiar" as she describes it. [9] This is because these texts were in many cases added to a pre-existent melody, and the number of syllables of the text had to match the number of pitches in the melody. Beyond this generic difference, one must keep in mind that the Latin language evolved during the course of the Middle Ages, thus is not the same in late as in early texts.[10] This plays a concrete role in the tropes, since newer pieces were constantly being added to the repertoire, but stand side by side with older ones in the manuscripts themselves.[11] In addition, there are regional differences in the quality and character of the Latinity one encounters in tropes that must be dealt with by the modern editor.[12]

Regarding the task of the editor of tropes, Iversen points out three fundamental problems, which are pertinent whether one is editing the texts by themselves or with their music.[13] The first is to establish what she calls the "main structure" of a chant and its tropes, presenting the combinations of the elements or verses that belong to a given trope and demonstrating the way the elements and the base liturgical text link together. The second problem is to present the edited text in such a way that variants are presented as readings that are just as valid as those of the edited text itself, a point to which I shall return below. Her final problem is one that is overarching, and plays perhaps an even more important role in preparing an edition of texts with music than one of the texts by themselves: namely, the problem of trying to ascertain who will use a given edition and how much and what kind of information that user will need.

In addressing the special problems of editing trope texts with music, I should like to begin by underscoring Iversen's point that in dealing with liturgical texts we cannot define "authenticity" in the same way that we would for editing literary texts. In the case of the latter we are dealing usually with a text by a known author, and the job of the editor is to produce a text that is as close as possible to the final state of the text by that author. In the case of liturgical texts, however, we rarely know the name of the author, Notker Balbulus and Tuotilo of St. Gall, along with Adémar de Chabannes being noteworthy exceptions.[14] But having the name of an author is not the deciding factor when one is dealing with liturgical texts and their music. As Iversen says:

> The most important thing is that each different version of a text as long as it belonged to a liturgical practice, is to be regarded as authentic. The most interesting task for us today is not to come back to and re-establish the first, the earliest text, which may be the natural editorial impulse, but to give as accurate a picture as possible of all the versions that were used in their own right in different regions.[15]

In accordance with that statement, she and the other editors of *Corpus Troporum* have adopted the principle of maintaining the text of a trope as it appears in the manuscript, "as long as there is the slightest possibility of making sense out of it."[16] This strikes me as an eminently sensible decision, and is one I plan to adhere to in my own edition of tropes to the chants of the Ordinary. Let me now turn to that edition, relating something of its history, and some of the problems it will have to solve.

I must preface my remarks by returning to the third of the problems Gunilla Iversen outlined under the tasks of an editor: namely, the problem of trying to ascertain who will use a given edition and how much and what kind of information that user will need. Here lies the biggest difference between editing trope texts by themselves and editing those same texts with music. The latter have to be presented in such a way that they can be *sung* (even if the potential user is tone-deaf!). All sorts of decisions flow from that simple and obvious fact. One cannot simply prepare an edition for silent reading or the comparison of textual variants. One has to make decisions that can be converted into sound.

The need to provide performable music is only appropriate, since the texts were clearly sung in their role as parts of the liturgy, but lacking an oral tradition that extends back to the ninth or tenth centuries, we must present them in a type of musical notation that a modern singer can read, i.e., in ordinary staff notation, using either tenor or bass clefs. This means that we are forced to prepare editions of the melodies using some form of diastematic, that is to say intervallically precise, musical notation. Since the advent of fully diastematic notation takes place only in the eleventh century, in particular as outlined in the *Prologus in Antiphonarium* of Guido d'Arezzo (ca. 1030),[17] virtually any manuscripts copied before that time are not likely to be useable as primary sources for an edition. We may consult them and perhaps even collate their neumatic readings for the melodies, but without clefs they must be considered non-diastematic, and their melodies transcribed only from later, fully diastematic concordant sources. As an example of this, please see Examples 1 and 2, below.

Example 1, to which I shall return below, presents Gunilla Iversen's edition of the texts of the trope set *Omnipotens aeterna Dei*, a trope that appears in a number of tenth- and eleventh-century sources from England, France, and northern Italy. Example 2 presents musical settings for the first element of *Omnipotens aeterna Dei* in four manuscripts dating from the tenth to the twelfth centuries. As one can see in the example, the Aquitanian manuscript settings —A, B, and C— are relatively well heighted, but without clefs; given this lack, one really cannot sing the melody from them. Fortunately, this set of tropes was also copied into several later sources, including the twelfth-century manuscript Paris, BnF, lat. 10508, from St Evroult, whose setting appears as Example 2 D.[18] This source presents the trope on lines and with clefs, thereby permitting a reliable transcription into modern notation.

Related to the necessity of transcribing from diastematically notated manuscripts is the fact that a number of tropes cannot be found in any diastematic sources at all, hence cannot be part of an edition of the music. By my count there are fourteen of the Agnus Dei tropes and fifteen Sanctus tropes in Gunilla Iversen's editions in *Corpus Troporum* volumes IV and VII whose melodies are not transcribable.[19] One has to lament this, because some of these tropes have quite attractive texts. The earliest tropes from St. Gall are a special case. They are written for the most part in good Latin, and have clearly legible melodic settings. But because the earliest manuscripts from St Gall are notated *in campo aperto* —not on a staff, but in open field— the only way we can make those tropes available is by offering them in transcription from a later manuscript, if a concordant source may be found at all. In this regard we are fortunate to have a late manuscript from St Gall, St Gall, Stiftsbibliothek, codex 546, copied in 1507, that offers diastematic readings of a number of early tropes from the monastery that would otherwise be completely lost to us today except for their texts.[20] St Gall 546 is a "collectaneum" compiled by Frater Joachim Cuontz, hence not a manuscript belonging to a specific liturgical tradition. One can question whether a melody copied in St Gall 546 is in fact the same as the one with which a given text was originally sung, but in this case, as long as the neumes concord with each other, having a melodic setting —even a late one— is better than having no setting at all. As examples, I would cite the St Gall Agnus tropes *Christe, theos agye* and *Patris factus hostia*, both of which have diastematic concordances only in St Gall 546.[21]

The need to resort to transcribing, say a ninth-century trope from a sixteenth-century source is indicative of yet another issue that concerns tropes to the Ordinary in particular. As we know, tropes begin to be composed no later than the early part of the ninth century, as the canon of the Synod of Meaux (845/6) witnesses, and continue to be written throughout the Middle Ages.[22] The great bulk of the repertoire, however, in particular Proper tropes, is made up of texts and music composed between the ninth and twelfth centuries. The decision of the editors of *Corpus Troporum* to establish 1100 as cut-off date for their editions of Proper tropes was a wise and practical one.[23] As Gunilla Iversen has pointed out in her editions of tropes to the Sanctus and Agnus Dei, however, the composition of tropes for these two chants of the Ordinary of the mass continued through the Middle Ages and on into the Renaissance. Accordingly, she included some "later" texts in her edition of Agnus Dei tropes,[24] and even more in the editions of those for the Sanctus[25] and the Gloria.[26] The problem I face, however, is that my edition will be an edition not just of tropes, but of the Ordinary

Example 1. The Agnus Dei Trope *Omnipotens aeterna dei / Verum subsistens / Optima perpetuae* (Gunilla Iversen, *Tropes de l'Agnus Dei*, Corpus Troporum IV, Acta Universitatis Stockholmiensis, *Studia Latina Stockholmiensia* XXVI (Stockholm: Almqvist & Wiksell International, 1980), pp. 63–64:

> *Agnus dei qui tollis peccata mundi, miserere nobis.*

A   Omnipotens aeterna dei sapientia, Christe,
>> *miserere nobis.*

B   Verum subsistens vero de lumine lumen,
>> *miserere nobis.*

C   Optima perpetuae concedens gaudia vitae,
>> *miserere nobis.*

I   Quem Iohannes in Iordane baptizavit
        ovans et dicens :

D   Rex regum, gaudium angelorum, Christe,

E   Agne dei vivi, qui tollis crimina mundi,
    dona nos omnes hic vivere pace quieta.

ABC	Cdg 473 Ox 775 Du 6 Pa 10508 Pa 7185 Pa 13252 Lei 60
	Pa 1087 Pa 1240 Pa 1132 Pa 1133 Pa 1134 Pa 1135 Pa 1136
	Pa 1137 Pa 909 Pa 1120 Pa 1119 Pa 1084b Pa 1871 Apt 18
	Vro 107 Mod 9 Ivr 60 RoC 1741 RoN 1343
AC	Pa 903 Pa 1118
BCA	PaA 1169
IABC	Lo 13
IBAC	Pa 887
ABCD	Pa 1177 Pa 1177 sec.
ABCE	Apt 17 Apt 17 sec.

I   *Introductio vagans, vide* Quem Iohannes (50a)

A   aeterna:aeterne *Pa 1240   Pa 1132   Pa 1133   Pa 1134   Pa 1135 Pa 1136   Pa 1137   Pa 909   Pa 1120   Pa 1119   Pa 1084b   Pa 887 Apt 17   Apt 17 sec.   Pa 1118   Apt 18, ex* aeterne *corr. Pa 1871*   dei:et dei *Pa 1118* deus *ex* dei *corr. Pa 887*

B   verum:*primam litteram om. Apt 18,* verbum *Pa 1084b*   vero:verum *Pa 1133   Pa 887*

C   optima:optimam *Pa 1120*   perpetuae:perpetua *PaA 1169   Pa 1177 Pa 1177 sec.   Pa 1240   Pa 1135   Pa 887   Pa 1871   Pa 1118   Vro 107 Mod 9,* perpetuam *Pa 1137   Pa 1120   Pa 1084b,* perspicue *Apt 17   Apt 17 sec.*   concedens:conced *Pa 1240,* conce *marg. absc. Pa 1136,* concede *PaA 1169   Pa 1132   Pa 1133   Pa 1134   Pa 1137   Pa 1120   Pa 1119   Pa 1871,* concedas *Lo 13,* concedat *Pa 1084b   Pa 887,* concedat *ut videtur Pa 1118,* concedat ad *Pa 903,* concedens ... vitae *propter detrimentum desunt Lei 60*

Example 2. Musical settings of *Omnipotens aeterna Dei* (CT 4, no. 41: *Omnipotens aeterna dei (Verum subsistens / Optima perpetuae)* in sources from the 10th– 12th centuries

2.1 Paris, BnF, lat. 1240, fol. 35bis *verso*:

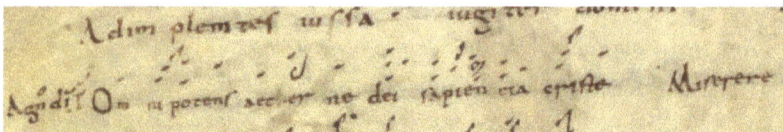

2.2 Paris, BnF, lat. 887, fol. 67 *verso*:

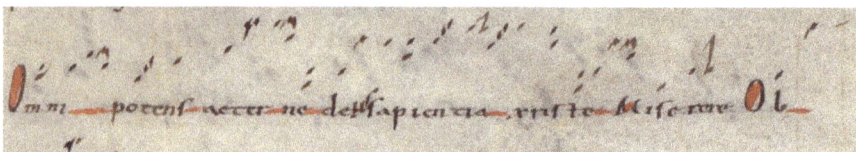

2.3 Paris, BnF, n.a. lat. 1871, fol. 55 *verso*:

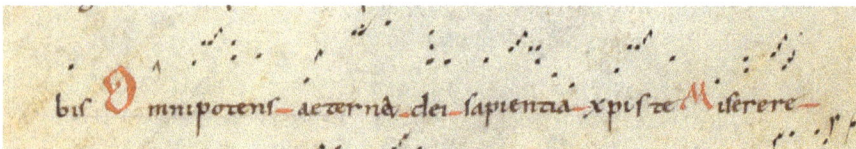

2.4 Paris, BnF, lat. 10508, fol. 126 *verso*:

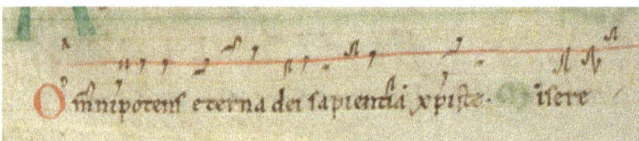

melodies themselves. And these continued to be written, even with newly composed tropes, into the sixteenth century.[27]

According to my own catalog of Sanctus and Agnus Dei melodies and tropes, based on the catalogs of Peter Josef Thannabaur[28] and Martin Schildbach[29] respectively, there are approximately 240 Sanctus tropes and 130 Agnus Dei tropes that were composed during the Middle Ages and early Renaissance. Gunilla Iversen's editions of Sanctus and Agnus Dei tropes contain 174 and 78 tropes respectively. That means that approximately 27 percent of the total repertoire of Sanctus tropes and 43 percent of Agnus tropes are not edited in *Corpus Troporum*, but will need to appear in my edition. This is a topic to which I shall return below.

Before proceeding further, I should perhaps now say something about the edition itself and its own history. As mentioned at the outset of this paper, Bruno Stäblein invited me to prepare an edition of the monophonic Sanctus and Agnus Dei for the series *Monumenta Monodica Medii Aevi*. That series was conceived by him as the counterpart to the great editions of polyphonic works edited under the general title of *Denkmäler* or "monuments" —*Denkmäler der Tonkunst in Österreich* and *Denkmäler deutscher Tonkunst* being two examples. One volume of tropes, those to the Introit, had been edited by Günther Weiss in *Monumenta monodica* volume 3 (1970), based exclusively on sources from Aquitaine.[30] I had just completed a dissertation on the earliest settings of the Agnus Dei and its tropes,[31] and Professor Stäblein thought it would be a relatively simple matter to edit both the Sanctus and Agnus Dei, since they often appear in manuscripts together. Of course, nothing about editing is simple, and certainly not editing a repertoire as diverse and problematic as the Sanctus and Agnus Dei, using manuscripts dating from the ninth through the sixteenth centuries.

My initial plan was to transcribe each of the melodies whose incipits appeared in Thannabaur's and Schildbach's catalogs, using the same sources from which the two earlier scholars had transcribed incipits. This would have involved transcribing the melodies from a colorful array of manuscripts, but without placing them in any specific liturgical context. It would also have meant transcribing one melody for each trope that appeared in manuscript together with the base melody that had already been catalogued —but it would also have meant that many of the tropes not appearing with those melodies in their manuscript sources would not have been edited at all. When I started collating sources for the tropes by themselves, the question became one of relating the tropes to their base melodies. Since some melodies can appear with a fairly large number of tropes, should one include the base melody along with every trope that appears with it? This is partly a philosophical question, but it is also a practical question of size.

The presentation of a printed version of a piece of music takes considerably more space than does the presentation of its text alone. Even the transcription of an Agnus Dei melody with a set of almost syllabic trope elements takes substantially more space on a printed page than would the transcription of the texts of the base chant and trope texts by themselves. We shall see evidence of this in the following examples.

Another problem that is raised by the musical settings of trope texts is that there can be several different melodies for a given text. Let me use as an example one of the trope sets that Gunilla Iversen used in her earlier article, the trope set "Omnipotens aeterna Dei." It may well be the best known of all tropes to the Agnus Dei, since it appears as the first in the series of such tropes in volume 47 of *Analecta Hymnica Medii Aevi*. I have provided the set as it appears in *Corpus Troporum IV* in Example 1 above. As one can see there, the text itself presents a number of questions, starting with the very first line. Is it *Omnipotens aeterna Dei* or *Omnipotens aeterne Dei*? Obviously, Iversen decided in favor of *aeterna*, modifying *sapientia*, but a large number of manuscripts read *aeterne*, modifying *Christe*.

The musical settings of this set of tropes add an additional layer — or perhaps several layers— of complexity to the task of preparing an edition. These problems arise in part because this trope complex appears with five different Agnus Dei melodies, numbers 64, 78, 119, 226, and 253 in Martin Schildbach's catalog. Even when a given trope verse or set of verses appears with a single melody, its melodic settings can differ somewhat among themselves. When a different base melody is involved, as is the case here, one can —and very often does— have different trope melodies as well. One can see this in Examples 3 and 4 below. As we shall discover, there are three different melodic traditions for the trope complex *Omnipotens aeterna*, one for melody 78, which we saw in Example 2 above, another for melodies 64, 119, and 253, and yet another for Melody 226. Let us take a closer look.[32]

Example 3 presents the first invocations of the Agnus Dei melodies associated with *Omnipotens aeterna dei* as presented in Schildbach's catalogue.

Example 3. Melodies with which *Omnipotens aeterna dei / Verum subsistens / Optima perpetuae* appears (melody numbers from Martin Schildbach, *Das einstimmige Agnus Dei und seine handschriftliche Überlieferung vom 10. bis zum 16. Jahrhundert* [Erlangen: Josef Hogl, 1967]):

3.1 Melody 78: Rome, Biblioteca Casanatense, 1741, fol. 42:

A - gnus___ de - i__ qui___ tol - lis__ pec - ca - ta__

mun - di. Mi - se - re - re___ no - bis.

3.2 Melody 119: London, British Library, Royal 2 B. IV, fol. 196v:

3.3 Melody 64: Paris, BnF, lat. 779, fol. 42:

3.4 Melody 253: Assisi, Biblioteca comunale, 695, fol. 52:

3.5 Melody 226: Apt, Archives de la Basilique Saint-Anne, 17, p. 327:

As one sees in Example 3, Melody 64 is a melismatic setting of the text, with a final on *D* and a range extending from the subfinalis *C* to the *c* an octave higher. (I call this "melismatic" because it frequently has five or more notes, or "melismas," over a single syllable of text.) It appears most often untroped, but it can also be prefaced by the introductory tropes *Haec festa precelsa,* and *Pro cunctis deductus.*[33] Melody 78, the melody with which *Omnipotens aeterna dei* most often appears, is a more modest, neumatic setting of the liturgical text —"neumatic" because it typically has between one and five notes over a single syllable, and hence is a bit less ornate than a melismatic chant such as Melody 64. Melody 78 begins on *G*, and has a range from *D*, a fourth below, to *e* a fifth above the opening pitch. Its final is on *a*, a fact that caused Schildbach to make the remark that "the final *a* does not correspond to the modal structure of this melody."[34] Schildbach also provides a version of the melody transposed down to start on *C*, with a final on *D*, and extending from the *A* beneath the initial *C* to the *a* an octave above it.[35] Although he does not catalog it as such, this transposed version is actually his Melody 253.[36] I have argued elsewhere that this is most probably the original pitch-level of this melody, which was transposed up to *G*, Schildbach's Melody 78, and also to *F* with a *B-flat*, which is Schildbach's Melody 119.[37] All three versions of the melody appear with *Omnipotens aeterna dei* as an internal set of tropes. As we shall see below, the upward leap of a fifth that occurs on the first syllable of the word *peccata* in melodies 78, 119, and 253 is a striking gesture that is actually reflected in the melodic ductus of the versions of *Omnipotens aeterna* that are sung with these melodies.

Finally, the two tropers from Apt set *Omnipotens aeterna dei* with Schildbach's Melody 226, the most widespread of all Agnus Dei melodies.[38] Like Melody 253, although somewhat less ornate, it is a neumatic setting that has its final on *D*; its range, however, is narrower than the other melodies, extending only a sixth from the subfinalis *C* to the *a* a fifth above the final.

We have already seen several of the earliest settings of the first verse of the set *Omnipotens aeterna/Verum subsistens/Optima perpetue* in Example 2 above; all of these appear with Schildbach's melody 78 in their respective sources. Given that all the settings but the last one are notated without clefs, it is impossible to know whether those appearing with Melody 78 are to be sung starting on *G* or on the *C* below it. This ambiguity of pitch level is only reinforced by the early diastematic settings. For example, Paris, BnF, lat. 10508 (D in Example 2) places the melody on C, which would correspond to Melody 253, the transposed version of Melody 78; other diastematic sources, such as Biblioteca Casanatense 1741 (in Example 3 above), place it a fifth higher on G, corresponding to the pitch level of Schildbach's Melody 78 itself.

Example 4 shows a sample of my collations of all three of the verses of *Omnipotens aeterna/Verum subsistens/Optima perpetue* as they appear with melodies 78 (on G), 119 (on F), 64 and 253 (on C), and 226 (starting on D) —here Examples 4A–D respectively.

The collations for lines 4A and C, melodies 78 and 253, are only partial; there is a substantially larger number of sources for this version of the trope than for the other two. What one sees at the top of each system of the example is a transcription from a reliably diastematic source —or at least as reliable a source as I could find. Beneath each of the transcriptions in 4A and 4C are my collations. In the cases of manuscripts with good heighting of neumes, but no clefs —here Paris, BnF, n.a. lat. 1871 and BnF, lat. 909— I chose to collate with Schildbach's Melody 78, as one can see in Example 4A. The exception to this decision is the setting in Apt 17. Since it appears with Melody 226, consistently pitched on D, I have transcribed it at that pitch level. The versions pitched on C are clearly indicated by clefs in their respective manuscripts.

In comparing the various versions in Example 4, one will notice that versions A and C are quite similar to each other in that the general melodic shape of the trope melody is fairly consistent, whether placed on C or G, and occurring with melodies 78, 64, or 253 as they appear in Example 4A and C. Example 4B, the version from London, BL, 2 B IV with Agnus Dei melody 119, has an incipit rather unlike the other two, but once it reaches the interval of a fourth above the initial pitch —on the syllables *-potens* of *omnipotens*— it continues in a manner very close to 4A and especially 4C. Particularly striking in all three settings 4A–C is the upward leap of a fifth on the first syllable of the word *Optima* that begins the third verse. This corresponds to the same leap that occurs in the melodies 78, 119, and 253 on the first syllable of the word *peccata* in the phrase *peccata mundi*, which I pointed out above in Example 3. Although it does not have a leap of a fifth on *peccata*, Melody 64 begins by traversing that same interval moving downwards.

The melodic kinship of the base melodies 78, 119, 64, and 253 and those of the trope verses set with them is clearly strong. One can say the same thing about the very different version of the trope in Apt 17, which sets the verses of *Omnipotens aeterna/Verum subsistens/Optima*

Example 4. *Omnipotens aeterna Dei* at 4 different pitch levels:

A (AD 78):

B (AD 119)
(Lo 2 B IV):

C (AD 64 & 253):

D (AD 226):
(Apt 17)

Example 4 (cont.). *Verum subsistens* at 4 different pitch levels:

A (AD 78):

B (AD 119)
(Lo 2 B IV):

C (AD 64 & 253):

D (AD 226):
(Apt 17)

Example 4 (cont.). *Optima perpetuae* at 4 different pitch levels:

A (AD 78):

B (AD 119)
(Lo 2 B IV):

C (AD 64 & 253):

D (AD 226):
(Apt 17)

perpetue with base melody 226. One can see Apt's setting of Melody 226 in Example 3 and the trope verses in Example 4D. As mentioned above, melody 226 moves only within the range of a sixth, *C* to *a*, rather than the more expansive range of an octave or a ninth of the other base melodies. And as one might expect, the trope melody moves only within this same range, hovering around the opening pitch for the first three words of the text before moving upward to *a* on the word *sapientia*.

The principal question raised by these versions is which ones to print in an edition, and according to what criteria. Were these to appear in an edition for *Monumenta Monodica* I would present one representative from each of the four versions presented in Example 4. Those from London, BL, 2 B IV and Apt 17 would be easy to justify, since they are each the only examples of their types —London, BL, 2 B IV because it appears with Schildbach's Melody 119 and Apt 17 because it is a unique melodic setting of the verses that appears with Melody 226. The others would not be quite so straightforward. Despite wanting to include a version from Aquitaine that was sung with Melody 78, I would feel compelled to use Rome, Casanatense 1741 as representative of those settings. This is because 1) the versions from Aquitaine might not actually have been sung with this melody and 2) because with *aeterne* instead of *aeterna* in the first verse, they are not as close to the text Gunilla Iversen established for this trope in *Corpus Troporum* IV. A similar rationale might lead me to choose Paris, BnF, lat. 10508 over Paris, BnF, lat. 1177 for the version in Example 4C, pitched on C. It has *perpetuae* in the third verse, modifying *vitae*; the other sources have *perpetua*, modifying *gaudia*. One could justify either choice, perhaps, but I would concur with Iversen on *perpetuae* as the preferred reading. Pa 10508 also has the slightly better *Optima* as the first word in this verse, as opposed to the *Obtima* in Paris, BnF, lat. 1177. In the final analysis, though, I would probably choose to present the version in Paris, BnF, lat. 1177 in the edition for the sake of completeness: it is the only setting of *Omnipotens aeterna dei* that also includes the verse *Rex regum, gaudium angelorum, Christe*.[39]

The musical edition in *Corpus monodicum*

The reader will have noticed that I have been using the subjunctive mood in my discussion of *Omnipotens aeterna dei*. This is because for various reasons my edition of Sanctus and Agnus Dei melodies with their tropes will not be appearing in the series *Monumenta Monodica Medii Aevi* after all. Instead, as mentioned above, it will be appearing in a new series conceived as the successor to *Monumenta Monodica*, namely the *Corpus monodicum*, the Project Director and Editor-in-Chief of which is Andreas Haug of the Universität Würzburg. Funded by a major grant from the Union of the German Academies of Science, *Corpus monodicum* has as its goal the edition of previously unedited repertoires of sacred medieval monophony.[40] Since one of the major repertories of sacred monophony that has not yet received a comprehensive edition of its music is the Ordinary of the mass, it made sense to place the edition of the Sanctus and Agnus Dei with their tropes in this new series and edit them together with both troped and untroped Kyrie and Gloria settings. I am delighted to report that Gunilla Iversen will be working with us on the texts of the tropes, insuring that the editions of the texts will be at the very highest level.[41]

The situation we have just seen and discussed with regard to one complex of tropes to the Agnus Dei is characteristic of the situation that obtains in the repertoire of Sanctus and Agnus Dei tropes as a whole. Hence, when Andreas Haug and I started to discuss how best to edit these trope complexes in the edition for *Corpus monodicum*, this was one of the foremost questions. My first thought was that we could give a representative version of each melodic tradition, in the manner just discussed, and provide information as to both textual and melodic variants in the critical apparatus. In order to test the viability of this approach, I collated all the manuscript settings of the Sanctus trope *Admirabilis splendor*, which is the very first in Gunilla Iversen's edition in *Corpus Troporum* VII and no. 4 in the catalog of tropes prepared by Peter Josef Thannabaur. One sees the tip of the iceberg in Example 5 below.

I have provided in Example 5 representative transcriptions of each of the three melodic versions of the trope, together with the Sanctus melodies with which they appear in their respective sources.

As one can see here, the three versions are quite different. The version with melody 111 (Example 5A) has the word *Admirabilis* beginning with an ascending *F*-major triad. The one with melody 74 (Example 5B) has the same word hovering around the pitch *G* until the melisma on the final syllable. The setting with melody 49 (Example 5C) is much more active than the other two, setting each syllable with 3- or 4-note neumes.[42] The textual edition and critical apparatus for both text and music of this trope complex take up 6 single-spaced pages, using a 12-point type font. If one adds the actual transcriptions of the three pieces, one has nine manuscript pages of material for this single trope. Multiply the 9 pages that this one complex requires by the 174 tropes that Gunilla Iversen includes in her edition, or the more than 300 Sanctus tropes that Thannabaur has catalogued —and that I plan to include in my edition— and one realizes that an entire forest of trees would have to be felled in order to provide enough paper! If the apparatus provided the kind of information that a scholar or performer could easily use to reconstruct the versions of the trope melodies as they appear in specific manuscripts, then 2,700 or so pages of manuscript would not

Example 5. The Sanctus trope *Admirabilis splendor* in its three different melodic versions, with Sanctus melodies 111 (A), 74 (B), and 49 (C).

A Madrid, Biblioteca Nacional, 19421, fol. 90:

B Benevento, Biblioteca capitolare, VI. 34, fol.20:

C Paris, BnF, n.a. lat. 3126, fol. 75v:

San - ctus. Ad - mi - ra - bi - lis splen - dor____ in -

es - ti - ma - bi - lis - que_____ lux_____ pa - ter

de - - us. San - ctus____ , Ver-bum_____

quod __ e - rat in prin - ci - pi - o____ a - pud __

be unreasonable. In our view, however, this method of presenting tropes and their variant readings seemed overly cumbersome, to the point of being unwieldy. Andreas Haug and I, along with other members of the team working on *Corpus monodicum*, have therefore decided to take a different approach.

We felt that it would best serve the needs of both performers and scholars to present editions of texts with their melodies as they appear in specific manuscripts representing specific geographical areas and liturgical traditions —i.e., an edition based on manuscript sources, not on genres of chant. A provisional list of sources grouped according to these criteria, appears as Example 6.

As one can see in Example 6, we are in essence following the same groupings as does *Corpus Troporum*. Each group of manuscripts will be divided into two subgroups: primary and secondary. Following procedures already established for the other five repertoires being edited in *Corpus monodicum*, we plan to present not just the settings of the Sanctus and Agnus Dei, but rather the complete corpus of Ordinary chants —Kyrie, Gloria, Sanctus, Agnus Dei— from each of the primary manuscripts in the order in which they appear in that source, complete with rubrics and cross references. Each individual chant will have its own "critical apparatus," but as Iversen suggested in "Problems in the Editing of Tropes," the reading in any given manuscript will be maintained "as long as there is the slightest possibility of making sense out of it."[43] Ordinary chants that do not appear in the primary sources

Example 6. Provisional list of core manuscripts for the *Corpus monodicum* edition of melodies of the Ordinary of the Mass with their tropes:

EAST

Aachen, Stiftsbibliothek der Münsterkirche, XII (12) (Gatzweiler-Kat. 13) (Rheinland)

Engelberg, Stiftsbitliothek, 314

Innichen, Stiftsbibliothek, VII a 7 (Austrian Benedictine)

München, Universitätsbibliothek, 2° 156 (Moosburg)

Prague, Metropolitankapitel St. Veit, Cim 4 (Prague)

St. Gallen, Stiftsbibliothek, 546 (St. Gall; Collectaneum, Frater Joachim Cuontz, 1507)

Wien, Österreichische Nationalbibliothek, 15501 (Kuttenberg, Böhmen)

NORTHERN FRANCE AND ENGLAND

Assisi, Biblioteca comunale, 695 (Reims/Paris)

Durham, University Library, Cosin V. II. 6 (England, non-Sarum)

London, British Library, Royal 2 B IV (St. Albans; non-Sarum; cf. Durham 6)

Madrid, Biblioteca Nacional, 289 (Palermo, Capella Palat.; Norman-Sicilian)

Madrid, Biblioteca Nacional, 19421 (Catania, Santa Agatha; Norman-Sicilian)

Paris, Bibliothèque de l'Arsenal, 135 (London ? Canterbury ?)

Paris, Bibliothèque nationale de France, n.a. lat. 1235 (Nevers)

SOUTHWEST

Apt, Archives de la Basilique Sainte-Anne, 17 (Apt)

Paris, Bibliothèque nationale de France, 3719 (Limoges)

Paris, Bibliothèque nationale de France, 778 (Narbonne)

Paris, Bibliothèque nationale de France, 909 (St. Martial – Adémar de Chabannes)

Huesca, Biblioteca de la Catedral, 4 (San Juan de la Peña)

Tortosa, Biblioteca del Cabildo de la Santa Iglesia Catedral, 135 (Tortosa)

NORTHERN AND CENTRAL ITALY

Bologna, Conservatorio Musicale G.B. Martini, Q 7 (north/central Italy)

Cividale, Museo archeologico, LXXIX (Aquileia; cf. Görz J)

Modena, Biblioteca Capitolare, 7 (Forlimpopoli)

Padova, Biblioteca Capitolare, 20 (Padova)

Pistoia / de Zayas, Biblioteca Capitolare, 121 (Pistoia)

Torino, Biblioteca Nazionale, F. IV. 18 (Bobbio)

SOUTHERN ITALY (Sanctus already in *BTC*; Agnus Dei, Kyrie, Gloria not)

Benevento, Bibl. capitolare, VI 34 (Benevento)

Benevento, Bibl. capitolare, VI 35, (Benevento)

Geneva, Bodmer GeB 74 (Rome, Sta. Cecilia in Trastevere)

Rome, Biblioteca Apostolica Vaticana, Urb. 602 (Montecassino)

---

from a given geographical area will be edited in their entirety from the secondary sources of that group; melodies that have already appeared in one or more of the primary sources will be given only via cross reference. Should there be items of the Ordinary sung in a given geographical area that do not appear in either the primary or secondary sources for that area, we shall edit them individually as they appear in other manuscripts from the same region.[44] The trade-off here (as it would have been in the edition for *Monumenta Monodica* as well) is that this edition cannot pretend to be a "complete critical edition," in the sense that the editions of the texts in *Corpus Troporum* certainly are. Our hope, however, is that even if it cannot present a picture of **all** the versions that were sung in a given tradition, it can at least provide a representative sample.

The way individual pieces might look in this edition can be gathered by considering the presentation of two versions of the Sanctus prosula *Clangat hodie vox nostra,* which appears with two different Sanctus melodies in manuscripts from two different geographical regions: one from the "Southwest" and the other from "Northern France and England" in the groupings given in Example 6. (See Examples 7 through 10):[45]

Example 7. Manuscript sources for *Clangat hodie vox nostra* (from "The Other Modus: on the Theory and Practice of Intervals in the Eleventh and Twelfth Centuries", in *The Study of Medieval Chant: Paths and Bridges, East and West, in Honor of Kenneth Levy,* ed. Peter Jeffery [Woodbridge, Suffolk, 2001]: 250):

Version I:

Manuscript	Provenance	Date	Sanctus	Rubric
Paris, BN, n. a. lat. 1871,	Moissac	s. XI/2	190	[no prose]
Paris, BN, n. a. lat. 1177, fo. 7v	Moissac	x. XI/2	[190]	
Madrid, Acad. de la Historia, 51, fo. 246	S. Millàn de la Cogolla	s. XI/2	190	PROSA
Huesca, Bibl. de la Catedral, 4, fo. 145–45v	San Juan de la Peña	s. XII	190	
Vic, Museo Episcopal, MS. 106, fo. 14–14v	Vic	s. XII/XIII	190	
Montpellier, Bibl. mun., MS 20,	Aquitaine	s. XIV	190	PASCHALE

Version II:

Manuscript	Provenance	Date	Sanctus	Rubric
Paris, BN, lat. 1139, fo. 74v	S. Martial	s. XI/2	112	
Madrid, Bibl. Nac., MS 289, fo. 95–95v	Norm. Sicily	s. XII	112	
Madrid, Bibl. Nac. 19421, fo. 88v-89	Norm. Sicily	s. XII	112	
Paris, BN, lat. 778, fo. 201–201v	Narbonne	s. XII/2	112	
Paris, Bibl. de l'Arsenal, 135, fo. 284	England	s. XIII/2	112	
Madrid, Bibl. Nac., MS M1361, fo. 192	Toledo	s. XIV	112	
El Escorial, Bibl. del Mon., J 17, fo. 344	N. Spain	s. XIV	112	
Burgos, Mon. de Las Huelgas, I, fo. 15–16	Las Huelgas	s. XIV	[112]	
Oxford, Bodl. Library, lat. lit b. 5	York	s. XV	[112?]	[De Omnibus Sanctis]
(=Summary Catalog no. 32940; *AH* 40:132)				

Example 8. Sanctus 190 with *Clangat hodie* (Version I : Huesca, Biblioteca de la Catedral, MS 4, fol. 145r-v):

: MS. cnmina
? MS. Quod

Examples 8 and 10 present two versions of *Clangat hodie*. Some readers will recognize it as a piece on which Gunilla Iversen and I have written complementary studies: she in "The Mirror of Music: symbol and reality in the text of *Clangat hodie*," and I in "Music and Meaning in *Clangat hodie*," both of which appeared in the Proceedings for the Madrid meeting of the International Musicological Society and its study group Cantus Planus in 1992.[46] Gunilla Iversen has also edited

Example 9. Text and Translation of *Clangat hodie:*

1a	Clangat hodie vox nostra melodum *simphonia,*	May our voice sound out today in a concord of melodies,
1b	Instant annua iam quia praeclara sollemnia.	for the brilliant annual feast is now here.
2a	Personet nunc tinnula *harmoniae organa* musicorum chorea.	May the ring of musicians now loudly make sound the clangorous instruments of *harmonia*
2b	*Tonorum* quam dulcia alternatim concrepet necne *modulamina!*	and in alternation make resound the modulations, so sweet, of the tones.
3a	*Diapason* altisona per *vocum discrimina tetracordis* figurarum alta conscendens culmina,	High-sounding at the octave, ascending in tetrachords through [seven] discrete pitches to the high summits of its contours,
3b	Substollat nostra *carmina* ad caeli fastigia, *hymnis* celestibus coherenda patri melodia,	may the melody lift our verses to heaven's pinnacles to join the angelic hymns for the Father,
4a	Quo nos mereamur ampla capere promissa,	So that we may merit to reach the rich promises,
4b	Sine fruituri meta sanctorum gloria,	to enjoy without end the glory of the saints,
5	Ad quorum collegia pia nos ducant merita	May our good works lead us to their community
	IN EXCELSIS	IN THE HIGHEST

the text of this prosula in *Corpus Troporum* VII.[47] The reader will see her edition of the text in Example 9, together with my translation.

Clangat hodie appears in some fifteen manuscripts dating from the eleventh through the fourteenth century. A list of these sources appears in Example 7. As one will see in that example, there are two versions of the piece. One, appearing in manuscripts from southwestern France and Spain, sets the text to an extended Osanna melisma for Sanctus 190 in Thannabauer's catalog of Sanctus melodies. A transcription of a representative setting of this version of *Clangat hodie,* taken from the twelfth-century manuscript Huesca, Biblioteca de la cathedral, codex 4, appears in Example 8.[48]

The second version of *Clangat hodie* appears in Example 10, transcribed from the twelfth-century Norman-Sicilian manuscript Madrid, Biblioteca Nacional 289.[49] This is the version one finds in

Example 10. Sanctus 112 with *Clangat hodie* (Version II: Madrid Biblioteca Nacional, MS 289, fol. 95r-v):

Sa - - - nctus. Sa - - - nctus. Sa - - - nctus

Do - - - mi - - nus de - us sa - - - ba - - oth.

Ple - ni sunt ce - - li et ter - ra glo - - ri - a tu - - a

O - - san - na _____ in ex - - cel - - sis

Be - ne - - dic - - tus qui ve - nit in no - - mi - ne do - mi - ni

O - - san - na.

Prosa: 1a. Clan - gat ho - di - e vox no - stra me - lo - dum sim - pho - - ni - u

1b. In - stant an - nu - a iam qui - a pre - cla - ra sol - lemp - ni - - a.

2a. Per - so - net nunc tin - nu - la ar - mo - ni - e or - ga - na mu - si - co - rum co - re - a

2b. To - no - rum quam dul - ci - a al - ter - na - tim con - cre - pe vo - ce mo - du - la - mi - na[1]

3a. Di - a - pa - son al - tis - so - na per vo - cum dis - cri - mi - na te - tra - cor - dis fi - gu - ra - rum al - ta con - scen - dens cul - mi - na

3b. Sus - tol - lat nos - tra car - mi - na ad ce - li fas - ti - gi - a hym - nis ce - les - ti - bus co - he - ren - da pa - tri me - lo - di - a

4a. Quo nos me - re - a - mur am - pla ca - pe - re pro - mis - sa.

4b. Si - ne 'flu - i - tu - ri[2] me - ta sanc - to - rum glo - ri - - a

5. Ad quo - rum col - le - gi - a pi - a[3] nos du - cant me - ri - ta in ex - cel - - sis

1 MS concrepet voce modulamine
2 MS futuri
3 MS quia

manuscripts from northern France and England, or what *Corpus Troporum* calls the "Northwest and Zone of Transition."

As one can see by comparing examples 8 and 10, the version in example 10 appears with a different Sanctus melody, melody 112 in Thannabauer's catalog. It is noteworthy that in its earliest settings, Melody 112 appears together with the prosula *Clangat hodie*, suggesting that this is a new composition of both text and melody.

I have posited elsewhere that this second version of the prosula with its associated Sanctus melody was newly composed in order better to reflect the meaning of the text, a text that is remarkable for the amount of musical imagery and terminology it contains.[50] That text, in Gunilla Iversen's edition and with my translation, appears in Example 9. With its references to *simphonia, organum, harmonia, tonorum modulamina, vocum discrimina, diapason* and *tetrachordum*, along with the more common *carmina* and *hymnus, Clangat hodie* stands almost alone in the Sanctus repertoire. Indeed, I know of no other Sanctus prose that makes such extensive and purposive use of technical musical terms.

The import of those terms is underscored by the use of the C mode for both Sanctus 112 and the prosula *Clangat hodie*. The C mode —or more accurately, the C scale— to which the text has now been set had first been discussed theoretically in the ninth-century *Scolica enchiriadis* and in the *De harmonica institutione* of Hucbald, in both cases being identified with instruments.[51] One cannot help but wonder whether there is any connection here with the *tinnula armonie organa* mentioned in line 2a of the prose. But there are yet other gestures that link this melody firmly with harmonic theory as presented on instruments: At the beginning of line 3b, the diapason really does ring out *altisona*, thanks to the octave leap that introduces it. This remarkable gesture had been prefigured by the octave leap between the end of line 1a and the beginning of 1b —introduced by the word *sinfonia*. In the Pythagorean mathematics underlying ancient Greek harmonic theory, the diapason, with its ratio of 2:1, was the most perfect *sinfonia*.[52] In his commentary on Martianus Capella, John Scottus even goes so far as to equate the diapason with *harmonia* itself.[53]

Moving further in line 3a of the prose, one finds that the diapason is reached *per vocum discrimina, tetrachordis...conscendens*. The first part of this phrase is of course a reference to the "seven discrete pitches" with which Orpheus plays in Book VI of the *Aeneid*.[54] The second part reminds us that these pitches are produced by a concatenation of tetrachords.[55] As if to render this scalar structure concretely, the melody for lines 3a and 3b of the prose divides into two disjunct tetrachordal strata (G-c, C-F) connected by the four-note figure on the word "tetrachordis." Underscoring this division even further is the fact that the upper tetrachord (G-c) is projected in stepwise motion at the beginning of lines 2a through 3b. Thus, the melody of *Clangat hodie* does indeed 'ascend in tetrachords through discrete pitches,' as the text says, and in a clear, yet subtle way.

I have discussed this piece in detail because it is one telling example —
among many that could be cited— of the importance of editing texts
with music. Some readers may know that in American musicological
circles in recent years there has been a tendency to denigrate the
preparation of editions as being old-fashioned, "positivist" musicology.
In her plenary lecture for the 1985 meeting of the four major American
musical societies, Margaret Bent pointed out that the making of editions
is an activity that demands not only a high level of philological skill, but
an equally high level of critical ability —precisely the kinds of skills that
have characterized the best musicology in the past and will continue to
do so in the future.[56] But there is even more to it than that.

In this paper I have focused mostly on the problems involved
with editing texts with music. They are indeed myriad —but not
insurmountable. And what they make possible, in a piece such as
Clangat hodie, is an example of *nuptiae bellae philologiae et musicae* —
a beautiful wedding of philology and music— that makes it possible to
bring these ancient texts to life in performance. Although performance is
not the only desired outcome of a scholarly edition, it is certainly one of
things that makes the preparation of editions of texts with music infinitely
fascinating and rewarding, and ultimately tremendously exciting.

Notes

1. *Monumenta Monodica Medii Aevi* (Kassel: Bärenreiter, 1956–). The series,
founded by Bruno Stäblein, began with his own edition, *Hymnen: I, Die
mittelalterlichen Hymnenmelodien des Abendlandes*.

2. The edition will now appear as part of *Abteilung I: Ordinariumsgesänge*,
in the series *Corpus monodicum, die einstimmige Musik des lateinischen
Mittelalters*, ed. Andreas Haug, published in Basel by Schwabe Verlag. Rather
than being an edition arranged according to genres, as was *Monumenta
Monodica, Corpus monodicum* is a *Quellen-Edition* ("source edition"), one
that presents repertoires as they appear in complete manuscripts. For more on
this, and its implications for my own edition, see below.

3. The Kyrie appears in two forms in the earliest manuscripts containing
it, both in melismatic versions exhibiting only the transliterated Greek text
(*Kyrie eleison* 3x, *Christe eleison* 3x, *Kyrie eleison* 3x), and in versions that
contain Latin texts underlaid to the same melismas in a syllabic fashion —one
syllable of text for every individual note of the melody. These latter are usually
referred to as "texted," "prosulated," (or "Kyrie with prosulae"), or simply
"Latin" Kyries. On this see Alejandro Planchart, 'Trope [ii] [a]', in *New Grove*

Dictionary of Music and Musicians, Revised Edition (London: Macmillan, 2002), v. 25, pp. 782–784; David Hiley, *Western Plainchant: A Handbook* (Oxford: Clarendon Press, 1993), pp. 209–213. There are also approximately 25 medieval Kyrie tropes (newly-composed texts with melodies added to the established chant text and its music; in the case of the Kyrie, the tropes can serve as introductions and also interpolations), which are catalogued and discussed by David Bjork in 'The Kyrie Trope', *JAMS*, 33 (1980), 1–41.

4. Charles M. Atkinson, *The Critical Nexus: Tone-System, Mode, and Notation in Early Medieval Music*, American Musicological Society Studies in Music 4 (Oxford/New York: Oxford University Press, 2009).

5. Since for most of its life this edition has been one of the Sanctus and Agnus Dei and their tropes and prosulae, I shall restrict myself to examples from those two chants of the Ordinary in the present discussion.

6. Gunilla Iversen, 'Problems in the Editing of Tropes', in *Text: Transactions of the Society for Textual Scholarship*, 1 (1981), ed. by D. C. Greetham and W. Speed Hill (New York: AMS Press, 1984), 95–132. The article began as a paper presented at the first meeting of the Society for Textual Scholarship in 1981.

7. Iversen, 'Problems', p. 95.

8. *Ibid.*, p. 96.

9. *Ibid.*

10. *Ibid.*, p. 97.

11. *Ibid.*

12. *Ibid.* In Iversen's words: "A text from Italy, for instance the Beneventan texts, or texts from Aquitania, often offer a very 'bad' Latin, while the tropes from Saint Gall are given in a very 'good' Latin with few 'unclassical' readings".

13. These are presented in Iversen, 'Problems', p. 97.

14. Notker identifies himself as the author of the *Liber hymnorum* in his famous Preface, see the ed. by Wolfram von den Steinen, *Notker der Dichter und seine geistige Welt* (Bern: A. Francke, 1948), vol. II, pp. 8–10. In his *Casus monasterii Sancti Galli* Ekkehard IV names Tuotilo of St Gall as the composer of several tropes (*Casus monasterii Sancti Galli*, ed. in MGH, *Scriptores*, ii, 1829, p. 101). The activities of Adémar de Chabannes as a composer of tropes, among other things, have recently been chronicled by James Grier in his book *The Musical World of a Medieval Monk: Adémar de Chabannes in Eleventh-Century Aquitaine* (Cambridge and New York: Cambridge University Press, 2006).

15. Iversen, 'Problems', p. 102.

16. *Ibid.*, p. 104.

17. Ed. Joseph Smits van Waesberghe, *Guidonis Aretini Prologus in Antiphonarium*, Divitiae Musicae Artis A.III (Buren: Frits Knuf, 1975) and in Dolores Pesce, *Guido d'Arezzo's Regulae rithmice, Prologus in antiphonarium, and Epistola ad Michahelem*, Wissenschaftliche Abhandlungen/ Musicological Studies 73 (Ottawa: Institute of Mediaeval Music, 1999), pp. 406–435. Pesce also provides a parallel translation into English; another translation into English may be found in Oliver Strunk, *Source Readings in Music History* (New York: W.W. Norton, 1950), pp. 117–120, and in its revised edition, ed. by Leo Treitler, transl. James McKinnon, *The Early Christian Period and the Latin Middle Ages* (New York: W.W. Norton, 1998), pp. 101–104.

18. Unless otherwise indicated, information as to provenance and date of all manuscripts discussed here, along with relevant bibliography, may be found in Gunilla Iversen, *Tropes du Sanctus*, Corpus Troporum VII, Acta Universitatis Stockholmiensis, Studia Latina Stockholmiensia, XXXIV (Stockholm: Almqvist & Wiksell International, 1990), pp. 53–60.

19. Gunilla Iversen, ed., *Tropes de l'Agnus Dei*, Corpus Troporum IV, Acta Universitatis Stockholmiensis, Studia Latina Stockholmiensia, XXVI (Stockholm: Almqvist & Wiksell International, 1980) and *Tropes du Sanctus*, Corpus Troporum VII (cited above).

20. Manuscript description from Beat Matthias von Scarpatetti, *Die Handschriften der Stiftsbibliothek St. Gallen*, Bd. 2: Abt. III/2: Codices 450–546, Liturgica, Libri precum, deutsche Gebetbücher, Spiritualia, Musikhandschriften 9.–16. Jahrhundert (Wiesbaden: Otto Harrassowitz, 2008), pp. 422–430. This description, along with a facsimile edition of the manuscript itself, is available on-line at the site *e-codices*.

21. These tropes are numbers 14* and 47* in Gunilla Iversen's edition, *Tropes de l'Agnus Dei*, CT IV.

22. The relevant passage in the canon of the Synod of Meaux appears in Gabriel Silagi, ed., *Liturgische Tropen: Referate zweier Colloquien des Corpus Troporum in München (1983) und Canterbury (1984)* (München: Arbeo Gesellschaft, 1985), vii.

23. On this, see Ritva Jonsson, *Tropes du propre de la messe, I: Cycle de Noël*, Corpus Troporum I, Studia Latina Stockholmiensia, XXI (Stockholm: Almqvist & Wiksell International, 1976), p. 18.

24. Iversen, *Tropes de l'Agnus Dei,* CT IV, p. 17.

25. Iversen, *Tropes du Sanctus*, CT VII, pp. 15 and 52.

26. Iversen, *Tropes du Gloria*, CT XII, vol. I, p. 67.

27. The principal source for editions of later tropes to the Ordinary is *Analecta hymnica Medii Aevi*, XLVII, *Tropi graduales: Tropen des Missale im Mittelalter, I: Tropen zum Ordinarium Missae*, ed. by Clemens Blume und Henry Marriott Bannister (New York: Johnson Reprint Corp., 1961/ reprint of ed. Leipzig, 1905).

28. Peter Josef Thannabaur, *Das einstimmige Sanctus der römischen Messe in der handschriftlichen Überlieferung des 11. bis 16. Jahrhunderts* (München: W. Ricke, 1962).

29. Martin Schildbach, *Das einstimmige Agnus Dei und seine handschriftliche Überlieferung vom 10. bis zum 16. Jahrhundert* (Erlangen: Offsetdruck-Fotodruck J. Hogl, 1967).

30. Günther Weiss, *Introitus-Tropen I: Das Repertoire der südfranzösischen Tropare des 10. und 11. Jahrhunderts*, Monumenta Monodica Medii Aevi 3 (Kassel: Bärenreiter, c1970).

31. Charles M. Atkinson, *The Earliest Settings of the Agnus Dei and its Tropes* (Chapel Hill, N.C.: Unpublished Ph.D. dissertation, University of North Carolina at Chapel Hill, 1975).

32. In the discussion that follows I use letter names to indicate pitches. Gamma (Γ) is equivalent to the G on the first line of the staff in bass clef. A represents the note a second above that; *a* the note an octave higher; and *aa* the note yet another octave higher.

33. *Haec festa praecelsa* and *Pro cunctis deductus* are trope sets 27 and 49 in Iversen, *Tropes de l'Agnus Dei*, CT IV. For Melody 64 see Schildbach, *Agnus Dei*, p. 92.

34. Schildbach, *Agnus Dei*, p. 95.

35. *Ibid.*, p. 163.

36. *Ibid.*, p. 160.

37. Atkinson, *The Earliest Settings of the Agnus Dei and its Tropes*, pp. 199–205.

38. Cf. Schildbach, *Agnus Dei*, pp. 149–153.

39. Cf. Example 1 above, where Pa 1177 is the only source with the verse order ABCD.

40. For a description of the state of the project as of 2012, see *Union der deutschen Akademien der Wissenschaften, vertreten durch die Akademie der Wissenschaften und der Literatur, Mainz: Musikwissenschaftliche Editionen, JAHRESBERICHT 2012* (Mainz: Akademie der Wissenschaften und der Literatur, 2013), pp. 54–57. The project encompasses six repertoires: I) Ordinary Chants of the Mass, II) Tropes, III) Sequences, IV) Antiphons, V) Songs, VI) Plays.

41. It almost goes without saying that the availability of excellent editions of the texts of tropes to the Gloria, Sanctus, and Agnus Dei, all prepared by Gunilla Iversen for the series *Corpus troporum* (volumes XII, VII, and IV respectively), will be of great benefit to this new edition of the texts with music.

42. In Example 5, neumes of the original notation that comprise two or more notes have been transcribed under slurs. Single note-heads correspond to *puncta* in the original, neumatic notation.

43. Iversen, 'Problems', p. 104. Cf. n. 16 above and the text associated with it.

44. This will be the case, for example, with the rather large number of both melodies and tropes for the *Sanctus* and *Agnus Dei* that are unica, and do not appear in the manuscripts we have selected as primary or secondary sources for each of the regions and orders, as given in Example 6.

45. Examples 7–10 originally appeared in my article, 'The Other *Modus: On the Theory and Practice of Intervals in the 11th and 12th Centuries*', in *The Study of Medieval Chant: Paths and Bridges, East and West: In Honor of Kenneth Levy*, ed. by Peter Jeffery (London: Boydell, 2001), pp. 233–256. I wish to thank the publishers of that volume, Boydell Press, an imprint of Boydell & Brewer Ltd., for their permission to reproduce these examples here.

46. *Actas del XV Congreso de la Sociedad Internacional de Musicología (Madrid, 3–10/04/1992)* «*Culturas Musicales del Mediterráneo y sus Ramificaciones*», ed. by Ismael Fernández de la Cuesta and Alfonso de Vicente [=*Revista de Musicología*, 16, no. 2 (1995)]. Our essays appear on pp. 771–789 ('Mirror of Music') and 790–806 ('Music and Meaning') respectively.

47. Iversen, *Tropes du Sanctus*, CT VII, no. 16, pp. 82–84.

48. On this manuscript, see German Prado, 'El Kyrial espanol', *Analecta Sacra Tarraconensia*, 14 (1941), 97–128, and 15 (1941), 53ff., and Heinrich Husmann, *Tropen- und Sequenzenhandriften*, RISM, vol. V¹ (1964), p. 86. For further bibliography see Iversen, *Tropes du Sanctus*, CT VII, p. 59, n. 26.

49. On this manuscript, see David Hiley, 'Quanto c'è di normanno nei tropari siculo-normanni?', *Rivista Italiana di Musicologia*, 18 (1983), 3–28 (esp. pp. 6–7), and 'Ordinary of Mass Chants in English, North French and Sicilian Manuscripts', *Journal of the Plainsong and Mediaeval Music Society*, 9/1 (1986), p. 6.

50. Atkinson, 'Music and Meaning in *Clangat hodie*', in *Actas del XV Congreso de la Sociedad Internacional de Musicología (Madrid, 3–10/04/1992)*, pp. 790–806; '*Ars musica* as *Ars cantica* in a Twelfth-Century Prose', in *Words and Music: Proceedings of the Seventeenth Annual Acta Conference, Center for Medieval and Early Renaissance Studies at the State University of New York at Binghamton, 30–31 March 1989*, ed. Paul Laird (Binghamton: State University of New York Press, 1993), pp. 1–30; and 'The Other *Modus: On the*

Theory and Practice of Intervals in the 11th and 12th Centuries', in *The Study of Medieval Chant*, ed. by Peter Jeffery, pp. 233–256.

51. For the description in the *Scolica enchiriadis* see Hans Schmid, ed., *Musica et scolica enchiriadis una cum aliquibus tractatulis adiunctis,* Veröffentlichungen der musikhistorischen Kommission, 3 (München: Bayerische Akademie der Wissenschaften, 1981), pp. 142–148; Engl. transl. in Raymond Erickson, *Musica and Scolica enchiriadis*, Music Theory Translation Series, ed. by Claude Palisca (New Haven & London: Yale University Press, 1995), pp. 86–89. For that in Hucbald, *De harmonice institutione*, see Yves Chartier, ed., *L'œuvre musical d'Hucbald de Saint-Amand,* Cahiers d'Études médiévales, Cahier spécial no. 5 (n.p.: Bellarmin, 1995), pp. 164–167; Martin Gerbert, ed., *Scriptores ecclesiastici de musica sacra potissimum* (Milan: Bollettino bibliografico musicale, 1931), vol. I, p. 110; Engl. transl. in Warren Babb, *Hucbald, Guido, and John on Music*, Music Theory Translation Series, ed. by Claude Palisca (New Haven & London: Yale University Press, 1978), pp. 24–25.

52. Cf. Anicius Manlius Severinus Boethius, *De institutione musica* I: 32, ed. Gottfried Friedlein, *De institutione arithmetica libri duo, De institutione musica libri quinque* (Leipzig: Teubner, 1867), 222; Engl. transl. in Calvin Bower, *Anicius Manlius Severinus Boethius: Fundamentals of Music*, Music Theory Translation Series, ed. by Claude Palisca (New Haven & London: Yale University Press, 1989), p. 49.

53. See *Iohannis Scotti Annotationes in Marcianum*, Cora Lutz, ed. (Cambridge, Mass.: Medieval Academy of America, 1939). In commenting upon the lemma 10, 22 [11]: MIRA SPECTACULA FORTUNATUM, John states: "si extremi soni sibi invicem ex dupla proportione iungantur, ut sunt duo ad unum, *diapason armoniam*, quae in simplicibus simphoniis maxima est effitiunt" (my italics).

54. *Aeneid*, Bk. 6, lines 645–646: "Nec non Threïcius longa cum veste sacerdos / obloquitur numeris septem discrimina vocum."

55. The ancient Greek Greater Perfect System, transmitted into the medieval Latin West by Boethius, consists of two pairs of conjunct tetrachords separated in the middle by a point of disjunction.

56. Margaret Bent, 'Fact and Value in Contemporary Musical Scholarship', in *The Musical Times,* 127 (1986), 85–89. Also printed in *CMS Proceedings: The National and Regional Meetings, 1985,* ed. by William E. Melin, 3–9 (Boulder, Colorado: College Music Society, 1986), pp. 1–7.

Bibliography

Analecta hymnica Medii Aevi, XLVII, *Tropi graduales: Tropen des Missale im Mittelalter, I: Tropen zum Ordinarium Missae*, ed. by Clemens Blume and Henry Marriott Bannister (New York: Johnson Reprint Corp., 1961/ reprint of ed. Leipzig, 1905)

Atkinson, Charles M., 'Ars musica as Ars cantica in a Twelfth-Century Prose', in Words and Music: Proceedings of the Seventeenth Annual Acta Conference, Center for Medieval and Early Renaissance Studies at the State University of New York at Binghamton, 30–31 March 1989, ed. Paul Laird (Binghamton: State University of New York Press, 1993), pp. 1–30

Atkinson, Charles M., The Earliest Settings of the Agnus Dei and its Tropes (Chapel Hill, N.C.: unpublished Ph.D. dissertation, University of North Carolina at Chapel Hill, 1975)

Atkinson, Charles M., The Critical Nexus: Tone-System, Mode, and Notation in Early Medieval Music, American Musicological Society Studies in Music, 6 (Oxford/New York: Oxford University Press, 2009)

Atkinson, Charles M., 'Music and Meaning in Clangat hodie', in Actas del XV Congreso de la Sociedad Internacional de Musicología (Madrid, 3–10/04/1992) «Culturas Musicales del Mediterráneo y sus Ramificaciones», ed. by Ismael Fernández de la Cuesta and Alfonso de Vicente [Revista de Musicología, 16, no. 2 (1995)], pp. 790–806

Atkinson, Charles M., 'The Other Modus: On the Theory and Practice of Intervals in the 11th and 12th Centuries', in The Study of Medieval Chant: Paths and Bridges, East and West: In Honor of Kenneth Levy, ed. by Peter Jeffery (London: Boydell, 2001), pp. 233–256

Babb, Warren, transl., Hucbald, Guido, and John on Music: Three Medieval Treatises, Music Theory Translation Series, ed. by Claude Palisca (New Haven & London: Yale University Press, 1978)

Bent, Margaret, 'Fact and Value in Contemporary Musical Scholarship', in The Musical Times 127 (1986), pp. 85–89. Also printed in CMS Proceedings: The National and Regional Meetings, 1985, ed. by William E. Melin, 3–9 (Boulder, Colorado: College Music Society, 1986), pp. 1–7

Bjork, David, 'The Kyrie Trope', Journal of the American Musicological Society, 33 (1980), 1–41

Bower, Calvin, transl., Anicius Manlius Severinus Boethius: Fundamentals of Music, Music Theory Translation Series, ed. by Claude Palisca (New Haven & London: Yale University Press, 1989)

Chartier, Yves, ed. and transl., L'œuvre musical d'Hucbald de Saint-Amand, Cahiers d'Études médiévales, Cahier spécial no. 5 (n.p.: Bellarmin, 1995)

Colette, Marie-Noël, and Gunilla Iversen, La Parole chantée, Temoins de notre histoire (Turnhout: Brepols, 2014)

Ekkehard IV, *Casus monasterii Sancti Galli*, MGH, *Scriptores*, ii (1829)

Erickson, Raymond, *Musica and Scolica enchiriadis*, Music Theory Translation Series, ed. by Claude Palisca (New Haven & London: Yale University Press, 1995)

Friedlein, Gottfried, ed., *De institutione arithmetica libri duo, De institutione musica libri quinque* (Leipzig: Teubner, 1867)

Gerbert, Martin, ed., *Scriptores ecclesiastici de musica sacra potissimum* (Milan: Bollettino bibliografico musicale, 1931)

Grier, James, *The Musical World of a Medieval Monk: Adémar de Chabannes in Eleventh-Century Aquitaine* (Cambridge and New York: Cambridge University Press, 2006)

Haug, Andreas, ed., *Corpus monodicum, die einstimmige Musik des lateinischen Mittelalters* (Basel: Schwabe Verlag, 2015–)

Hiley, David, 'Ordinary of Mass Chants in English, North French and Sicilian Manuscripts', *Journal of the Plainsong and Mediaeval Music Society*, 9/1 (1986), pp. 1–128

Hiley, David, 'Quanto c'è di normanno nei tropari siculo-normanni?', *Rivista Italiana di Musicologia*, 18 (1983), 3–28

Hiley, David, *Western Plainchant: A Handbook* (Oxford: Clarendon Press, 1993)

Husmann, Heinrich, *Tropen- und Sequenzenhandriften*, RISM, vol. V^{57} (1964)

Iversen, Gunilla, 'The Mirror of Music: Symbol and Reality in the Text of *Clangat hodie*', in *Actas del XV Congreso de la Sociedad Internacional de Musicología (Madrid, 3–10/04/1992) «Culturas Musicales del Mediterráneo y sus Ramificaciones»*, ed. by Ismael Fernández de la Cuesta and Alfonso de Vicente, [=*Revista de Musicología*, 16, no. 2 (1995)], pp. 771–789

Iversen, Gunilla, 'Problems in the Editing of Tropes', in *Text*: Transactions of the Society for Textual Scholarship 1: For 1981, ed. by D. C. Greetham and W. Speed Hill (New York: AMS Press, 1984), pp. 95–132

Iversen, Gunilla, *Tropes de l'Agnus Dei*, Corpus Troporum IV, Acta Universitatis Stockholmiensis, Studia Latina Stockholmiensia, XXVI (Stockholm: Almqvist & Wiksell International, 1980)

Iversen, Gunilla, *Tropes du Sanctus*, Corpus Troporum VII, Acta Universitatis Stockholmiensis, Studia Latina Stockholmiensia, XXXIV (Stockholm: Almqvist & Wiksell International, 1990)

Iversen, Gunilla, *Tropes du Gloria*, Corpus Troporum XII:1–2, Studia Latina Stockholmiensia, LXI (Stockholm: Stockholm University, 2014)

Jonsson, Ritva, *Tropes du propre de la messe, I: Cycle de Noël*, Corpus Troporum I, Studia Latina Stockholmiensia, XXI (Stockholm: Almqvist & Wiksell International, 1976)

Lutz, Cora, ed., *Iohannis Scotti Annotationes in Marcianum* (Cambridge, Mass.: Medieval Academy of America, 1939)

McKinnon, James, *The Early Christian Period and the Latin Middle Ages*, in *Source Readings in Music History*, ed. by Oliver Strunk, revised edn. by Leo Treitler (New York: W.W. Norton, 1998)

Monumenta Monodica Medii Aevi (Kassel: Bärenreiter, 1956–)

Pesce, Dolores, *Guido d'Arezzo's Regulae rithmice, Prologus in antiphonarium, and Epistola ad Michahelem*, Wissenschaftliche Abhandlungen/ Musicological Studies, 73 (Ottawa: Institute of Mediaeval Music, 1999)

Planchart, Alejandro, 'Trope [ii] [a]', in *New Grove Dictionary of Music and Musicians*, rev. edn. (London: Macmillan, 2002), vol. 25, pp. 782–784

Prado, German, 'El Kyrial espanol', *Analecta Sacra Tarraconensia*, 14 (1941), 97–128, and 15, (1942), 43–63

Scarpatetti, Beat Matthias von, *Die Handschriften der Stiftsbibliothek St. Gallen*, Bd. 2: Abt. III/2: Codices 450–546, Liturgica, Libri precum, deutsche Gebetbücher, Spiritualia, Musikhandschriften 9.–16. Jahrhundert (Wiesbaden: Otto Harrassowitz, 2008)

Schildbach, Martin, *Das einstimmige Agnus Dei und seine handschriftliche Überlieferung vom 10. bis zum 16. Jahrhundert* (Erlangen: Offsetdruck-Fotodruck J. Hogl, 1967)

Schmid, Hans, ed., *Musica et scolica enchiriadis una cum aliquibus tractatulis adiunctis*, Veröffentlichungen der musikhistorischen Kommission, 3 (München: Bayerische Akademie der Wissenschaften, 1981)

Silagi, Gabriel, ed., *Liturgische Tropen: Referate zweier Colloquien des Corpus Troporum in München (1983) und Canterbury (1984)* (München: Arbeo Gesellschaft, 1985)

Stäblein, Bruno, ed., *Hymnen: I, Die mittelalterlichen Hymnenmelodien des Abendlandes*, Monumenta Monodica Medii Aevi I (Kassel: Bärenreiter, 1956)

Steinen, Wolfram von den, *Notker der Dichter und seine geistige Welt* (Bern: A. Francke, 1948)

Strunk, Oliver, *Source Readings in Music History* (New York: W.W. Norton, 1950)

Thannabaur, Peter Josef, *Das einstimmige Sanctus der römischen Messe in der handschriftlichen Überlieferung des 11. bis 16. Jahrhunderts* (München: W. Ricke, 1962)

Union der deutschen Akademien der Wissenschaften, vertreten durch die Akademie der Wissenschaften und der Literatur, Mainz: Musikwissenschaftliche Editionen, Jahresbericht 2012 (Mainz: Akademie der Wissenschaften und der Literatur, 2013)

Waesberghe, Joseph Smits van, *Guidonis Aretini Prologus in Antiphonarium*, Divitiae Musicae Artis A.III (Buren: Frits Knuf, 1975)

Ars computistica ancilla artis editionum

Modern IT in the service of editors of (Greek) texts*

Charalambos Dendrinos and Philip Taylor
Royal Holloway, London, Great Britain

Almost two decades ago, a *Festschrift* was published in honour of the distinguished Hellenist, Byzantinist and Palaeographer, the late Robert Browning (1914–1997), whose work on Greek manuscripts and editions of Byzantine texts has left an indelible mark in our field. In his important article included in that volume, Professor Evangelos Chrysos

---

This lecture was given on 3 April 2014 at Stockholm University.

* This article was written with the cooperation of Philip Taylor for the technical part (see Part II). The work presented above is the result of close and fruitful collaboration. Grateful thanks are offered to the following institutions: the British Library for their co-operation and support in providing us with high-resolution digital images of the Royal MS 16 C X, and for their kind permission to reproduce them in our edition; the *Thesaurus Linguae Graecae® Digital Library Project* at the University of California, Irvine, the *Perseus Digital Library Project* at Tufts University, and *The Archimedes Digital Research Library Project*, a joint endeavour of the Classics Department at Harvard University, the Max Planck Institute for the History of Science (MPIWG) in Berlin, the English Department at the University of Missouri at Kansas City, and the aforementioned *Perseus Digital Library Project*, for their kind permission to link our edition with entries in their online Liddell-Scott-Jones, *Greek-English Lexicon* and Lewis and Short, *Latin Dictionary*. We are pleased to gratefully acknowledge the financial help we have received for this phase of the Project from the Hellenic Institute and the Faculty of Arts and Social Sciences Research Initiative Fund at Royal Holloway, University of London, and from a donor who wishes to remain anonymous.

Our deepest thanks go to the members of our team, whose dedication, enthusiasm and hard work on both scholarly and technical aspects made the timely completion of this project possible: Dr Annaclara Cataldi Palau, Michalis Konstantinou-Rizos, Dr Konstantinos Palaiologos, Dr Vasos Pasiourtides, Rob Turner, and Dr Christopher Wright. We would also like to express our warmest thanks to Dr Scot McKendrick, Head of History and Classics at the British Library, for his co-operation and scholarly contribution, and to Professor Caroline Macé for her co-operation and support in the preliminary phase of the project.

How to cite this book chapter:
Dendrinos, C. and Taylor, P. 2016. *Ars computistica ancilla artis editionum*: Modern IT in the service of editors of (Greek) texts. In: Crostini, B., Iversen, G. and Jensen, B. M. (eds.) *Ars Edendi Lecture Series, vol. IV*. Pp. 85–116. Stockholm: Stockholm University Press. DOI: http://dx.doi.org/10.16993/baj.e. License: CC-BY 4.0

reflected on the use of Information Technology as an educational and research tool in Byzantine Studies from the beginning of computing applications up to that point in time.[1] Describing the response by the scholarly community to the use of computers at that early stage, he distinguished various attitudes, ranging from the 'virgin's stance', reflecting fear and suspicion towards technological tools, considered unsuitable for traditional, serious scholarship; the 'Sisyphus syndrome', describing a sense of *impasse* in the endless struggle to reconcile incompatible hardware and software technologies; the 'Eleusinian syndrome', shared among the devotees of a close circle of scholars, whose expertise in informatics elevated them to the status of 'initiators to modern mysteries'; to the 'grab's motion', representing those who felt that only slowly perhaps some software applications could eventually be used in, or even created for, the humanities; the 'publish *in print* or perish' view, which degraded the production of electronic and multimedia applications and databases in terms of scholarly value; and finally, what Professor Chrysos called the 'Trithemius attitude'.

Trithemius is not an unfamiliar name to readers of the present Lecture Series. It was Professor Jan M. Ziolkowski who mentioned Johannes Trithemius (John of Trittenheim, 1462–1516) in his article included in the first volume of this Series.[2] Both Professor Chrysos and Professor Ziolkowski, among other scholars,[3] drew attention to Trithemius's treatise *De laude scriptorum manualium*, which he wrote in 1492, almost four decades after Johannes Gutenberg printed the Bible in Mainz (1454/5) using a movable-type press. In his treatise, the Benedictine abbot reflected on the spiritual and practical value of writing and copying for the monk as opposed to the production of the printed book. Ironically, the treatise does not survive in manuscript form but only in printed copies; it was first published in 1494, while a revised edition appeared in 1497.[4] As Professor Ziolkowski judiciously remarked, Trithemius's case is analogous to the 'posting online, or blogging, or tweeting [of a] stout defence of conventional publication' today. Trithemius eventually realised the potential benefits of typography for education and scholarship, and changed his mind, openly expressing his appreciation of printing, which he elevated to '*ars illa mirabilis & prius inaudita imprimendi & characterizandi libros*'.[5]

Trithemius is an enlightened guide for scholars who, though holding old-fashioned scholarship close to heart and mind, are prepared to make good use of the advantages of the rapid advances in technology for the pursuit of learning and teaching, combining tradition and innovation. Judging from the ever-increasing number of on-going projects in digital humanities being conducted at present, as if foreseeing the future Trithemius was entirely justified to include, among the major disciplines a monk ought to master, '*theologia, musica, iura et ars computistica*' (the latter actually in the sense of chronology).[6] Let us see how, in our case, the *ars computistica* (in its modern sense) can act as *bona ancilla* to the *ars editionum*. In other words, how modern Information Technology can help us in responding to the challenges of editing and publishing texts, especially mediaeval, and Greek in particular.[7]

At the invitation of Dr Antonia Giannouli (University of Cyprus) and Dr Elisabeth Schiffer (Austrian Academy of Sciences), a group of scholars met at the *International Workshop on Textual Criticism and Editorial Practice for Byzantine Texts* held in Vienna in December 2009. Among the various issues discussed were the progress of digital humanities and the potential benefits of online electronic editions, especially of autograph Greek texts, in terms of interactive presentation and wide dissemination.[8] The task of exploring the possibilities and limitations of such an approach was subsequently undertaken by a team of scholars, postgraduate students and technical advisors at the Hellenic Institute of Royal Holloway, University of London, in close collaboration with the British Library. It was suggested at the time that this edition should be presented to H.M. Queen Elizabeth II as part of the celebrations of her Diamond Jubilee. For this reason, the text selected combines a number of elements: it is unpublished, autograph and written in Greek, it survives in a unique manuscript in the Royal Collection in the British Library (MS 16 C X), and is related to the history of Hellenic Studies in Britain. In addition, it is dedicated to Queen Elizabeth II's distinguished homonymous predecessor, Queen Elizabeth I. What we had not anticipated at this early stage were the circumstances in which the edition would be finally presented to our Royal honorand, as we shall see.

   The text is an Encomium on King Henry VIII (1509–1547), addressed to his daughter Queen Elizabeth I (1558–1603) with the intention of presenting it to her on the occasion of her Royal Visit to Oxford in 1566. Another important manuscript related to this event is preserved in the Bodleian Library in Oxford, MS Bodley 13a, which gives a unique account of the famous buildings of the University, illustrated by a series of pen drawings by John Bereblock, Fellow of Exeter College.[9] Composed in Latin verse by Thomas Neale, Regius Professor of Hebrew, the account is presented in the form of a fictitious dialogue between Elizabeth and the Chancellor of the University, Robert Dudley, Earl of Leicester, who guides her on an imaginary tour around Oxford Colleges, and takes the opportunity to praise their founders for their generosity, thus encouraging the Queen to imitate them. Though Elizabeth was not persuaded to establish a College in Oxford, this manuscript gives us an insight into the workings of patronage and endowment in Elizabethan times.

A vivid description of the Royal Visit was also given by Penry Williams.[10] Among the representatives of the city and the university who gave a series of orations in honour of Elizabeth during the course of her stay at Oxford was Giles Lawrence (1522–1584/5), a native of Gloucester and Regius Professor of Greek at Oxford University (1551–1553 and 1559–1584/5). His oration, delivered to the Queen in Greek, received a short response by Elizabeth, also in Greek. Lawrence's oration, however, is not the text being edited here. The text chosen for editing is an oration that *would* have been delivered by George Etheridge, former Professor of Greek at Oxford (1547–1550 and 1553–1559), had he not been expelled from this post seven years earlier (1559).

George Etheridge was born in Thame, Oxfordshire, in 1519, and received his education at the University of Oxford.[11] He studied under John Shepreve at Corpus Christi (1534–1539). After he received his BA he was appointed a probationary Fellow and in 1541 his post was made permanent. A master of the three humanistic languages —Greek, Latin and Hebrew—, Etheridge published a number of works including a Greek translation of the second book of the *Aeneid*, a Latin translation of the works of Justin Martyr and a devotional text on Saint Demetrios. He also composed verses in Hebrew based on the Psalms, and in Greek on Thomas Wyatt's Protestant conspiracy and revolt against Mary I, clearly an attempt on Etheridge's part to win royal favour and revealing of his strong Catholic convictions. The last book Etheridge published, in 1588, is a Latin medical textbook based on Paul of Aegina. This work, which reflects his interest in medicine, is accompanied by an introduction in Greek and verses in Latin and Greek, where he expresses his appreciation to the learned physicians of Oxford for the help he had received from them and for their knowledge of Greek.

From an early stage of his academic life, Etheridge was involved in religious controversy. Though he was prepared to accept Henry's breach with Rome in order to secure his University post at the beginning of his career, with the advance of the Protestant Reformation he refused the return of the Royal Supremacy under Elizabeth, as did other scholars. His religious convictions led to his arrest and questioning in 1561. Expelled from his post, receiving no regular income and persecuted by the authorities, Etheridge composed his Encomium on Henry in an attempt to win Elizabeth's favour during her Royal Visit to Oxford (1566). Whether the Queen ever read this Encomium remains unknown. What is certain is that its purpose was never fulfilled, as Etheridge was not restored to his post.

The autograph Encomium is composed in blank verse, written in classical and primarily Homeric Greek which reflects the epic character of its subject, the heroic deeds and virtues of Henry. It is directly addressed to Elizabeth. In his preface, Etheridge praises the Queen's education and knowledge of Greek (ff. 1r-v). The preface is followed by a summary of its content in Latin (ff. 5r–6r). Apart from quotations from the *Iliad*, and to a lesser extent from the *Odyssey*, Etheridge alludes to the Platonic philosopher king (f. 20v), a most appropriate image of the ideal monarch, and Plutarch's *Life of Artaxerxes* (ff. 4r, 36v–37r). He also makes extensive use of Scriptural quotations, refers to Greek theological works of Justin Martyr (f. 31r), which he had translated into Latin, and lists other Church fathers including Cyprian, John Chrysostom, Basil of Caesarea and Gregory of Nazianzus (f. 19v).

The encomium devotes a large part to Henry's military achievements, including the two campaigns against the French, both of which he commanded in person (ff. 8v–13v). Henry is presented as the synthesis of the four Platonic virtues (courage, justice, prudence and wisdom) and the qualities of a peaceful ruler (including clemency, moderation and *philanthropia*) (ff. 8r-v, 22v–27r), which complement his martial prowess —themes typical of *Mirrors of Princes*. Remarks on Henry's preferment of obedience through reason and persuasion rather than fear (f. 15r) reflect Etheridge's concerns regarding his own situation. By stressing the value of education and commending Henry as a patron of academia and of the author himself —even mentioning what salary he used to receive as Regius Professor (f. 19r)— Etheridge serves his own aims and at the same time invites Elizabeth to continue her father's legacy promoting scholarship (ff. 18r–21r, 24r, 25r, 35v–37r).

In the latter part of the text, Etheridge appeals to Elizabeth, touching upon the sensitive issue of her succession, voicing the national concern relating to the security of the kingdom through an heir to the throne, thus confirming his own allegiance to her and her successors (ff. 28v–30r). [http://www.rhul.ac.uk/Hellenic-Institute/Research/Etheridge/Author-and-Text/Text.html - ftn39] He closes the encomium by exhorting Elizabeth to continue her father's legacy by supporting and promoting scholarship, and by acting mercifully towards him.

This short autograph rhetorical text adds to our knowledge of Greek Studies in Tudor England in general and of George Etheridge and Henry's cultural politics in particular. By editing this Encomium electronically, we aimed at offering a new resource to the academic community while at the same time providing a useful educational tool accessible also to the general public, free of charge. Although aware of existing work in the field, especially The Codex Sinaiticus Project at the British Library,[12] we opted to begin from scratch in order to explore the possibilities free from the constraints that would have been imposed by any attempt to replicate or perhaps just improve existing methods. In the process, we have been developing new ideas and techniques and addressing numerous questions, not all of which have yet found a satisfactory answer. Similarly, not all ideas and suggestions we have received from colleagues and students have been fully explored or applied. It is essential for the success of our project to continue developing, experimenting, sharing and inviting new approaches and practices concerning both conventional and electronic editing of texts.

Turning now to the technical aspects of our edition, the Encomium which forms the basis of this project, as mentioned above, survives in a unique autograph manuscript. This considerably simplifies some of the technical issues involved in its electronic presentation. In particular, we have not had to address the complications which would have arisen had we been forced to present more than one manuscript variant. The online edition quite deliberately makes use of only well-established and proven non-proprietary web technologies (HTML 4.01, CSS and JavaScript) and should therefore be accessible from any modern web browser; a "debug" option is provided to facilitate the reporting and diagnosis of any errors encountered.

In the opening web page we have placed (on the left-hand side) navigation aids that expand to allow access to the supplementary material and (on the right-hand side) the image of the first folio of the manuscript which gives access to the edition (Figure 1).[13] If we start by looking at the electronic edition of the manuscript, we see that the facsimile image of the manuscript is presented on the left-hand side of the screen, while on the right is displayed either the transcription of the text, or an edition of the text, with or without line numbers, and with different possible reflows. We also provide an English translation of the text.

The benefits of juxtaposing the digital images of the manuscript with the transcription and edition, and to a lesser extent with the translation, are, we believe, self-evident, and we take advantage of this parallel presentation by providing a two-way visual linking between a word or phrase in the manuscript and the corresponding word or phrase in the text. This technique is intended to help the user in interpreting the script, with its many ligatures and abbreviations. If we move the mouse cursor over any word in the image, both that word and the corresponding word in the facing text are highlighted in red, and if we move the mouse over any word in the text, exactly the same behaviour occurs. In the case of the translation, it is not possible to achieve this kind of precise word-for-word matching, as we have deliberately produced an idiomatic translation rather than simply translating mechanically on a word-to-word basis; the linking within the translation is therefore on a phrase-by-phrase basis.

In order to aid palaeographical training, we have opted for a diplomatic transcription exactly matching the style of script of the manuscript; so, for example, where letters or words have been written as superscript in the manuscript, this disposition is replicated in the transcription. An example can be seen at f. 4r, where we have the interlinear addition of the two words μᾶλλον μιμεῖσθαι on line 5. The fact that an electronic presentation enables us to offer different variants of the text alongside the facsimile means that we can emphasise this visual correspondence in the transcription, reserving normalisation of the text solely for the edition. However, in order to clarify the meaning of the text, we have intervened in the transcription by expanding abbreviations as, for example, in the case of the word καὶ in line 11, thus following normal editorial practice.

The edition is equipped with an *apparatus criticus* and an *apparatus fontium*. Words with *apparatus criticus* entries attached to them are identified by being displayed in a different colour; this colour is currently green, but we may change this in the future in order to improve access for those with red-green colour blindness. If we hover the mouse pointer over such a region for more than a moment, a small pop-out appears containing an editorial note. In line 2, for example, Etheridge has written the word ἡγοῦμαι with a smooth rather than a rough breathing, and the editorial emendation is glossed in the accompanying note. In the case of the *apparatus fontium*, we use a footnote-type mark. If we click on such a mark, it will cause the corresponding note to be displayed in the footnote area, while a second click will dismiss it. *Apparatus fontium* notes also accompany the translation, and can be displayed in exactly the same way.

In addition, the translation is accompanied by a commentary which sets out to elucidate the text, and this appears in a separate sequence of notes which are triggered in a similar manner. In f. ɪv, for example, we see a note (ᵃ) with information on Elizabeth I's education: she was taught by William Grindall and Roger Ascham, and her study of Greek texts included Sophocles and Isocrates as well as the Greek New Testament. According to Asham, Elizabeth spoke her Greek 'frequently, willingly and *moderately* well'!

Apart from these aspects, we try to assist the user in interpreting the text by supplying each word in the transcription and edition with a brief lexicographical analysis. If we click on any Greek word (for instance, παιδείας in f. ɪv, line 3) a note appears at the bottom of the page. This note shows the form in which the word appears in the text, parses it and also indicates its lemma form. In addition, it offers links to corresponding entries in three online dictionaries (Archimedes Lexicon, the online Liddell-Scott Jones Lexicon provided by Perseus, and the same lexicon from the *Thesaurus Linguae Graecae*), whose administrators have kindly allowed us to hot-link to their content in this way. A click on the link will display the entry on the left-hand side of the screen, temporarily overlaying the manuscript image. The latter two online dictionaries are themselves linked with the cited Greek texts, for those who wish to explore further.

In designing the infrastructure to support the electronic edition, we had a number of desiderata in mind; these, and the accompanying code fragments illustrating how they were accomplished, are presented here as succinctly as possible, as it is appreciated that these aspects of the project may be of interest to only a minority of readers of this volume. Nonetheless, we feel that the details *are* worth recording, as they may save others considerable time if they decide to attempt a similar project (see Appendix below).

Returning to the project as a whole, supplementary material is provided on the website to help to place the manuscript, the text and our edition in the wider context. This material includes an article by Dr Scot McKendrick on the Greek manuscript collections of the British Library, providing links to descriptions and digital images of a number of manuscripts they contain.[14] Dr Christopher Wright's articles on the

Author and the Text shed light on Etheridge's life, personality and work, and analyses and evaluates the Encomium.[15] The Royal MS 16 C X is described by Dr Annaclara Cataldi Palau, including links to specific folia and to other related manuscripts and sites.[16] A separate option gives access to the British Library Digitisation page, which includes a zoomable image of the manuscript.[17] Other options offer guidelines on how to use the edition,[18] a presentation of our editorial principles,[19] and implementation details for those who would like to know more about the technical aspects of the methods employed.[20]

We view this work very much as an on-going exploratory, interactive editorial project which, as with all such projects, has assumed a life of its own. Our hope is that in the future it will keep growing, developing and maturing, with the help of experts and non-experts alike, who will be willing to share their thoughts and work with us in order to help improve it further. It is just as important for us that members of the public are involved in this project, with the ability to offer their comments, ideas and suggestions on how to make this and similar editions more accessible, readable, useful and indeed more enjoyable, without compromising quality in terms of scholarship. For this reason, as mentioned above, we have provided a semi-automated feedback feature. In order to send feedback, all that is necessary is to highlight the word or phrase on which one wishes to comment, and click [Feedback]. The text is automatically copied into the appropriate field of the web form, so all one has to do is to add a comment and the commentator's e-mail address and click [Submit feedback] to send it to us.

The next step in our Project will be to convert the written text into the spoken word, completing a full circle from its inception, to its written composition, and to its oral delivery, something of which we hope that Etheridge himself might have approved. This aspect raises questions concerning pronunciation, which was a matter of considerable controversy in sixteenth-century English academia. At that time, the scholarly world was divided between the advocates of the traditional pronunciation of Greek, which is virtually the same pronunciation still used by Greeks today, and which was at that time associated with Catholic and conservative circles; and the advocates of the then-new 'Erasmian' system, which was adopted by the humanists and Protestant reformers and which became established in England with Elizabeth's accession to the throne in 1558.[21] Etheridge's own convictions, and internal evidence in the text (in particular, errors of *itacisms* and faulty breathings), suggest that he almost certainly used the traditional pronunciation, which, rather confusingly, is also called the 'modern' pronunciation.

Even when all issues of pronunciation have been resolved, to produce a synchronised recording of the text is not an easy task. The main reason for this is that it requires the automated determination of word boundaries in spoken Greek, something which we believe has never previously been attempted. However, with the advice, assistance and encouragement of Professors Jiahong Yuan and Mark Liberman (University of Pennsylvania), and Professor Amalia Arvaniti (University of Kent), we have made a successful start at this.[22] Looking to the future, a major step will be to experiment with the edition of a Greek text transmitted in more than one manuscript, which has so far proved a major challenge.

PART II

Desiderata (presentation)

- Simple and flexible navigation, with consistent placement and appearance of navigation aids
- Parallel presentation: MS facsimile left; text (edition, transcription or translation) right
- Interlinked highlighting: corresponding words (or phrases) highlighted simultaneously in MS facsimile and in text on mouseover
- Brief lexicographical analysis of word displayed in footnote area when word is clicked in text
- Lexicographical analyses linked to one or more external e-lexica for additional information
- E-lexicon content should temporarily overlay MS facsimile, and be dismissed by either [View MS] button or further click on lexicon link
- Existence of scholarly *apparatus* indicated by text colour (*apparatus criticus*) or superscript (*apparatus fontium, apparatus referentium, apparatus scholiarum*)
- Stretch of text to which scholarly *apparatus* applies indicated by underlining in text while *apparatus* is displayed
- Simple feedback mechanism that automatically embeds any highlighted text, together with current view state
- View state can be bookmarked (required for above)
- Optional line-numbering
- Vertically and horizontally centered display that gracefully accommodates varying degrees of zoom

Desiderata (technical)

- Standards-compliant code (Validated HTML 4.01 Strict, CSS 2/3, JavaScript)
- Browser independence: coded to perform as near as possible identically in all modern browsers
- Minimal markup (DOM analysis on page load, attributes added dynamically where possible)
- Use AJAX (XMLHttpRequest) wherever possible (i.e., other than cross-domain requests)
- Minimal dependence on libraries; no use of large libraries such as jQuery or similar

Desiderata (edition)

- Tri-state reflow: none, normal, full
- Editorial interventions (with concealed *apparatus criticus*) indicated by change of text colour (currently green)
- *Apparatus criticus* displayed as temporary boxed overlay ("tooltip") on mouseover of marked text
- Existence of *apparatus fontium* indicated by superscripted Arabic number, *apparatus* displayed in footnote area when callout clicked
- Existence of *apparatus referentium* indicated by superscripted lower-case Roman number, *apparatus* displayed in footnote area when callout clicked

Desiderata (translation)

- Simultaneous highlighting by phrase rather than by word
- Phrases that span folio boundaries set off by chevrons
- Existence of *apparatus fontium* indicated by superscript Arabic number, *apparatus* displayed in footnote area when callout clicked
- Existence of *apparatus referentium* indicated by superscript lower-case Roman number, *apparatus* displayed in footnote area when callout clicked
- Existence of commentaries ("*Apparatus scholia*") indicated by superscript lower-case letter, commentary displayed in footnote area when callout clicked

Desiderata (adjunct material)

- Uniform style of presentation, enforced by use of Macromedia Dreamweaver template
- "Accordion"-style menu with bi-stable expansion/contraction
- When jumping to a footnote, individual footnote should be discreetly highlighted to enable it to be easily identified, and a return from the footnote should be possible by clicking on the footnote itself rather than requiring, for example, the use of the browser "Back" button

The methods by which some of the more important of these aims were accomplished can be summarised as follows:

Simultaneous highlighting (image)

- The visible (sepia) MS facsimile is overlaid with a number of invisible identical red clones
- Each word in the transcription and edition is tagged with line- and word-number (in the translation, phrases are tagged)
- During DOM traversal, an "onmouseover" event handler is grafted onto each of these elements
- When the event handler fires, the rectangular region(s) in the hidden graphic overlays which correspond to the active line- and word-number (or active phrase) are revealed
- A subsequent "onmouseout" event restores the *status ante bellum*

The markup used to accomplish this is shown below. Note that the <B> elements, corresponding to words in the transcription and edition and to phrases in the translation, are not rendered in bold; the <B> element is (ab)used simply because its tag is as short as possible, consisting of a single letter, and the element is not otherwise needed (modern semantic markup uses <strong>).

Folio 1 recto (transcription)

```
<DIV id="Transcription" class="Transcription">
   <P>
      <SPAN>
         <B class="L2 W1" style="content: Ἐλισάβετ
         (dative)'">Ἐλισάβετ</B>,
         <B class="L2 W2">τοδὶ</B>
```

```
            <B class="L2 W3">τοὔνομα</B>
         </SPAN>
      </P>
      . . .
</DIV>
```

Folio 1 recto (translation)

```
   <DIV id="Translation" class="Translation f1r">
      <P>
         <B class="R1">To the most honoured and famous Elizabeth</B>,
         <B class="R2">First of that name</B>,
         <B class="R3">Queen of England, France, Ireland, etc</B>:
         <B class="R5">act rightly and prosper</B>!
         <B class="R4">George Etheridge, physician</B>.
      </P>
      . . .
</DIV>
```

Simultaneous highlighting (text)

- Each word in the MS facsimile is partitioned into a number of (possibly overlapping) rectangular areas
- Each area contains a part or the whole of exactly one word, and is tagged with line-, word- and region number
- Taken together, the set of areas constitutes an HTML <MAP> element
- During DOM traversal, an "onmouseover" event handler is associated with each area
- When the event handler fires, the word in the text that corresponds to the active line- and word-number has its current colour recorded, and its colour is then set to red
- A subsequent "onmouseout" event restores the *status ante bellum*.

The process can most easily be visualised by examining each of the four pairs of plates below:

Folio 1r, showing map areas

- (Figure 2) f1r.jpg
- (Figure 3) f1r-mapped.jpg

Fol. 1r (detail), showing map areas
- (Figure 4) f1r-detail.jpg
- (Figure 5) f1r-detail-mapped.jpg

Fol. 1r (detail), showing mask
- (Figure 6) f1r-detail-mask.jpg
- (Figure 7) f1r-detail-mapped-mask.jpg

Fol. 1r (detail), one word highlit
- (Figure 7) f1r-detail-mapped-mask.jpg
- (Figure 8) f1r-detail-highlit.jpg

Simultaneous highlighting (inter-linking of text and image)
- In addition to changing the colour of the corresponding word in the facing panel, an "onmouseover" event in the graphics pane changes the colour of the active word in the graphics pane using the same procedure as was outlined above in "Simultaneous highlighting (image)"
- In addition to changing the colour of the corresponding word in the facing panel, an "onmouseover" event in the text pane changes the colour of the active word in the text pane using the same procedure as was outlined above in "Simultaneous highlighting (text)"

The JavaScript which accomplishes this is as follows:

Mouse handler for text

```
Mouse.Active.Over.Text = function (Element)
    {
        Global.LastEvent = "Mouse.Over.Text"
        Element.onmouseout = function ()
            {
                Global.LastEvent = "Mouse.Out.Text"
                Conceal (Element)
                Restore (Element)
            }
        Highlight (Element)
        Disclose (Element)
    }
```

Mouse handlers for folio image

```
Mouse.Active.Over.Folio = function (Element)
    {
        Global.LastEvent = "Mouse.Over.Folio"
        Disclose (Element)
        Highlight (Element)
    }
Mouse.Active.Out.Folio = function (Element)
    {
        Global.LastEvent = "Mouse.Out.Folio"
        Restore (Element)
        Conceal (Element)
    }
```

Lexicographical analyses

- During initialisation, a lexicon (for the Greek) and a *dictionarium* (for the Latin) are read into internal data structures
- Each entry in these contains a headword, lexicographical analysis, and keywords that allow it to be looked up in external lexica
- During DOM traversal, an "onclick" handler is grafted onto each word in the text
- When the handler is invoked, a content-addressable search of the data structures is conducted, and the record returned is used to populate a region in the footnote area
- A further "onclick" on the same word conceals the entry in the footnote area, while an "onclick" on a different word causes the lexicographical information for that word to replace the former information.

External lexica

- When a lexicographical record is retrieved, HTML elements are wrapped around the external lexica components of the record to render them active and to associate an "onclick" handler with each
- In addition, the Unicode used internally is dynamically converted to Betacode for those external lexica that are still dependent on this encoding
- When the "onclick" handler is invoked, an attempt is made to retrieve the corresponding record from an external lexicon by

making the associated URL the "src" attribute of an <IFRAME> element contained within an otherwise concealed <DIV> that overlays the MS facsimile; this <DIV> is then made visible
- A further click on the link (or on the [View MS] button) renders the <DIV> invisible again, re-disclosing the MS facsimile

Apparatus criticus

- When the text for the edition of a folio is prepared, editorial emendations are wrapped in <SPAN class="*Apparatus criticus*"> elements
- During initialisation, an external file containing the *apparatus criticus* for the entire MS is read in and used to populate an internal data structure
- During DOM traversal, the <SPAN . . .> elements have an "onmouseover" handler associated with them
- When this handler is activated, the corresponding entry is retrieved using folio, face and *AC* ordinal as keys, HTML elements are interpolated, and the record is displayed as a tooltip using Erik Bosrup's "Overlib" library
- When the mouse leaves the region of the <SPAN . . .> element, the *status ante bellum* is restored

Markup and data for *apparatus* criticus

```
<P>
    <B class="L9 W1">Ἀμφοτέρων</B>
    <B class="L9 W2">ἕνεκα</B>,
    <B class="L9 W3">ὦ̃</B>
    <SPAN class="Apparatus criticus">
    <B class="L9 W4">ἐντιμοτάτη</B>
    </SPAN>
</P>
```

["foo1r", "AC-1", "<I>corr.: </I>ἐμφανέστατη<I> cod.</I>"],
["foo1r", "AC-2", "<I>corr.: </I>ἐντιμωτάτη<I> cod.</I>"], . . .

Apparatus fontium

- When the text for the edition of a folio is prepared, direct quotations from other authors are wrapped in <SPAN class="*Apparatus fontium*"> elements

- During initialisation, an external file containing the *apparatus fontium* for the entire MS is read in and used to populate an internal data structure
- During DOM traversal, the <SPAN ...> elements have a trailing superscript with associated "onclick" handler grafted on
- When this handler is activated, the corresponding entry is retrieved using folio, face and *AF* ordinal as keys, HTML elements are interpolated, and the record is displayed in the footnote area
- If the superscript is clicked a second time, the *status ante bellum* is restored

Markup and data for *apparatus fontium*

```
<P>
    <B class="L4 W1">Ἀρταξέρξῃ</B>
    <B class="L4 W2" style="content: 'τὸ (accusative)'">τὸ</B>
    <SPAN class="Apparatus fontium">
        <B class="L4 W3">μῆλον</B>
        <B class="L4 W4">ὑπερφυὲς</B>
        <B class="L4 W5">μεγέθει</B>
    </SPAN>
</P>
```

["f004r", "AF-1", "Author=Plutarch; Work=Life of Artaxerxes; Locus= IV:5"], . . .

Apparatus referentium

- When the text for the edition of a folio is prepared, references to works by other authors are wrapped in <SPAN class="*Apparatus referentium*"> elements
- During initialisation, an external file containing the *apparatus referentium* for the entire MS is read in and used to populate an internal data structure
- During DOM traversal, the <SPAN ...> elements have a trailing superscript with associated "onclick" handler grafted on
- When this handler is activated, the corresponding entry is retrieved using folio, face and *AR* ordinal as keys, HTML elements are interpolated, and the record is displayed in the footnote area
- If the superscript is clicked a second time, the *status ante bellum* is restored

Markup and data for *apparatus referentium*

```
<P>
    <SPAN class="App ref" style="content: 'Set: 1; parts: 2'">
        <B class="L2 W7">laudemus</B>
        <B class="L2 W8">viros</B>
    </SPAN>
    </P>
    <P>
    <SPAN class="App ref" style="content: 'Set: 1; parts: 2'">
        <B class="L3 W1">gloria</B> . . . <B class="L3 W8">sua</B>
    </SPAN>,
</P>
```

["foo5r", "AR-1", "Book=Ecclesiasticus; Locus=44:1"], . . .

Feedback mechanism

- If a stretch of text in the edition, transcription or translation is selected and the [Feedback] button clicked, a partially pre-populated web-mail form is displayed with the selected text occupying the "Text" field
- To accomplish this, the selected text must be captured *before* the [Feedback] button is clicked, as any click cancels the selection
- The [Feedback] button therefore has an "onmouseover" handler associated with it that retrieves any selected text and stores it in an internal data structure
- When the [Feedback] button is clicked, the contents of the internal data structure are retrieved and used to pre-populate the "Text" field of the web-mail form

Markup for [Feedback] button

```
<TH>
    <INPUT
        name="Feedback"
        type="button"
        value="Feedback"
        class="active"
        onMouseOver="CaptureSelectedText ()"
        onClick="SendFeedback (Global.SelectedText)"
        src="../Feedback/SendMail.aspx"
    >
</TH>
```

Capturing the view state

- When any aspect of the view state is changed, the change is recorded in the query string component of the URL
- The query string records the folio, text variant, line numbering, reflow and debug states

```
function BookmarkCurrentState ()
    {
        var folio = document.getElementById ("Folio-selector").value
        var variant = document.getElementById ("Text-selector").value
        var linenos = document.getElementById ("Lineno-selector").value
        var reflow = document.getElementById ("Reflow-selector").value
        window.location.search = "?" + "folio=" + folio + ";" + "text=" +
        variant + ";" + "linenos=" + linenos + ";" + "reflow=" + reflow + ";" +
        debug=" + Global.Debug
    }
```

Restoring the view state

- If a query string is found in the URL from which the page is loaded, the view state is retrieved from the query string and used to re-construct the original view state

```
function RestoreState ()

    {
        Dim ()
        GetParameters ()
        document.getElementById ("Folio-selector").value = Global.Folio
        SelectFolio (Global.Folio)
        document.getElementById ("Text-selector").value = Global.
        Textclass
        SelectText (Global.Textclass)
        document.getElementById ("Lineno-selector").value = Global.
        Linenos
        SelectLinenos (Global.Linenos)
        document.getElementById ("Reflow-selector").value = Global.
        Reflow
        SelectReflow (Global.Reflow)
        Brighten ()
    }
```

Optional line numbering

- Space is reserved in the left margin of the text pane for possible line numbers
- All lines of a single text page are embedded in a surrounding <DIV> element
- When line-numbering is selected, this <DIV> is dynamically made a member of the "linenos" class in addition to any pre-existing class(es) such as "Edition", "Transcription" or "Translation"
- CSS rules prepend the current value of the CSS counter "linecounter" to each line within an element of class "linenos", and cause that counter to be incremented at each line boundary
- A further CSS rule causes that counter to be reset by the surrounding <DIV> element

Selecting line numbering

```
<TH>
    <SELECT id="Lineno-selector" name="Lineno-selector"
    onChange="Dim (); BookmarkCurrentState ()">
        <OPTION value="Off" selected>Line-nums: off</OPTION>
        <OPTION value="On">Line-nums: on</OPTION>
    </SELECT>
</TH>
```

Reflow

- The surrounding <DIV> of a text page indicates the class of the page ("Edition", "Transcription" or "Translation")
- If reflow is selected (possible only for Editions), the class is dynamically changed to reflect the reflow variant desired ("Reflowed-edition", "Fully-reflowed-edition")
- For both "Reflowed-edition" and "Fully-reflowed-edition", CSS rules change the "display" property of each line from "block" to "inline-block", thus allowing consecutive lines to run-on
- For "Reflowed-edition", a further CSS rule interpolates a red solidus between line boundaries and appends a red double-solidus to the last line

Selecting a reflow variant

```
<TH>
    <SELECT id="Reflow-selector" name="Reflow-selector"
    onChange="Dim (); BookmarkCurrentState ()">
        <OPTION value="None" selected>Reflow: none</OPTION>
        <OPTION value="Normal">Reflow: normal</OPTION>
        <OPTION value="Full">Reflow: full</OPTION>
    </SELECT>
</TH>
```

Commentaries and footnotes

- Unlike the *apparatus criticus, fontium* & *referentium*, commentaries (in the translation) and footnotes (in the supplementary material) are embedded in the page, not loaded from external files
- In the source of a translation, a stretch of text for which a commentary is available is embedded in a <SPAN class="*Apparatus scholia*"> element
- During DOM traversal, a superscript with associated "onclick ()" handler is grafted on whenever such an element is encountered
- Clicking the superscript will result in the commentary being displayed in the footnote area, and clicking it a second time will restore the *status ante bellum*

Markup for commentaries

```
<DIV id="Translation" class="Translation f1v-4r">
    <B class="R1">both because you do not consider such . . . </B>
    <SPAN class="Apparatus scholia">
        <B class="R2">having been very well educated in it both in
        itself</B>
        <B class="R3">and as you are accustomed to engage
        also . . . </B>;
    </SPAN>
    <B class="R4">and because your father the most famous . . . </B>,
</DIV>

<DIV class="Commentary">
    Elizabeth's education had benefited from the skills of a talented
    circle of humanist . . . saying that she spoke the language
    'frequently, willingly and moderately well'.
</DIV>
```

Footnotes

- Footnotes proper occur only in the supplementary material such as "The Author" rather than in the Electronic Edition *per se.*
- As the supplementary material is not subject to DOM traversal, explicit markup is required to indicate a footnote callout
- When the callout is clicked, the browser repositions the content to force the corresponding fragment to the top of the viewport, while a CSS rule ":target {background: #ffffc8; color: black; border: dotted 1px}" causes the target <LI> element to be discreetly highlit
- The JavaScript "onclick" event handler "SetReturn" receives the full URL of the target element as sole parameter and adds an "onclick" handler to the target element which, when activated, removes itself as "onclick" handler, and then calls "history.go (-1)" to return to the footnote callout

Markup for footnotes

Having received his BA in 1539 . . . two years later.^{<A href="#ftn1" onClick="return SetReturn (this)">[1] </A>}

<OL style="">
    <LI id="ftn1" title="">Anthony Wood, <EM>Athenae Oxonienses: an exact history of all the writers and bishops . . . 1690</EM> (London 1691), p. 191; Alfred B. Emden, <EM>A Biographical Register of the University of Oxford, A.D. 1501 to 1540</EM> (Oxford 1974), p. 194.</LI>
    <LI id="ftn2" title=""> J. S. Brewer, James Gairdner and R. H. Brodie (eds.), . . .</LI>
. . .
</OL>

Full centering

- Horizontal centering of web content is well understood and trivial to implement
- Vertical centering of such content, particularly when the height of the content is *a priori* unknown, is far less well understood and distinctly non-trivial to implement
- There are a number of mooted solutions, with all of which the one selected appears to compare favourably

- The only known downside is that unless hidden from Dreamweaver (at least at version 8.0.2), it reliably causes the latter to crash from resource exhaustion
- The method chosen is based on prior work by Julien Cabanès, Chris Coyier and Michał Czernow
- The basis of the method is the use of the CSS property "display: inline-block" applied to the <BODY> element, together with use of the CSS pseudo-element ":before" to generate further "display: inline-block" content with "vertical-align: middle"
- The implementation is hidden from Dreamweaver by loading a subsequent stylesheet that over-rides the problematic properties
- This latter spreadsheet is then disabled by JavaScript, for which Dreamweaver has no interpreter
- As stylesheets cannot have an ID attribute, the "disabled" property is accessed via the stylesheet's index in the "document.styleSheets []" array

Implementing full centering

```
<STYLE type="text/css">
    body {width: 99.9%; overflow: auto; white-space:nowrap}
    body:before, div.MainContent {vertical-align: middle}
    body, body:before, div.MainContent {display: inline-block}
    body:before {content: ''; height: 99.9%}
    body, div.MainContent {text-align: center}
    html, body {height: 100%}
</STYLE>

<SCRIPT type="text/javascript">
    document.styleSheets [4].disabled = true // Allow page to centre
</SCRIPT>
```

Problems encountered during development

- Highlighting very occasionally "sticks" in Internet Explorer, possibly as a result of a race hazard
- The inconsistent use of *tonos* and *oxia* caused much lost time
- Supporting the Chrome browser required the addition of one "!important" CSS rule
- Current browsers tend to inhibit use of "XMLHttpRequest ()" by default if files are requested from the local file system

- MIME-type over-rides are also necessary if files are to be locally accessed
- Further problems resulting from local file access remain to be resolved (e.g., apparent corruption of HTML in dynamically loaded files)

Further desiderata

- Synchronised audio (or even audio/video), with each word highlit in MS and text as it is spoken (proof of concept already exists for audio; see below, n. 22)
- Simplify markup even further
- Generalise methodology to allow it to be easily applicable to other MSS
- Examine if/how methodology could be extended to accommodate multiple variant MSS
- Re-examine event handling to establish whether a race hazard is causing highlight sticking in IE

As mentioned above, Etheridge's *Encomium* was not delivered to Elizabeth I during her Royal Visit to Oxford in 1566 and it is doubtful whether she ever received it. This does not apply, however, in the case of our own electronic edition of the *Encomium*, which was presented to H.M. Queen Elizabeth II as a reminder of her and H.R.H. Prince Philip's Royal Visit to Royal Holloway, University of London on 14 March 2014, when she graciously conferred a Regius Professorship in the Department of Music. This was one of twelve Regius Professorships bestowed on British Universities to mark the celebrations of the Diamond Jubilee on the occasion of the 60th anniversary of Her Majesty's accession to the throne of the United Kingdom. In this way Etheridge's wish was somehow fulfilled, as his Encomium was at last received, amazingly enough on a similar occasion, by Elizabeth I's distinguished and homonymous successor almost 450 years later —better late than never!

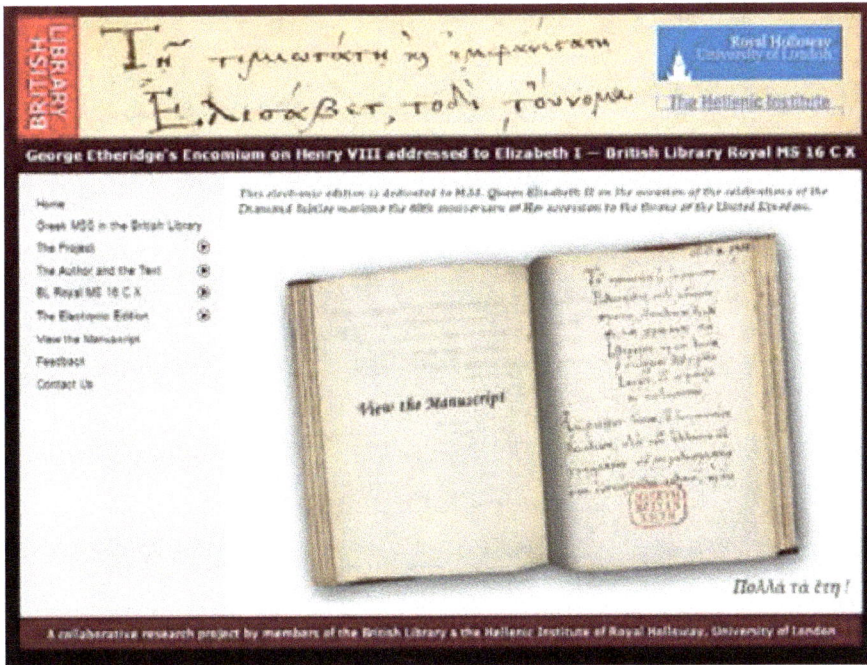

Figure 1. Hagiographical Texts in the Dominican Communication System.

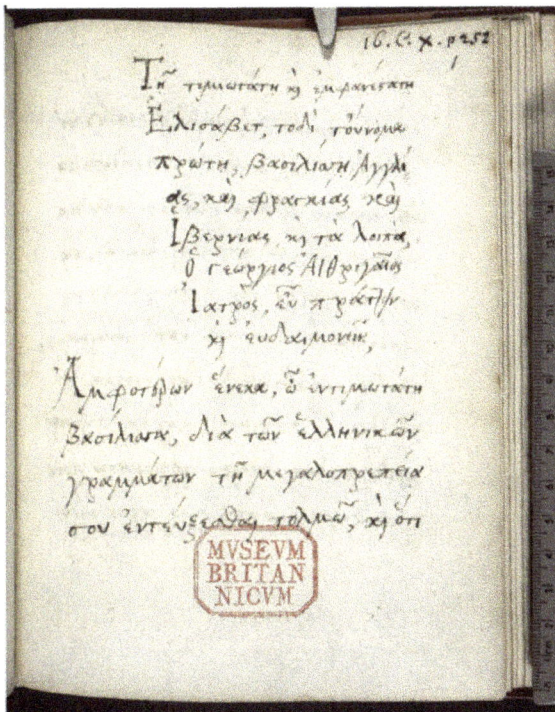

Figure 2. f. 1r (f.1r.jpg)

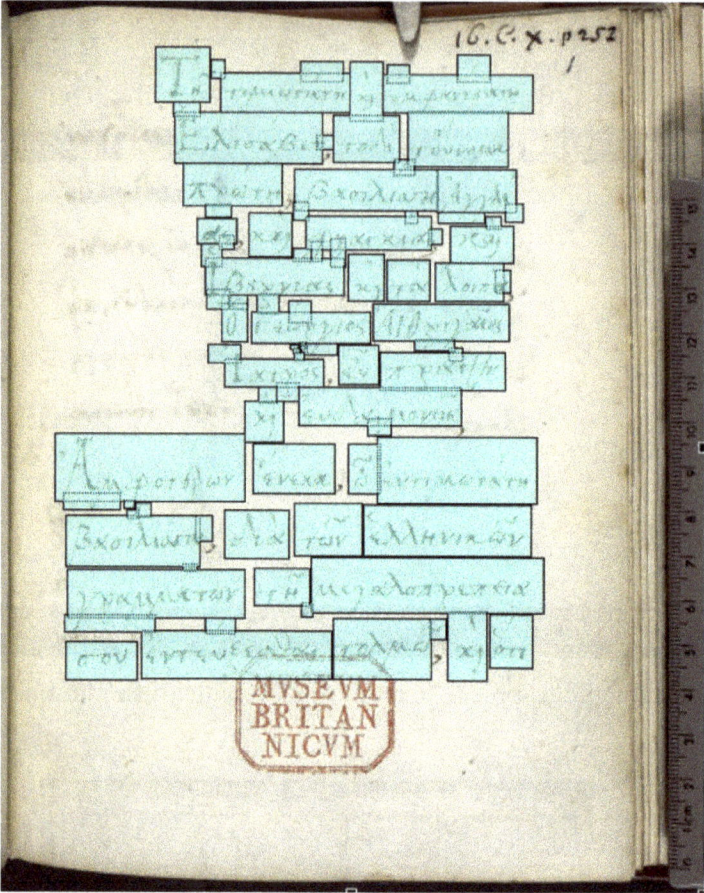

Figure 3. f. 1r, showing map areas (f.1r-mapped-jpg)

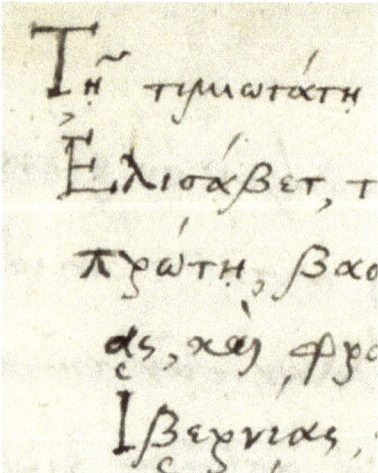

Figure 4. f. 1r (detail) (f.1r-detail.jpg)

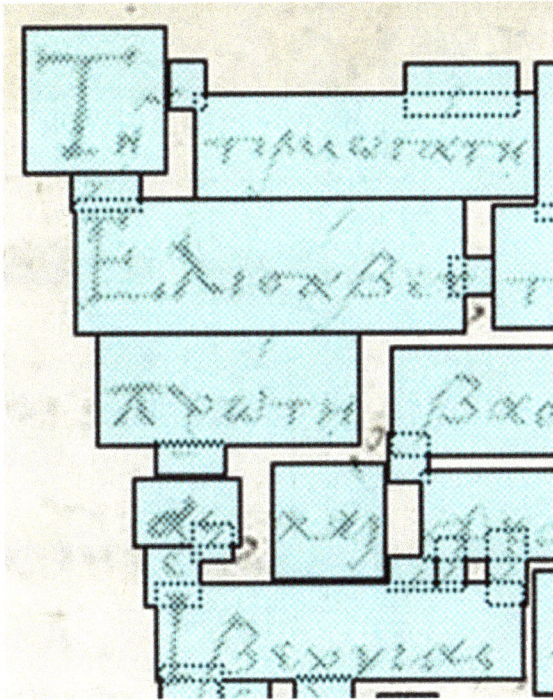

Figure 5. f. 1r (detail), showing map areas (f.1r-detail-mapped.jpg)

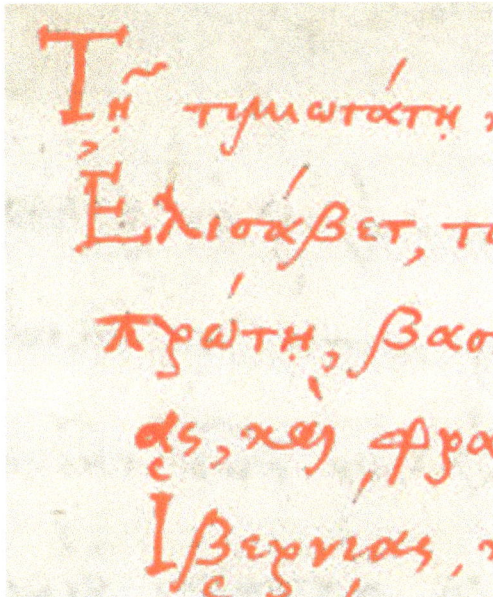

Figure 6. f. 1r (detail), showing red mask (f.1r-detail-mask.jpg)

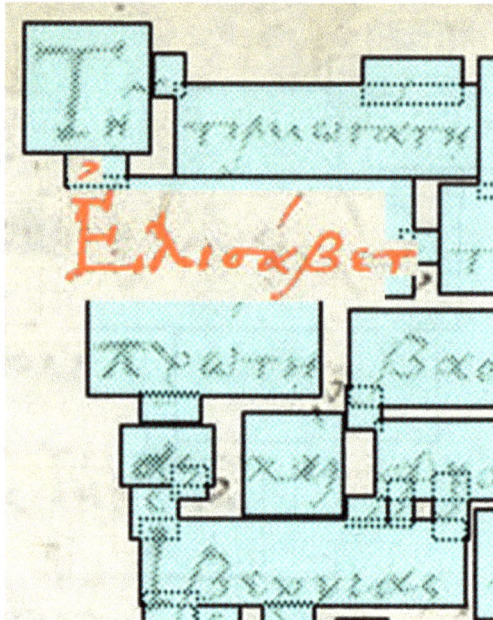

Figure 7. F. 1r (detail), showing mapped red mask (f.1r-detail-mapped-mask.jpg)

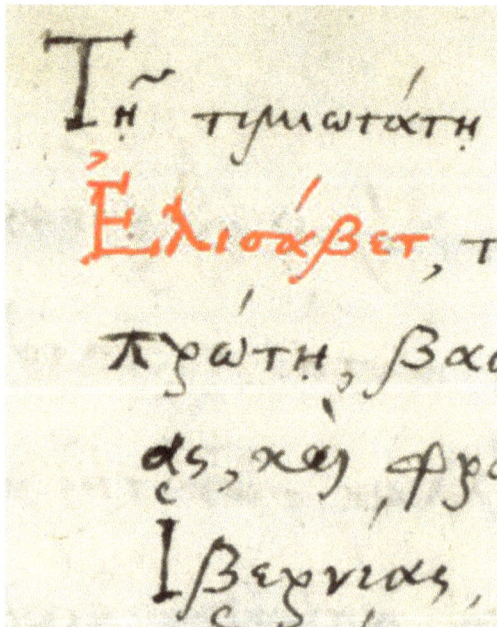

Figure 8. F. 1r, one word highlighted (f1r-detail-highlit.jpg)

Notes

1. Evangelos Chrysos, 'Information Technology and Byzantine Studies', in Φιλέλλην: *Studies in Honour of Robert Browning*, ed. by Costas N. Constantinides, Nikolaos M. Panagiotakes, Elizabeth Jeffreys and Athanasios D. Angelou, Istituto Ellenico di Studi Bizantini e Postbizantini di Venezia, Bibliotheke, 17 (Venice, 1996), pp. 43–53.

2. Jan M. Ziolkowski, '*De laude scriptorum manualium* and *De laude editorum*: From Script to Print, From Print to Bytes', in *Ars edendi Lecture Series*, vol. 1, ed. by Erika Kihlman and Denis Searby, Studia Latina Stockholmiensia, 56 (Stockholm, 2011), pp. 25–58.

3. For example, Elizabeth L. Eisenstein, *The Printing Press as an Agent of Change: Communications and Cultural Transformations in Early-Modern Europe*, 2 vols (Cambridge, 1979), vol. 1, pp. 14–15; Noël L. Brann, *The Abbot Trithemius (1462–1516): the Renaissance of Monastic Humanism*, Studies in the History of Christian Thought, 24 (Leiden, 1981).

4. *De laude scriptorium pulcherimus tractatus domini Johannis Tritemij abbatis Spanbemensis ordinis sancti Benedicti de observancia Burkfeldensi ad Gerlacum abbatem Tuiciensem* (Mainz, 1492; revised edition, 1497); ed. and German trans. by Klaus Arnold, *Johannes Trithemius, De laude scriptorum: Zum Lobe der Schreiber*, Mainfränkische Hefte, 60 (Würzburg, 1973); English trans. by Roland Behrendt, *Johannes Trithemius, In Praise of Scribes: De laude scriptorum* (Lawrence, Kansas, 1974); Italian trans. by Andrea Bernardelli, *Giovanni Tritemio, Elogio degli amanuensi* (Palermo, 1997).

5. *Joannis Trithemij, Spanheimensis, et Postea Divi Jacobi apud Herbipolim Abbatis, Viri suo ævo doctissimi, Tomus II. Annalium Hirsaugiensium, Opus nunquam hactenus editum, & ab Eruditis semper desideratum. Complectens Historiam Franciæ et Germaniæ, Gesta Imperatorum, Regum, Principum, Episcoporum, Abbatum, et Illustrium Virorum. Nunc primum in gratiam, & utilitatem Eruditorum è Manuscriptis Bibliothecæ Monasterij S. Galli public luci datum, Cum licentia Superiorum, Typis ejusdem Monasterij S. Galli, Anno MDCXC, Excudebat Joannes Georgius Schlegel*, p. 421; quoted and trans. by Brann, *The Abbot Trithemius*, p. 146.

6. Johannes Trithemius, *De laude scriptorum*, 10, 24, ed. Arnold, *Johannes Trithemius*, p. 72.

7. This explains why we opted for *editionum* rather than *edendi* in the title of this paper, as *editio* covers the meanings of both *editing* and *publishing*.

8. See Charalambos Dendrinos, 'Palaiologan Scholars at Work: Makarios Makres and Joseph Bryennios' Autograph', in *From Manuscripts to Books. Proceedings of the International Workshop on Textual Criticism and Editorial Practice for Byzantine Texts (Vienna, 10–11 December 2009) – Vom Codex*

zur Edition. Akten des internationalen Arbeitstreffens zu Fragen der Textkritik und Editionspraxis byzantinischer Texte (Wien, 10.–11. Dezember 2009), ed. by Antonia Giannouli and Elisabeth Schiffer, Veröffentlichungen zur Byzanzforschung, Band XXIX (Vienna, 2011), pp. 36–38.

9. For a facsimile edition of the entire manuscript see Louise Durning ed. and Sarah Knight transl., *Queen Elizabeth's Book of Oxford* (Oxford, 2006). Digital images of certain folios are accessible online at: http://bodleian. thejewishmuseum.org/?p=50.

10. Penry Williams, 'Elizabethan Oxford: State, Church and University', in *The History of the University of Oxford,* vol. 3: *The Collegiate University*, ed. James McConica (Oxford, 1986), pp. 397–440.

11. Biographical information is based on Christopher Wright's articles, 'The Author' and 'The Text', both accessible at: http://hellenic-institute.rhul.ac.uk/ Research/Etheridge/Author-and-Text/Author.html and http://hellenic-institute. rhul.ac.uk/Research/Etheridge/Author-and-Text/Text.html.

12. Accessible at: http://codexsinaiticus.org/en/manuscript.aspx.

13. Accessible at: http://hellenic-institute.rhul.ac.uk/Research/Etheridge/.

14. Accessible at: http://hellenic-institute.rhul.ac.uk/Research/Etheridge/ British-Library/Greek-MSS.html.

15. See above, note 11.

16. Accessible at: http://hellenic-institute.rhul.ac.uk/Research/Etheridge/ Manuscript/BL-Royal-MS-16-C-X.html.

17. Accessible at: http://www.bl.uk/manuscripts/FullDisplay.aspx?ref=Royal_ MS_16_C_X.

18. Accessible at: http://hellenic-institute.rhul.ac.uk/Research/Etheridge/ Electronic-Edition/User-Guide.shtml.

19. Accessible at: http://hellenic-institute.rhul.ac.uk/Research/Etheridge/ Electronic-Edition/Editorial-Principles-and-Conventions.html.

20. Accessible at: http://hellenic-institute.rhul.ac.uk/Research/Etheridge/ Electronic-Edition/Technical-Aspects.html.

21. See W.S. Allen, *Vox Graeca* (Cambridge, 1991³), pp. 125–134.

22. A foretaste of the synchronised audio-textual rendition of the opening words of Etheridge's manuscript is accessible at: http://hellenic-institute.rhul. ac.uk/Research/Synch/Greek.html.

Bibliography

Allen, W.S., *Vox Graeca* (Cambridge, 1991³)

Brann, Noël L., *The Abbot Trithemius (1462-1516): the Renaissance of Monastic Humanism*, Studies in the History of Christian Thought, 24 (Leiden, 1981)

Chrysos, Evangelos, 'Information Technology and Byzantine Studies', in Φιλέλλην: *Studies in Honour of Robert Browning*, ed. by Costas N. Constantinides, Nikolaos M. Panagiotakes, Elizabeth Jeffreys and Athanasios D. Angelou, Istituto Ellenico di Studi Bizantini e Postbizantini di Venezia, Bibliotheke, 17 (Venice, 1996), pp. 43–53

Dendrinos, Charalambos, 'Palaiologan Scholars at Work: Makarios Makres and Joseph Bryennios' Autograph', in *From Manuscripts to Books. Proceedings of the International Workshop on Textual Criticism and Editorial Practice for Byzantine Texts (Vienna, 10–11 December 2009) – Vom Codex zur Edition. Akten des internationalen Arbeitstreffens zu Fragen der Textkritik und Editionspraxis byzantinischer Texte (Wien, 10.–11. Dezember 2009)*, ed. by Antonia Giannouli and Elisabeth Schiffer, Veröffentlichungen zur Byzanzforschung, Band XXIX (Vienna, 2011), pp. 36–38

Durning, Louise, ed. and Sarah Knight transl., *Queen Elizabeth's Book of Oxford* (Oxford, 2006)

Eisenstein, Elizabeth L., *The Printing Press as an Agent of Change: Communications and Cultural Transformations in Early-Modern Europe*, 2 vols (Cambridge, 1979)

Johannes Trithemius, *De laude scriptorium pulcherimus tractatus domini Johannis Tritemij abbatis Spanbemensis ordinis sancti Benedicti de observancia Burkfeldensi ad Gerlacum abbatem Tuiciensem* (Mainz, 1492; revised edition, 1497)

Johannes Trithemius, De laude scriptorum: Zum Lobe der Schreiber, ed. and German transl. by Klaus Arnold, Mainfränkische Hefte, 60 (Würzburg, 1973)

Johannes Trithemius, In Praise of Scribes: De laude scriptorum, English trans. by Roland Behrendt (Lawrence, Kansas, 1974)

Giovanni Tritemio, Elogio degli amanuensi, Italian transl. by Andrea Bernardelli (Palermo, 1997)

Williams, Penry, 'Elizabethan Oxford: State, Church and University', in *The History of the University of Oxford*, vol. 3: *The Collegiate University*, ed. James McConica (Oxford, 1986), pp. 397–440

Wright, Christopher, 'The Author' and 'The Text', at: http://hellenic-institute.rhul.ac.uk/Research/Etheridge/Author-and-Text/Author.html and http://hellenic-institute.rhul.ac.uk/Research/Etheridge/Author-and-Text/Text.html respectively

Ziolkowski, Jan M., '*De laude scriptorum manualium* and *De laude editorum*: From Script to Print, From Print to Bytes', in *Ars edendi Lecture Series*, vol. 1, ed. by Erika Kihlman and Denis Searby, Studia Latina Stockholmiensia, LVI (Stockholm, 2011), pp. 25–58

How to Read and Reconstruct a Herculaneum Papyrus*

Richard Janko
University of Michigan, USA

There is no simple, practical guide in English to the mechanics of reading and reconstructing the carbonized papyrus-rolls from Herculaneum.[1] Literally hundreds of texts await the application of the methods of reading and reconstruction that have been developed since the 1980s, not to mention the approximately 280 rolls or parts thereof that may soon become legible by the use of high-energy rays (Figure 1).[2] However, few scholars have had the courage or hardihood to undertake this arduous but extraordinarily rewarding work, which offers our best hope of obtaining new texts from antiquity; hence I have often been asked to record these principles in writing so that they are better known. The reconstruction of the carbonized Derveni papyrus necessarily follows the same principles.[3] Part I will discuss how to read such papyri; even this is not as simple as it sounds. Part II will review how to reconstruct whole *volumina* from Herculaneum; several aspects of this will be useful for the reconstruction, whether actual or digital, of non-carbonized papyrus-rolls.[4]

This paper was given on 28 April 2014 at Stockholm University.

* I thank Denis Searby for his kind invitation to Stockholm and the other participants at the seminar, and Justin Barney for reading a draft of this article. I also presented versions of this material the previous week at the University of the Peloponnese, Kalamata, where I thank Prof. Georgia Xanthaki-Karamanou, and at the University of Athens, at a seminar at American Philological Association Annual Meeting in Philadelphia in 2012 (jointly with J. Fish), and at the Center for the Tebtunis Papyri, University of California, Berkeley, in 2011. All figures marked 'B.N.N.' are reproduced by courtesy of the Ministero per i Beni è le Attività Culturali, Italy (copyright, all rights reserved).

How to cite this book chapter:
Janko, R. 2016. How to Read and Reconstruct a Herculaneum Papyrus. In: Crostini, B., Iversen, G. and Jensen, B. M. (eds.) *Ars Edendi Lecture Series, vol. IV.* Pp. 117–161. Stockholm: Stockholm University Press. DOI: http://dx.doi.org/10.16993/baj.f. License: CC-BY 4.0

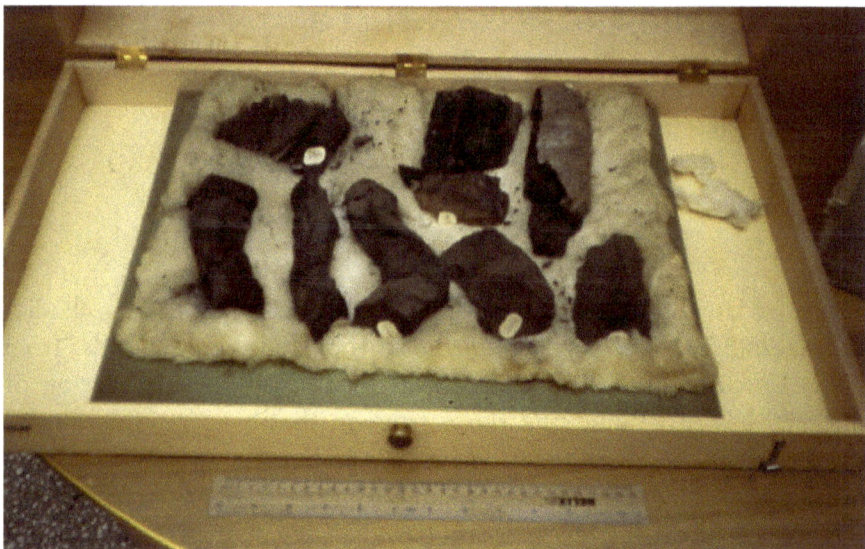

Figure 1. Unopened papyrus-rolls from Herculaneum (photo R. Janko/B.N.N., copyright, all rights reserved)

Any qualified person can study a Herculaneum papyrus upon application to the Soprintendente of the Officina dei Papiri at the Biblioteca Nazionale di Napoli, but the conservators rightly require academic credentials and letters of introduction. The *Cronache Ercolanesi* publishes annually a list of which scholars are working on which papyri;[5] it is only proper that access to them should be controlled, so that years of work by one scholar are not duplicated or preempted by the premature publication of an interloper. On the other hand, as is true of all collections of papyri, if for many years or even decades scholars give no sign of working on a text which has been assigned to them, it should eventually be transferred to someone who will bring it out. There is, regrettably, no internationally agreed statute of limitations, to prevent the fortunate (or the greedy) from hoarding papyri and depriving the next generation of the opportunity to make their own discoveries. Shame or loss of reputation seem not to be effective sanctions. The allocation of papyri is among the tasks of the *Consiglio* of the *Centro Internazionale per lo Studio dei Papiri Ercolanesi* (CISPE), to whom all researchers should write.[6] Decisions are taken by the Biblioteca, which is in regular consultation with the CISPE.

The location of particular papyri and *disegni* within the Officina is recorded in catalogues produced by its recent Superintendents,[7] which give much other helpful information about these artefacts. These catalogues are not to be confused with the *Catalogo dei Papiri Ercolanesi*,[8] produced by the CISPE (as are its successive updates[9]), which is the indispensable starting-point and lists exhaustively references to each papyrus in published sources. Note, however, that this work often repeats Domenico Bassi's inaccurate and outdated deductions about the history of the unrolling of any particular papyrus. The catalogue of the copious Archive of the Officina is also kept there. A card catalogue gives access to the publications held there, which include copies of nearly every printed item on the Herculaneum papyri that has ever appeared. A computer gives access to the digitized MSI images.[10]

Reading the Papyrus

Most of the papyri from Herculaneum are not conserved between glass, since this would crush the delicate fibres of these carbonized rolls. Instead, they were unrolled and held together with a backing of gold-beater's skin (*battiloro*).[11] This is visible as a wispy grey film behind the papyrus, or stretched across the gaps where it has perished. Its presence is sometimes a useful proof that fragments were in a given spatial relationship, but this impression can also be deceptive. The rolls were cut during unrolling into pieces about 30 cm wide, which were lightly glued at their corners to a backing sheet of thicker paper (*cartoncino*). Since the 1970s each segment (*cornice*) has been stored flat, in frames with a transparent lid, from which they are removed for reading.[12] If the *cartoncino* is white, coarse, attached with drawing pins to a thin wooden board, and signed with the name 'Conforti', the artisan who did the pinning for Domenico Bassi in the 1910s, it is an original *cartoncino*, which may bear precious annotations in ink such as the date of unrolling, the identity of the unroller and the number of the *cornice*, given as a large letter of the alphabet. If the *cartoncino* is white or blue and glued to a cardboard backing, it dates from the remounting of the papyri in the 1860s, when those papyri judged worthy of display were framed and hung up on the walls of the Archaeological Museum.[13] The latter classes of *cartoncini* may have had their original numbers changed during remounting, and their corners must be scrutinized for signs of a prior numeration in pencil; to establish the original numbers will require measurement of the *sezioni* (see Part II). In the 1910s Bassi either discarded the old *cartoncini* or turned them over and reused them for mounting other papyri.[14]

In the 1960s Anton Fackelmann separated the layers of other fragments and remounted them onto blotting-paper between sheets of glass,[15] using much the same methods that he applied to the Derveni papyrus.[16] These are almost impossible to read by eye without lifting the upper sheet of glass, which cannot be lowered again without crushing the papyrus badly (this applies to the Derveni papyrus too). Hence such papyri must be read either from images carefully photographed with an oblique light-source or, to far better effect, through a small digital microscope with a cold light-source which is in almost direct contact with the glass;[17] otherwise the reflections are just as impossible as with the naked eye, and mean that one can hardly even keep one's gaze on the same place. These are the only papyri in the collection that are deteriorating rapidly, because their fibres have been crushed; this confirms that the old system for conserving carbonized papyri that are curved and/or corrugated is better than mounting them between glass. Pieces obtained by the Kleve-Fosse method of dismantling papyri are again mounted on rice-paper, not under glass, and are stored flat in trays like the older papyri.[18]

Our ability to read carbonized papyri depends in the first instance on our eyes; these must be good. An excellent student of mine, who misread papyri badly because of an astigmatism, read them far better when I suggested that he do so with one eye closed; I suffer myself from a milder version of the same disability, which makes it difficult to see depth and therefore to distinguish layers of papyrus that lie one above the other (for an illustration of the layers as they appear to the eye see Figure 3). One needs to know one's limitations. Some find contact lenses useful for reading with the microscope; my insistence on spectacles has cost me much time, since these have to be put aside whenever I peer through the microscope.

Reading the papyri depends crucially on the types of images and technology that are available. Methods improved over time, at first slowly but more rapidly of late. Whether a papyrus needs reediting normally depends on the date of the prior edition, but **most papyri edited before 1995 probably need to be redone.** From their first unrolling, lenses and bright sunlight must have been used to read and draw them. Sunlight is still essential for reading the papyri in Naples, which are kept in a room with a glass ceiling; despite the heat that this generates, the overhead sunlight is essential. Transcriptions made on a sunny day will not be replicable when the sky is overcast, even with the best microscopes. **What is seen in sunlight is so invisible in poor light that you will doubt that you ever saw it,** and you risk erasing correct readings from your notes (*experto crede*). Because of the low angle of the sun,

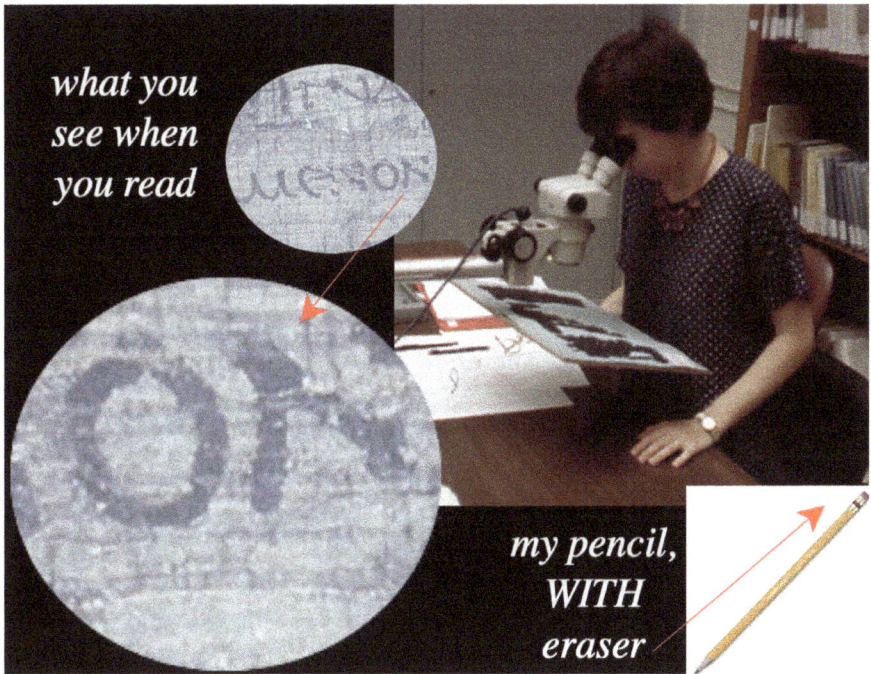

Figure 2. What you see through the microscope, *P. Herc.* 460 cr. 1 fr. 1 (photos with ring-flash R. Janko/B.N.N., copyright, all rights reserved)

the light in winter is inferior to that in other seasons; study in Naples is best undertaken between May and October. Eric Turner introduced binocular microscopes in about 1981. These earliest models relied on reflected sunlight as a light-source, but the shadow of the apparatus through which one looked drastically reduced the visibility of the papyrus. Better microscopes, with an annular light around the lens, were introduced in 1995; this counteracts the shadow from the apparatus, but of course the lenses still show only a small extent of the surface (Figure 2). In 2013 even better models, with cold light-emitting diode (LED) light-sources, were brought in. Digital microscopes are usable only on those few pieces still mounted between glass. I will return at the end of this section to the difficulties, and the dire necessity, of working by autopsy from the original papyri, and will explain how best to do so.

The earliest method for reproducing papyri was of course drawing either in ink, as was practised by Piaggio himself, or (normally) in pencil, since no other method then existed.[19] This resulted in four types of drawings (*disegni*), which almost always bear the number of the papyrus and the name of the draughtsman, a useful detail for establishing their date.

(i) First is the Oxonian set on single sheets, now bound into nine volumes and kept in the Bodleian Library at Oxford;[20] this set consists of almost all the pencil drawings that had been made down to January 1806, including those made before John Hayter arrived in 1802; the latter may be in ink, and drawings in ink usually predate 1800.[21] Those made in Hayter's time bear in their lower left corners the original numbers that he assigned; as these are close to the binding, they are rarely visible in reproductions.[22] Hayter's system of numbering is complete, distinctive, reliable and useful, because each *cornice* is assigned a capital letter of the alphabet (with J omitted), and then each column is numbered with a lower case letter; thus H:a means the first column of the eighth *cornice*, and the drawing is labelled H even if the preceding *cornici* were never drawn. The same letters appear on the original *cartoncini*, where these survive.

(ii) The second set of *disegni* is the Neapolitan, which are made on the first recto of a bifolium: these were begun in 1807 in order to replace the Oxonian drawings after the latter had been removed from Naples, but were then expanded to include other, newly opened papyri. They ceased to be made after the unification of Italy in 1861. These are kept in the Officina. They bear no *cornice*-number, but only a fragment number or column number (the term 'column' was used when the draughtsmen thought the columns formed a continuous sequence). Their numbering is not reliable, as they were subject to later changes which were often mistaken (see Part II).

(iii) A small group of *disegni*, made in 1819 under the supervision of Sir Humphry Davy and annotated by the Rev. Peter Elmsley, are bound and kept separately in the Bodleian Library;[23] others from this same group, including some duplicates, are among the Neapolitan *disegni*. They bear, as usual, the papyrus-number and the name of the draughtsman. A version of some of these (the 'King's Book'), painted in *gouache* by Sir William Gell and presented to the Prince Regent, is now in the Queen's Library in Windsor castle.[24] However, I have eliminated it as an apograph.[25]

(iv) A few more drawings were made by Domenico Bassi and his draughtsman Mario Armani in the 1910s; these are kept with the Neapolitan *disegni*, and add little to our knowledge.

The early drawings are never wholly accurate transcriptions of the papyri, but also contain many traces, which have since disappeared; this is particularly true of the Oxonian set, which may show detached fragments in the margins and, where they exist, are generally better than the Neapolitan. Where outer parts of papyrus-rolls that were opened by *scorzatura* are involved (see Part II for what this means), the Neapolitan *disegni* are the primary witnesses to the text, since after the layer was drawn it was destroyed in order to reveal and to draw the layer beneath: such drawings usually bear the note 'non esiste l'Originale'. The early drawings should be read with the microscope, since this sometimes reveals traces of original readings that have since been falsely corrected.

The *disegni* in Oxford have suffered no modification since they were made. The Neapolitan *disegni*, however, were subject to some later annotation or supplementation, often anonymously. They were verified shortly after their creation by an *interprete*, who, unlike the draughtsmen, actually knew some Greek. He approved the accuracy of the drawings, marked them 'Visto buono', and signed his name;[26] sometimes his supervisor did so too. The first use of the Neapolitan drawings was to serve as the basis for a transcript by an *interprete*. Many transcripts have been lost or were never made, but many more survive in the archive of the Officina, as I discovered.[27] Hayter himself transcribed some of the Oxonian *disegni*; his transcripts are in Oxford.[28] The transcripts are valuable for three reasons: they sometimes show lost letters (but one must exercise caution, since the *interpreti* supply lost letters without using brackets), they occasionally record lost fragments, and they are the first scholarly work on these pieces.

The next step was to engrave the Neapolitan drawing onto a copper plate; this action was authorized by the leading *interprete*, who signed the drawing with the command *s'incida*. Beginning in the 1830s, the engraver countersigned and dated the second recto of the bifolium that bears the drawing; he also put his name and that of the *disegnatore* onto the plate. Proofs ('prove di stampa') of these engravings were then made; these too are kept in the Officina. If the drawing is lost, which is occasionally the case, the *prove* become its primary source; in any case they must always be checked, because they may contain valuable information like original fragment-numbers (often under erasure themselves, with one number in ink and the other in pencil), which on the drawings themselves may have been deleted without trace or otherwise altered; these details matter for the reconstruction (see Part II). Lastly, the copper-plates were printed in the *Herculanensia Volumina* series 2, sometimes with bad 'corrections' initialled by Minervini and Fiorelli, who often introduced errors into the plates in HV^2. Even the plates must be collated, because the gradual deterioration of the papyri sometimes brought to light letters that were previously covered by the layer above, and could be added to the plates in later stages of engraving. However, as one would expect, the plates normally introduce error rather than improvement.[29] Lastly, Theodor Gomperz' copy of the HV in the library of the University of Vienna contains valuable marginal material,[30] as does the archive of Christian Jensen and Wolfgang Schmid held in the Papyrussammlung at the University of Cologne.[31]

Photographs of the papyri taken with ordinary wavelengths of light are almost always unsatisfactory.[32] The first set of them was published in Milan in 1914 as HV^3, containing papyri 1050 and 1457. Ordinary photographs have two defects: the contrast rarely suffices to reveal all the details, and the folding of the surface obscures many of the traces. However, colour photographs taken in ordinary light through a binocular microscope with a ring-flash around the lens, a technique developed by Knut Kleve, produce extraordinarily good images of an area perhaps averaging 4 cm high by 6 cm wide. These will show you perhaps seven lines with a width of eighteen letters in each; they still have shadows where the gradients of the papyrus are steep, but the ring-flash reduces the effects of folding. Since the area photographed is small, the technique is laborious, but the results are excellent (Figure 3). The image can of course be magnified by digital enhancement.

Infra-red photographs increase the contrast between the ink and the background, which can be further enhanced by digital processing; thus the original infra-red photographs of the Derveni papyrus, which were taken before it was mounted between glass sheets, are still one of the best ways to read its text.[33] The 'multi-spectral' images (MSI) produced by the team of Steve Booras from Brigham Young University, mostly at wavelengths of about 940 nanometers, used excellent lighting from multiple directions.[34] This too helps to 'flatten' the papyri. Even so the folding and the superposed layers still cause distortions and a high risk of false readings. Holes in the papyrus that are too small to allow the backing to become visible are indistinguishable from traces of ink (Figure 4).[35] Unfortunately the MSIs were taken without a scale, which makes them rather hard to use for reconstructing the *volumina* (see Part II). Each image shows an area about two columns wide by sixteen lines high (14 cm wide by 8 cm high). The individual images can be stitched digitally into larger images of whole *cornici*; the stitching very

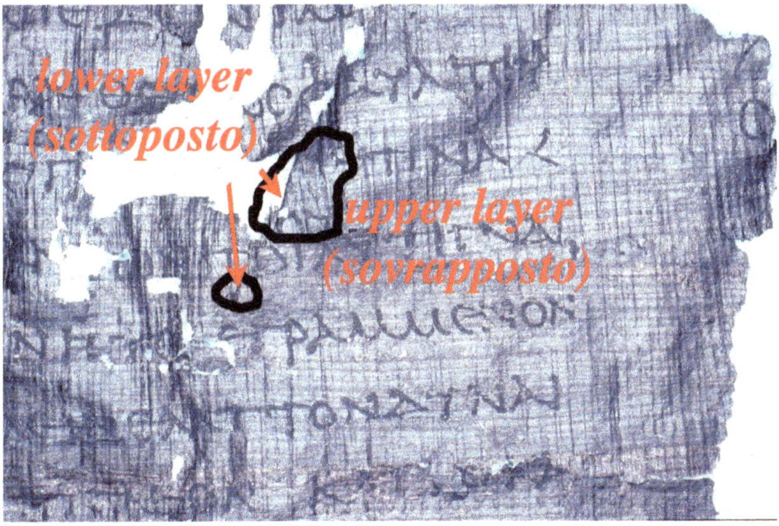

Figure 3. Detail of *P. Herc.* 460 cr. 1 fr. 1 of Philodemus' *On Poems* 1, showing layers (photo with ring-flash R. Janko/B.N.N., copyright, all rights reserved)

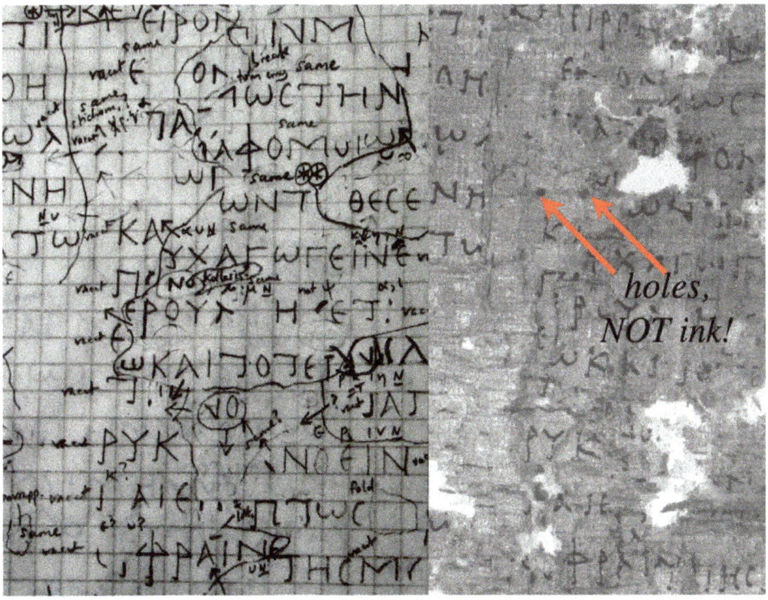

Figure 4. Detail of notebook showing notations of vacant space, layers, variants in *disegni*, date and time (photo R. Janko), with MSI image of *P. Herc.* 994 cr. 11 showing holes that appear as ink (photo Brigham Young University/B.N.N., copyright, all rights reserved)

rarely causes problems. They can be profitably studied on very large computer-monitors. Studying infra-red images alongside photographs taken in ordinary wavelengths of light with a ring-flash is a good approach, but studying them along with drawings corrected against the original papyrus is in my view the best method; the extra time it takes is rewarded with a higher degree of reliability in the results.

The most recent advance, pioneered by Kathryn Piquette from the University of Cologne (Piquette forthcoming), is Reflectance Transformation Imaging (RTI) at infra-red wavelengths. In this method, multiple images are taken from different angles and combined digitally. The viewer can alter the direction of the light to make it rake across the surface; a still photograph yields a very imperfect recreation of the extraordinary effect (Figure 5). This is the best approximation to looking through the microscope that I have experienced, since different layers are clearly visible in full perspective. However, it has the same drawback as microscopic study, viz. that only a small portion of the curved portions of the papyrus is fully visible at once. At the time of writing there are other difficulties: the making of such images is highly labour-intensive, and the file-sizes are enormous.

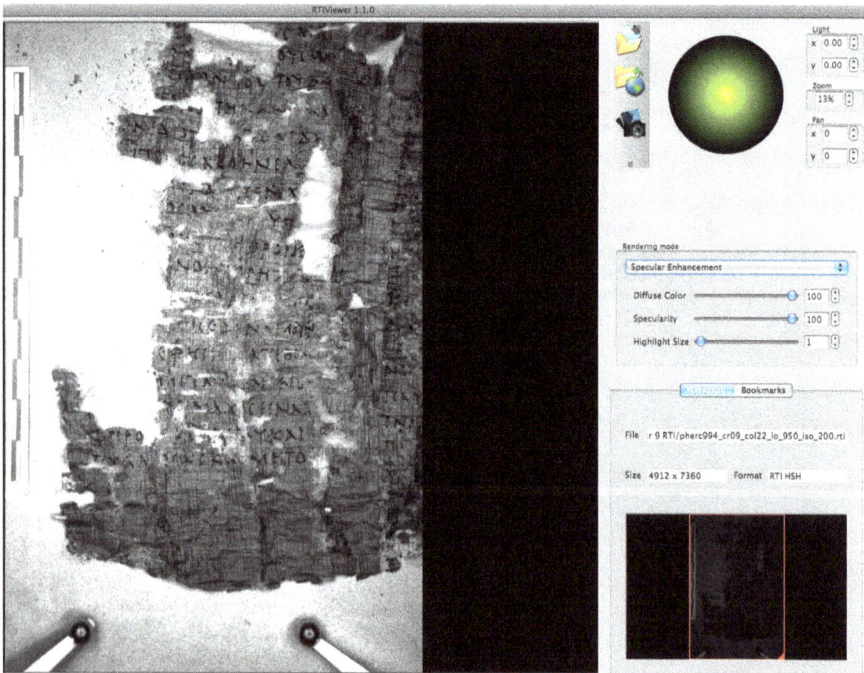

Figure 5. RTI image of *P. Herc.* 994 cr. 9 displayed with RTIViewer v.1.1 (RTI image Kathryn Piquette/B.N.N., copyright, all rights reserved)

To return, finally, to reading the papyri by autopsy through the microscope, this is an utterly enthralling task, but not a simple one. It is expensive to stay in Naples, and time in the Officina is at a high premium. One must plan visits carefully so as to avoid holidays. Generations of scholars have lamented that the gates of their paradise are open for so few hours —from 8.30 a.m. until 1.30 p.m. on weekdays; a passport is required for entry, and the Officina now closes on Saturdays. It is worth asking in the Officina whether items from the archives can be transferred to the Sala dei Manoscritti downstairs, so that they can be read there after the Officina has closed. It is crucial to start early each day and to bring to the library without fail all the necessary items — passport, pencils, pencil-sharpeners, rulers, pens, notebooks, and a large bottle of water. Forgetting even one minor item can cost much time, since it takes so long even to traverse the library from its entrance, where one must leave one's bag in the lockers, to the Officina, let alone to retrieve something from one's lodging.

Since at least a day is needed to verify even one column of papyrus, every effort must made to enhance what can be done there by preparation in advance. The papyrus cannot be read simply by leaving it to lie flat under the microscope, since this reveals almost nothing. Instead, the reader must support with one hand the *cornice* on which the papyrus is mounted, and take notes with the other. Only a few letters from a couple of lines are visible at a time, and at higher magnification only three or four letters, with just the edges of the line above or below (this applies too to imaging the Derveni papyrus with the USB microscope). Thus one is in constant danger of losing one's place. Doing so is worse than an annoyance, since regaining one's bearings takes precious time. There are two ways to reduce that risk.

First, one should bring to the Officina a set of print-outs of the *cornici*, not so much for the sake of the traces as for the pattern of holes in the papyrus; when one looks at the papyrus with the naked eye, as one must when trying to find one's place, holes of a particular shape are easier to locate than are individual letters. The print-outs can also be used for recording measurements (see below).

Secondly, for the difficult task of recording one's results, it is crucial to use only pencils with erasers at the opposite end, so that the implement can be reversed with one hand without either putting it down or taking one's eye off the microscope; one needs constantly to alternate between writing and erasing (mostly erasing). Employing such pencils reduces the risk of getting lost in the papyrus; the use of a separate eraser takes far too much time, as it increases that risk. Many pencils should be brought, all sharpened in advance, with erasers that are not worn down and graphite that rarely breaks.

The best method for recording results is NOT by making a drawing from scratch by autopsy. That approach carries a great danger of inaccuracy and is extremely time-consuming —a major disaster in the Officina, given its limited hours of opening. Instead, one must prepare in advance a drawing in pencil, and then correct and annotate it by autopsy, always in pencil (Figure 4). I have found it best to use MSI images as the basis of drawings on squared paper, bound together in the type of A4 exercise-books that Italian schoolchildren use; loose sheets get lost too easily. One must begin the drawing where there will be enough paper to finish it, perhaps at the upper left corner of an opening, and leave a blank line between each line of writing. It is also important, if having to turn a page, to indicate where the next column begins by drawing in the first letter of each line, so that the successive columns can be aligned and the intercolumnium is carefully checked. Readings derived only from the *disegni* or other sources should be written in lightly between the lines, so that one remembers to verify them. Where textual deletions are proposed, one should add a note to check whether there are expunction-points ('cancel dots') above the letters, as these are particularly easy to miss. Paragraphi should be marked for verification, since they are often confused with fibres. Vacant papyrus at line-ends should be marked 'vacat' so that one is not tempted later, when away from the papyrus, to suggest that a letter is lost there. The same is true for upper and lower margins and spaces left by the scribe as punctuation, which can provide crucial help for reconstructing a given passage, as can diacritical signs. Changes of layer are marked with arrows, indicating up or down; surprising readings should be marked 'sic' to show that they have been verified; traces to be checked can be marked as such, and the notation erased after verification. Crowding of letters towards the right margin must be noted, as it may betray the presence of that margin when it is lost. The time, date, and light should all be recorded. The time is important, because one needs to know how long it takes to verify the column; this helps with planning future visits to the Officina. The date matters because it can be correlated with the print-outs that I will discuss below. The light is important because, as we have seen, verifications carried out in bad light can be disastrous, leading to the abandonment of the true reading. One must always recheck work that is done in such conditions, and never erase or discard results that were obtained in good light.

The drawings will need to be revisited several times until one is fully satisfied with the text that they yield. I have learned from painful experience never to alter them when I am not in the presence of the original. Others make notes on large printouts of the MSI images; this may seem less laborious at first, but has the serious disadvantage that such annotations need for legibility to be in ink, but will inevitably need correction, which is certain to become both messy and dangerously confusing. Annotating printouts of the text while looking at the digital image on one's computer-screen and only checking the original from time to time seems to work for some scholars, but I worry about the accuracy of their results. In my experience reflections from the glass ceiling make the screen hard to see. In addition, a slow and microscopic perusal of the entire surface yields many unexpected and valuable surprises, such as annotations in apparently blank upper or lower margins, stichometric signs or points in the left margin, punctuation, faint supralinear corrections, faint deletion-lines through letters, expunction-points, abortive or unfinished letters at line-ends where the scribe was slow to realize that he needed to start a new line, and alignment dots at the top of the left margin for column-layout.[36] One must constantly watch for all these phenomena.

Print-outs of the stitched digital images are essential not only for finding one's place, but also for recording measurements (Figure 6). These can be written directly onto the printout, preferably in a red or blue pen with a very fine point. No drawing of one's own will be accurate enough for recording such measurements, whereas on printouts one can mark the beginning and end of every measurement that is noted. Yardsticks and digital calipers are kept in the Officina for this purpose; the digital calipers are better, since yardsticks cause serious parallax errors. Every possible measurement should be recorded, from the height of the letters, height of the interlinear spacing, width of the lines, and width of the intercolumnium to the height of whole columns and of the upper and lower margins: one never knows what will be needed later. Others prefer to annotate the digital images on their computers. At least this is less fraught with risk than is relying on them for reading the ink.

Above all, the exact height and width of the entire *cornice* must be established and checked, since this is needed for scaling the digital images, which do not have a scale in the picture. For the purposes of reconstruction, an equally important measurement is the distance from the left margin of one column to the left margin of the next. The column-

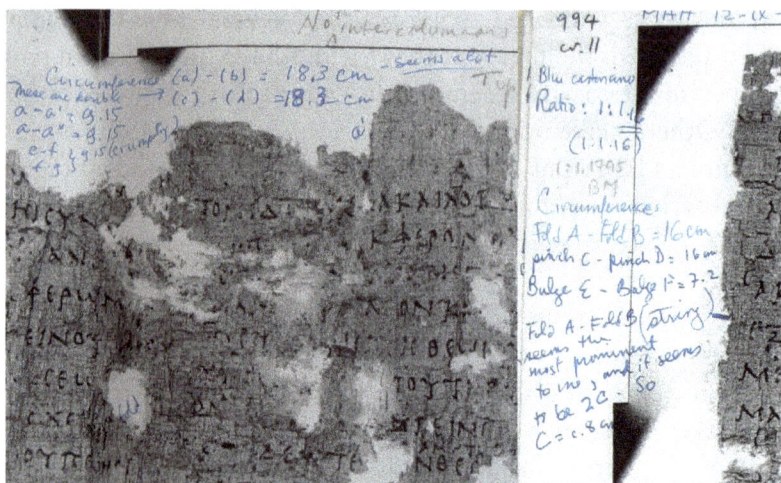

Figure 6. Measurements recorded on print-outs of MSI images of *P. Herc.* 994 crr. 10 and 11 (photos R. Janko/B.N.N., copyright, all rights reserved)

to-column width is normally fixed in prose texts.[37] Since this number will be multiplied by a large factor when the entire roll is reconstructed, it is vital to establish the average with the greatest possible exactitude. In prose texts written in short lines (13–23 letters), as is usual in the Greek texts from Herculaneum, this dimension should vary hardly at all, but be almost exactly fixed, as if the scribe used a mark on his pen-box each time he wished to place the left margin of the following column. However, it must always be verified, since any variations will affect the reconstruction profoundly (see Part II).

Equally important, the distances between successive *sezioni* and circumferences must be determined.[38] One must distinguish between *sezioni*, i.e. repeated distances of half a circumference or less into which papyrus roll tends to fracture, and full circumferences, in which there are at least two *sezioni*. Indeed, if the cross-section of the papyrus was not round or elliptical, but pentagonal or hexagonal, as could happen if it was part of a stack of rolls stored horizontally, there may be five or six narrow *sezioni* in a single circumference. The circumferences were burned into the papyrus when it was carbonized. They can be found only by study of the original; in future one might be able to use Reflectance Transformation Images with a scale in them, if these can ever be stitched together. To find circumferences, one needs to search for recurrent patterns of damage and/or of elevation and depression, and measure the horizontal distances between them as exactly as possible, marking on the print-out the points where the distance begins and where it ends. Circumferences can be very difficult to isolate. Multiple measurements at the top, middle and bottom of the columns will be needed to verify that they have been found. Successive dimensions should always diminish fairly steadily towards the end of the roll. Such measurements need to be tabulated and collated to ensure that they do so decline. They are particularly difficult to make across a break between *cornici*. Although the Officina will permit two *cornici* to be studied at once, this hardly helps the calculation; the final result has to be determined by careful addition and subtraction, since the lateral margins of the *cornici* prohibit taking the measurement in a single operation. The outermost, widest circumference will be almost impossible to determine (unless the initial title of the roll survives), because the exterior of the roll is usually in worst condition. The innermost, on the other hand, is likely to be knowable. Many papyri were wound upon themselves and therefore have very small final circumferences, while others had a central rod (ὀμφαλός or *umbilicus*) around which the innermost circumference was rolled.[39]

Lastly, papyrus-rolls were composed of separate sheets or *kollemata*, which were glued together with an overlap.[40] The line where the two sheets join is called the *kollesis* (Figure 7). The finding of *kolleseis* is very difficult in carbonized papyri, since the eye tends to focus either only on the letters, or only on the fibres, and the latter are hard to follow under the microscope. The search for *kolleseis* requires a completely different kind of looking from that which is involved in searching for traces of ink. Sometimes a *kollesis* can be seen with the naked eye, because the upper layer overlies the lower, or the scribe tries to avoid writing over it. But often the digital images suggest a *kollesis* where none exists: the phenomenon is simply a crack. A separate horizontal scanning of the entire *cornice*, in which one's eye follows the horizontal fibres, is needed, with particular attention to places where the surfaces are unbroken. Reading the ink is so fascinating, and finding the *kolleseis* so tedious, that it is wise to note on the drawing that the latter task too needs to be done.

Kolleseis can usually be found by exercising great persistence, except in pieces were multiple layers are present. There are two clues. (i) Diagonal fibres are often present near a *kollesis*, where they were glued down by the *glutinator* as he put the roll together. (ii) There should be a *vertical* crack or break in the papyrus some 1–1.5 cm before the *kollesis*, which one often mistakes for the *kollesis* itself (Figure 7). The fibres will in fact be found to run on. This vertical break in fact corresponds to the

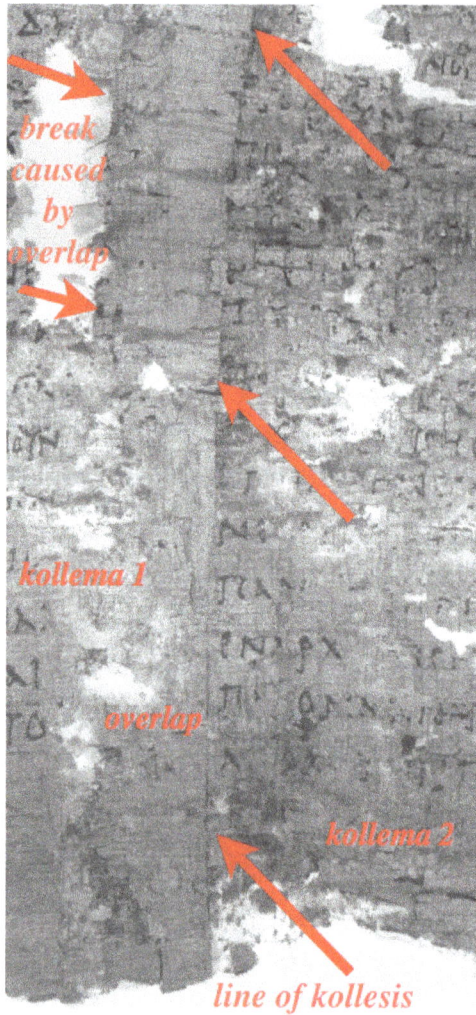

Figure 7. Join between *kollemata* at left margin of *P. Herc.* 994 cr. 9 fr. 23, with crack preceding the *kollesis* (MSI image Brigham Young University/B.N.N., copyright, all rights reserved)

beginning of the underlying (rightward) sheet, which only becomes visible where the overlying (leftward) sheet runs out. But this latter transition is the only one that is directly visible, and this is where the *kollesis* is said to occur and whence the next *kollema* is measured. Once a *kollesis* is found, it should be verified at multiple heights in the column, and the location marked on the drawing and on the print-out of the digital image. Its distance from the left and right edges of the *cornice*, and from the next or previous *kollesis*, if known, should be measured in several places with the digital calipers. The measurements will vary slightly, since the sheets of papyrus from which the roll is made were cut manually, but the average width of the *kollema* can readily be determined. Knowing the average also helps one to discover further *kolleseis*, since one can work out roughly where they should fall and search for them there. The distances need to be measured precisely, since the *kollemata* can play an important role in reconstructing the *volumina* (see Part II).

After the papyrus has been drawn and the drawing has been verified, there begins the multi-stage process of establishing the text, which loops back into drawing the papyrus and forward into the process of reconstructing the roll. Often I am able to establish the readings accurately long before I can understand the text. I create a double-sided print-out of the preliminary text bound with a cover to protect it, since it will suffer a lot of wear. The text must be in columnar format, with a date and title (Figure 8). Each line is annotated at the right with a count of letter-widths, because I find that if I do not count the letters I fall into error in proposing supplements at the ends of lines. Also, if the scribe does justify the right margin and uses filler-signs based on the asteriscus (✳ or :<), one must be careful to supply these where the line is broken

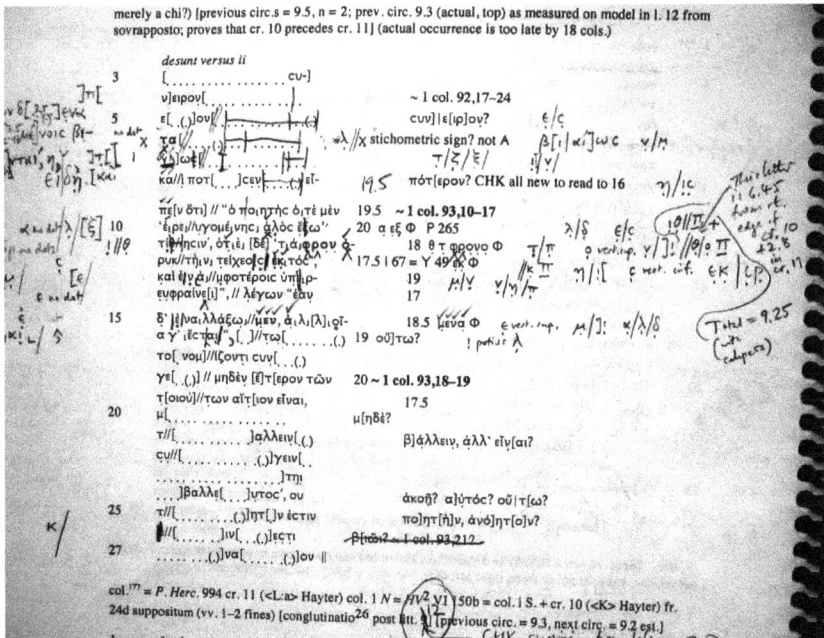

Figure 8. Detail of printout of Philodemus' *On Poems* 2 col. 178 (= *P. Herc.* 994 cr. 10 fr. 24c + cr. 11 col. 1 fr. suppositum) with counts of letter-widths and verifications (photo R. Janko)

at the right and a letter or two short; they are often a valuable clue that one's initial supplement is wrong. One must also apply correctly the Greek rules of word-division.[41] Letters which need to be rechecked are temporarily printed in bold type,[42] and the other possibilities are recorded in the right margin, together with suggested supplements. These must be verified from autopsy, because quite often traces emerge which confirm or disprove them. The apparatus records previous scholarly conjectures (if any) and possible readings of uncertain letters; this is kept current on my laptop computer, but is not taken to the Officina (nor do I carry my computer there, since there is neither need for it nor time to use it). When I return to the Officina, I annotate the bound text as well as the drawing. I mark each verification as it is made, noting the alternative readings of each trace in the right margin, and updating the drawing too as necessary; the double system reduces inaccuracy. I record in the print-out the date, the time and the quality of the light. I note in the right margin suggestions for supplements. All these notes are in pencil. After the Officina closes I work the changes into the text on my computer, and update the apparatus at the same time, recording the possible alternative readings of the damaged letters; this normally takes almost as long as the five hours spent in the Officina itself.

When further ideas occur to one, whether by free thought, from books[43] or from digital searches of the *Thesaurus Linguae Graecae* (*TLG*), *LSJ*, or other sources,[44] they must be marked as needing verification the next morning, along with any uncertainties in one's notes from the morning's work. Only once such queries have been clarified can forward progress through the text resume. The print-out, being bound, can be read and pondered even in places that are inhospitable to study, like trains and aeroplanes; but changes made when one is away from Naples must be marked in ink and verified later. Every rereading in Naples of the same parts of the papyrus requires a clean, new print-out, on which this process of verification is repeated until the text seems satisfactory. One's original notebooks will need to be checked many times before the text is finished, to see whether one did once confirm a given letter in Naples; *it is unwise to go against what was recorded there, even if the digital image seems to show something else*, although about half the time it does not mislead.

Reconstructing the Papyrus

Camillo Paderni tells us that 800, or perhaps 815, book-rolls of papyrus were found in the Villa dei Papiri at Herculaneum.[45] However, many

N 1081b set D (2 layers, 2πr = 20.9) [peeled off before 1763, *scorzatura* 1823] ¶ ::	—::
P. Herc. 994 cr. 1 fr. A (3 layers, 2πr = ??) [= *N* 1081b *ultimo foglio*, peeled off before 1763]::	*P. Herc.* 994 cr. 1 fr. B (3 layers, 2πr = 20.3) [= *N* 1074b *ultimo foglio*, peeled off before 1763]::
N 1081b *scorze*, sets A + B (9 layers, 2πr = 19.2 → 17.6) [1823] + *P. Herc.* 1677a frr. 3–4 [1763–5]::	*N* 1074b *scorze* (7 layers, 19.0 → 17.9) [1823] + *P. Herc.* 1677a fr. 4 [1763–5]::
P. Herc. 1676 cr. 1 (2 layers, 17.6 → 17.1) + *N* 1081b set C fr. 12 (17.3) ¶ *P. Herc.* 1676 cr. 2 (3 layers, 17.1 → 16.9) ¶ *P. Herc.* 1676 crr. 3–5 (7 layers, 16.9 → 16.2) [1763–5]::	*P. Herc.* 1676 cr. 1 (3 layers, 17.6 → 17.1) ¶ *P. Herc.* 1676 cr. 2 (3 layers, 17.1 → 16.9) ¶ *P. Herc.* 1676 crr. 3–5 (7 layers, 16.9 → 16.2) [1763–5]::
P. Herc. 1419c cr. 2 (3 layers, 2πr = 15.7 → 15.4) [1763–5]::	*P. Herc.* 1419c cr. 2 (3 layers, 2πr = 15.7 → 15.4) [1763–5]::
P. Herc. 1677a crr. 3–4 (7 layers, 15.4 → 14.5) [1763–5]::	*P. Herc.* 1677a crr. 3–4 (7 layers, 15.4 → 14.5) [1763–5]::
P. Herc. 994 crr. 3–19 + 2 (104 layers, 14.5 → 1.3) [1802–3]::	*P. Herc.* 994 crr. 3–19 + 2 (104 layers, 14.5 → 1.3) [1802–3]::

Figure 9. Table of the 'papyri' of Philodemus' *On Poems* 2, showing stages of unrolling and decline in circumferences (table R. Janko)

were broken up before or during their opening, with the result that about 1,830 items are currently inventoried as a *P. Herc.* In theory this yields an average of 2.3 items per roll; in practice this is not a helpful guide, as the standard deviation is large. A great number of items correspond to only one roll. However, many rolls were divided into many items: thus Philodemus' *On Poems* 2 consists of six different and very dissimilar *P. Herc.* numbers (Figure 9). On the other hand, some items contain pieces from more than one roll: *P. Herc.* 1419 comprises parts of at least six. No catalogue was made for the first thirty years after the discovery, as there seemed no reason to do so, when nothing had been opened or read. Later the difficulty of tracking so many equally illegible objects introduced considerable confusion into the collection.[46]

The old catalogues are an essential guide to how a given papyrus was unrolled.[47] The process may well have been more complicated than at first appears, or is suggested in the *Catalogo dei Papiri Ercolanesi* of 1979; understanding it can be decisive for the reconstruction, since it is vital to know the sequence in which pieces of a roll were opened and/or read. The earliest work on them is the least well recorded.[48] Piaggio compiled the earliest catalogue in March to June of 1782;[49] its surviving portion lists and describes papyri numbered 312–1695, which was the highest number then used.[50] Historical work to establish exactly which papyri he unrolled in which order and between what dates has progressed significantly in recent years.[51] One can easily trace work on a given papyrus down to *c.* 1810 via the contemporary lists of papyri, which have all been published.[52] However, three subsequent inventories have not: (i) that of 1819–23,[53] (ii) Castrucci's inventory of 1824,[54] and that of 1853.[55] These are essential sources for the massive opening of *scorze* that began in *c.* 1820. Unfortunately they are full of erasures and additions by unidentified hands of unknown date, and can be inaccurate. However, by combining these with other sources one can often correct serious errors.

The records of the storage of the papyri reveal the sequence and approximate dates when they were unrolled, since the call-number of any particular papyrus, which is recorded in the inventories, can be correlated with the date of construction of the cabinet in which it was stored.[56] Lastly, the signatures of the draughtsmen, engravers, *interpreti* and superintendents on the Neapolitan *disegni* and engravings are a useful source for chronology, since the dates of employment of the personnel of the Officina are in principle knowable from the archives,[57] and a particular pairing of employees may provide chronological precision.

The task of reconstruction is hard to undertake in Naples, where few of us have the basic necessities for it. These are an oblong table large enough to support a two-metre length of a paper model of the roll at actual size, excellent light, tranquillity, and plenty of time. But the basis for this task must be laid in the Officina, above all by reading the papyrus accurately, measuring the *sezioni* and circumferences, recording the annotations on the *cornici* and *disegni*, and investigating all the old catalogues and relevant archives.

The first desideratum is to link the text to a particular scribal hand and to gather together all the pieces on the same topic that are written in that script. There is no complete inventory of the hands in the collection. A start on classifying them was made by Cavallo in 1983. His work revealed the useful heuristic principle that the scribes who copied Epicurean authors are often represented in the collection more than once, even for different works by the same author, but that the other texts, e.g. those of Chrysippus, are in hands that do not recur, as if these items were copied elsewhere and added to the collection at different times.[58] Thus the reconstruction of Philodemus' *On Poems* 2 was simplified by the fact that all the items in Cavallo's hand 'Anonimo VIII' are about poetry and in fact belong to one and the same roll. Subsequent identifications of hands have been made piecemeal and are mostly published in *Cronache*

Ercolanesi, the main journal for this field of study. Further information can be found via the multimedia catalogue of the Herculaneum papyri, *Chartes*;[59] this contains low-quality images of (in principle) all the different hands in the collection.

The approximate location of pieces of papyrus within a given roll can be found in several ways. Which methods apply depend on whether the fragment is from a *scorza* or a *midollo* (see Figure 10). These terms derive from the earliest days of Herculanean papyrology. They denote (a) a stack of pieces from the outer layers of the roll (*scorza*, 'bark' as of a tree, plural *scorze*) and (b) its cylindrical interior, still rolled up (*midollo*, 'marrow' as in a bone). This distinction also applied to the Derveni papyrus, where frame (πλαισίο) I, called A by its editors, contains the *midollo*.[60] I will begin with (a), the reconstruction of the outer parts, which is known as the Delattre–Obbink method.

(a) The Delattre–Obbink method for reconstructing detached fragments

When carbonized scrolls are first opened, at least two stacks of *scorze* are peeled off from the outsides of the roll, one from each side of it, to yield **two hemicylinders**; if, in order to open the roll, it had to be cut in half, there would be at least **four stacks of *scorze***, and any particular stack might separate into more than one distinct 'stack' (Figure 10). These stacks retain the original curvature of the roll from which they derive; the interior surface displays a layer of writing, and the exterior surface should represent the exterior either of the stack or of the roll itself. Since, at Herculaneum, the layers in the *scorze* were often stuck together, for a long time they were left untouched.

Once all the usable *midolli* and other material that could be opened without destroying it had been exhausted, in about 1820, the unrollers turned to the stacks of *scorze*. These they 'opened' as follows: they made a *disegno* of the uppermost (innermost) layer of writing that was exposed, numbering it '1'; they then scraped away that layer, destroying it in the process and thereby exposing another layer of writing; they then copied the next layer, numbering it '2', and continued to repeat this process until the lowest (outermost) layer in the stack was attained. This lowest layer, which they called the *ultimo foglio*, i.e. the 'last leaf', ought in principle to survive, but was sometimes destroyed in a vain effort to separate further layers. The whole process is called *scorzatura*; its result is a series of drawings, often many drawings (up to thirty or

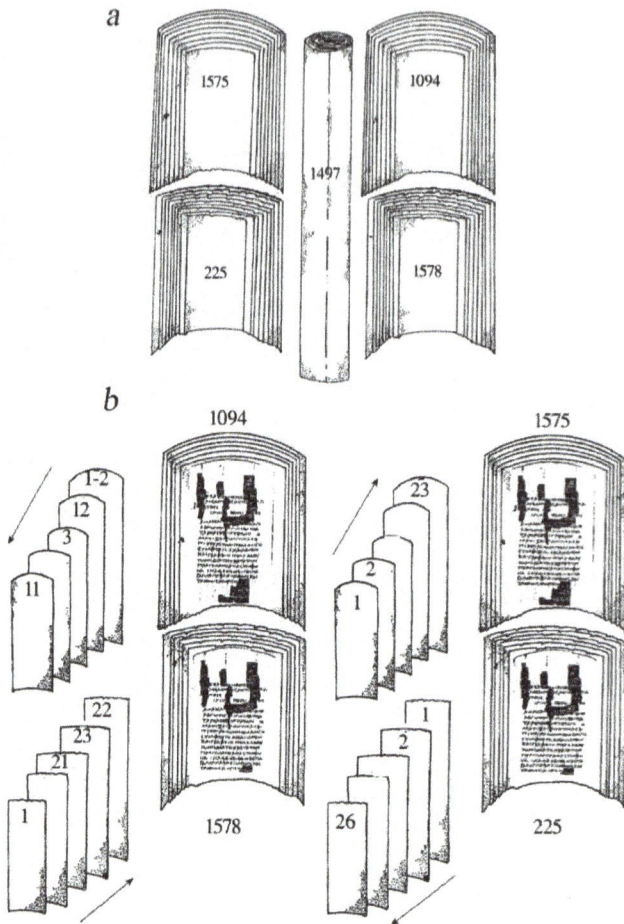

Figure 10. Diagram to illustrate the Delattre-Obbink method (reproduced by permission from Delattre 2006, Planche 5)

so), the last of which ought to depict the surviving *ultimo foglio*. Joins within each set of *scorze* are impossible, unless between small pieces of overlying and underlying layers (*sottoposti* and *sovrapposti*).[61] By thinking in three dimensions, one can use this method to reconstruct a cross-section of the roll (Figure 11).

For at least a century, the way in which the *scorze* were opened was forgotten. Nobody understood that the first *disegno*, i.e. the item numbered '1', would be the last in the series, because the interior of the roll would contain the end of the text, whereas the drawing of the *ultimo foglio*, which would have the highest number, would actually be the

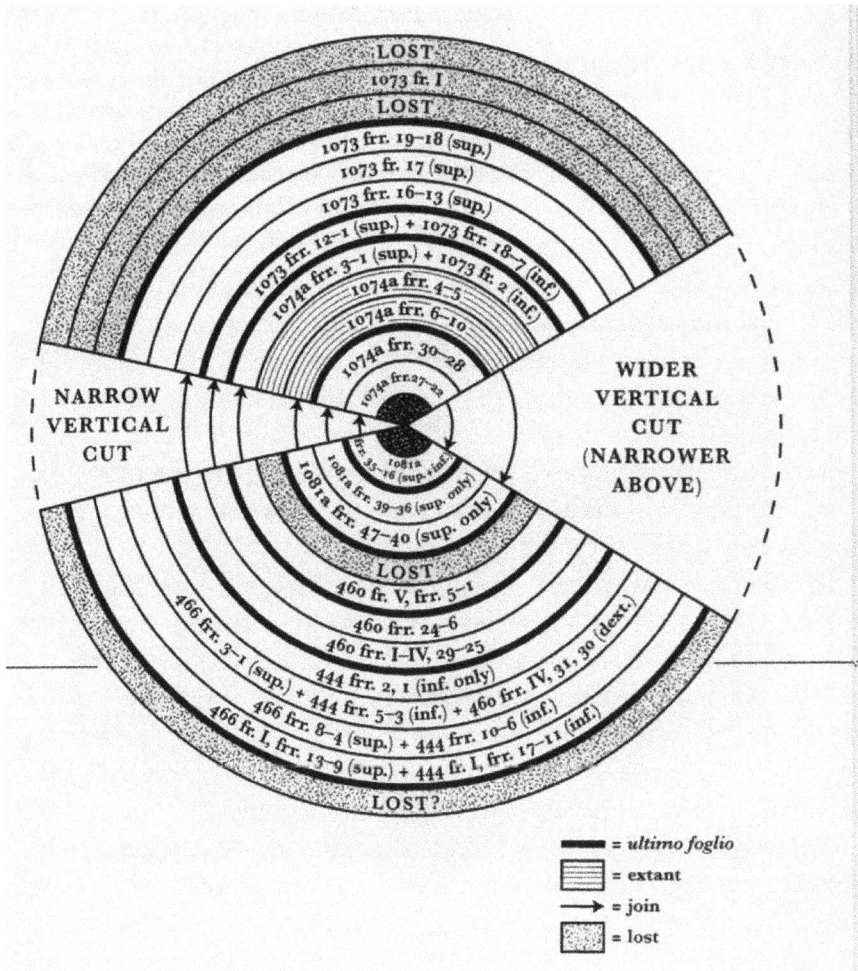

Figure 11. Cross-section of the roll of Philodemus' *On Poems* I (diagram R. Janko)

first in the series and form the outermost layer, bearing on it the start of the text (Figure 10). To restore the original sequence of fragments, the separate sets of *scorze* need to be reintegrated in **alternating backwards order**. Schober had some inkling of this is his unpublished edition of Philodemus' *De pietate*,[62] but Delattre, in preparing his edition of *De Musica* IV, was the first to comprehend and publicly explain this principle.[63] Obbink intuited it independently in editing *De pietate*.[64]

One obstacle to the Delattre–Obbink method is that the draughtsmen (*disegnatori*) did not follow scientific principles. They did annotate the drawings to indicate that 'the original does not exist' (*non esiste l'originale*), but often they did not draw all the pieces or layers. They might omit a layer that contained a few letters from the end of one column, the usual intercolumnar space, and the first few letters of the next column, or they might omit just one of the two columns, normally whichever contained fewer letters. Layers showing the edges of columns are invaluable for discovering the correct sequence, since they can be joined to a piece that contains the remaining width of the column, but they are often missing. Again, if parts of two columns appeared in the same layer, the draughtsmen sometimes drew them separately and gave them separate numbers, but sometimes drew them as a single *disegno*. If the edge broke off a larger stack, the resultant small stack might be given a separate sequence of drawing-numbers within the same set. Thus in those drawings in N 1081 that are from *On Poems* 2 a stack of three fragments forms the right-hand upper edge of the main stack. Often the shapes of different stacks from the same roll will be uniform, so that they can be sorted out.

Problems in the sequence can be surmounted by close attention to the shape of successive fragments. Is each a left or a right edge? Does it have an upper or lower margin? How many letters does it preserve? On this basis, one should aim to reconstruct the shape of the original stack of *scorze*, and the surviving *ultimo foglio* can be used to determine its original exterior dimensions. These should be compared, where possible, with the dimensions in Piaggio's catalogue.

A second complication is that the draughtsmen sometimes depicted two or more layers in a single drawing. If the same layer appears in two successive drawings, the same letters will appear in them as *sovrapposti* or *sottoposti* (i.e. layered above or below); this can be a valuable clue to the correct sequence. In N 1081 of Philodemus' *On Poems* 2 the unroller missed the fact that the *scorza* was cracked across horizontally, and rarely exposed the upper and lower parts of the same layer at the same time. When the left margins of the upper and lower layers coincided, he drew the upper and lower parts of different layers as if they were the same layer. The problem was insoluble until I treated the upper and lower parts of each *disegno* as two separate sub-series, with a system of numeration to reflect this situation. Once such a situation is understood, the separate fragments then count as *sovrapposti* and *sottoposti* relative to each other, a fact which is vital to the reconstruction.

A third obstacle to the method is that the pencilled numbers on the *disegni* were sometimes changed after the operation of *scorzatura*, normally by erasure and writing a new number over the old one; sometimes the numbers were altered more than once. Such renumbering can ruin the prospects of reconstruction. The drawings themselves must always be inspected under the microscope; one can usually see that an erasure has been made, but it is often hard to determine the original reading. Sometimes two sets of unrelated drawings have been combined; one common technique for combining them was to prefix a '1' to the original number, so that '2' becomes '12' and so on. Minute inspection of the palaeography of the draughtsman can sometimes reveal renumbering. The solution to this problem may lie in the archives of the Officina. The drawings were meant to be engraved as copperplates, but this often happened only years later. Proof copies of the engravings (*prove di stampa*) were produced, which the Officina has preserved; these normally bear the number which they then had. This too may well be changed, but since the annotations are usually in ink, and the corrections are often in pencil, they are easy to decipher (Figure 12). Also, after *c.* 1836 the *Registro de' rami incisi*[65] records not only the engraver's identity but also specific fragment-numbers; by elimination and comparison with the *Herculanensia Volumina*, which identify the engraver, one can often determine which fragment is meant. In addition, the transcriptions of the *interpreti* may also disclose earlier numbering-systems. Tabulation of all the data will make any patterns in them easier to discern. On very rare occasions, renumbering conceals the blending

Figure 12. Detail of *prova di stampa* of *P. Herc.* 1081 fr. 9, to show changed numeration (photo R. Janko/B.N.N., copyright, all rights reserved)

of different hands within the same 'papyrus', where drawings of two rolls in two different scripts have been mixed up. Thus there are two sets of fragments within N 1081, since this set of *disegni* contains pieces from two rolls in two different hands.

I discovered a fourth complication when I noticed that some of the sequences of fragments in Delattre's reconstruction of *On Music* 4 ran forwards rather than backwards, and that these same fragments were the only ones that actually survived. I deduced that Piaggio made some experiments at lifting layers one by one from the outside or exterior of the roll, a process which I called *sollevamento* 'lifting off';[66] in theory this should yield a series of extant pieces from one side of a roll in the correct sequence, separated by equivalent pieces from the opposite side of each circumference. In practice, however, more than one layer would often separate at the same time, and the upper layers would then be removed by *scorzatura*, a process that would destroy any such piece. Hence the pieces resulting from *sollevamento* sometimes contain unexpected reversals of sequence that are owed to *scorzatura*. Within a set of fragments that were removed by *sollevamento*, pieces which were subjected to *scorzatura* will survive only as a *disegno*.

As for the Derveni papyrus, the layers in the stacks of fragments, which fill frames II–VII, called B–G by editors (there are also remnants of stacks in frames VIII–IX, but these are even more jumbled), did not adhere to each other. This fact enabled Fackelmann to preserve them. Their sequence, as determined by the sense, shows that he removed pieces now from the front (interior) of the stacks, now from the back (exterior), without any system; sequences of fragments run now forwards, by *sollevamento*, now backwards, as if by *scorzatura*, but all the pieces survive, regardless of the sequence in which they were removed or mounted.

If two or more sets of stacks (*scorze*) are thought to derive from a single roll, their relation to each other must be determined. One needs to try to classify them in terms of whether they come from the same side of the roll or from the opposite side. Similarities in the shapes of different stacks can be tabulated in order to see whether they resemble each other. If they have upper or lower margins, one may be able to find joins in the sense between the end of one column and the beginning of the next. **However, these are subject to error, since they depend on a single linkage only.** Joins where two halves of a column are in different stacks of *scorze* are more reliable, since these will have linkages within each line of writing and will yield a complete text. One needs to try every possible method for finding joins: matching up photocopies to scale of each piece, examining print-outs of the texts for possible similarities, and so on. The process needs repetition many times, since a change elsewhere in the reconstruction may allow a combination that had at first seemed impossible. One needs to persist until any oddities are resolved. As in the rolls from Herculaneum, pieces from different hemicylinders of the Derveni papyrus need to be arranged alternately in order to recover the original order. If pieces from the same hemicylinder are juxtaposed, the reconstruction must be wrong, as in the first edition of that papyrus.[67]

To establish the position of a piece from a hemicylinder, it helps greatly to know the width of its *sezione*. However, it is extremely hard to deduce measurements from fragments that are known solely from *disegni*.[68] Any extant *ultimo foglio* must be measured carefully, since in the *disegni* the draughtsmen spread the letters out for the sake of greater clarity, and did not draw broken edges exactly to scale; one can approximate by counting the number of standard letter-widths and comparing the width of that number of letter-widths on the original. If the column-to-column width can be determined from surviving pieces (see Part I), and the order can be tested by placing the fragments on a model, the distances from one layer to the next must be consistent, as measured from the start of one column to the start of a column in the next circumference; the circumference should always diminish towards the end of the roll. If the number of layers can be determined, the circumferences can yield approximate measurements, and indeed the approximate measurements can help to determine the number of circumferences; however, one must bear in mind that the tightness with which rolls were wound will vary unpredictably, at least at a few points.

Most rolls contain both *scorze* and a *midollo*, but in a few cases no *midollo* has been identified, as in Philodemus' *De poematis* i. This was reconstructed entirely from six sets of *scorze*, of which only the *ultimo foglio* survived in most cases. Let us turn to reconstructing the *midolli*, and to the tricky problem of how to reconstruct the transition from *scorze* to *midollo*.

(b) Reconstructing continuous parts of rolls

This part of the process of reconstruction might seem straightforward, but in fact has many pitfalls.[69] First, although a *midollo* was unrolled continuously, the separate frames (*cornici*) into which it was cut may have had their original order altered. Hayter's system of numbering (A–Z, without J) was used down to 1806 at least; these letters were later replaced by numbers. The letters were also written on the original *cartoncini* on which the papyri were first mounted. Many papyri, however, were remounted in the 1860s on new *cornici* of blue or white cardboard, numbered in ink under the new system (see Part I). The number of these *cornici* might differ from the number of original *cartoncini*. In the case of Philodemus' *On Poems 4*, the original numeration appeared in pencil on the corners of the new *cornici*, where they were hidden (as the unfaded blue reveals) under the frames in which the papyri were hung on the wall until 1910.[70]

Many rolls have the entire *midollo* under a single inventory-number, but the *midolli* of others were unrolled sequentially at various times and received different numbers, as in Philodemus' *On Poems 2*. Four stretches of papyrus from this roll were given four largely unrelated numbers. Since their dates of unrolling were not clearly recorded in the archives, their relative sequence became clear only via the careful measurement of the *sezioni* and circumferences; **even the sequence of the *cornici* within each number needs to be confirmed by such measurements.**

Constructing a table of fragments and circumferences (Figure 13), in which each fragment is assigned to the correct hemicylinder and to an appropriate circumference (certainty is not always possible), is an essential step towards the reconstruction of the roll; this needs to

volute no. (no. of total whole cols.)	next $2\pi r$ (est.)	*sezione* A (W. = 53.3%) (measurements from extant pieces are bold)	*sezione* B (W. = 46.7%)	*kollesis* and distance to next; actual and estimated distance; changes to W. of cols.
1 (3)	21.0	<***> + <*>//	//<*> + <***>	?
2 (6)	20.9	1081b fr. 23 (olim fr. B12) ~ 1677a fr. 12 (olim fr. 1?) + 1081b fr. 20 (olim fr. B11) ~ <*>// **20.9**	//<*> + 994 **cr. 1 fr. Ba** ~ <***>	?
3 (9)	20.6	1081b fr. 17 (olim fr. B10?) + fr. 15 (olim fr. B9)//	//<*> + 994 cr. 1 fr. Bb ~ 1677a fr. 3 col. i (olim fr. 2) + <*> ~ col. ii// **22.0?**	?
4 (11)	20.5	//<*> + <*>//	//<*> + 994 cr. 1 fr. Bc ~ <*>//	?
...	...	...	...	...
100 (195)	7.9	994 col. 13// **7.9**	//994 col. 13 + col. 14//	994 col. 13 litt. 3: 16.0 to next
101 (196)	7.8	//994 col. 14// **7.8**	//994 col. 14 + col. 15//	none
102 (197)	7.7	//994 col. 15//	//994 col. 15 + col. 16// **7.6 (cr. 14)**	994 col. 15 litt. 9: 16.2 to next
103 (198)	7.5	//994 col. 16//	//994 col. 16 + col. 17//	none

Figure 13. Extracts from table of layers and circumferences in Philodemus' *On Poems 2* (R. Janko)

contain a calculation by dead reckoning of the expected circumferences, together with a record of the circumferences that have been reliably measured. It must be kept in mind that **the length of the circumference diminishes even within a single circumference.** Since the column-to-column width, as measured from the left margins of successive columns, is nearly always fixed, whereas successive circumferences must decline by a smaller or occasionally a larger amount, Essler used the relation between successive circumferences and the left edges of columns to calculate, using modular arithmetic, the probability that successive left edges belong to successive circumferences.[71] His spread-sheet by which that probability is calculated is a valuable tool for reconstruction (Figure 14).[72]

If the exact circumference is not known, it can be extrapolated from circumferences further away. The reduction in successive circumferences is necessarily limited by the thickness of the material of which the scroll is made; each circumference must decline by an amount given by the

	Excel File Edit View Insert Format Tools Data Window $ Help							

maße_italiano sovr.xls

	A	B	C	D	E	F	G	H
1	Distanza fra due margini							
2								
3	Largezza della colonna più intercolumnio					70		
4	Circonferenza					152		
5	Diminuizione di circonferenza per voluta					1		
6	Distanza del primo margine dall'inizio della circonferenza					0		
7	Distanza del secondo margine dall'inizio della circonferenza					79		
8								
9	Margine di errore					10		
10								
11	Di quale colonna fa parte il secondo margine							
12								
13	Colonna	0 (la stessa)	1	2	3	4	5	6
14	Vero/Falso	FALSE	TRUE	FALSE	FALSE	FALSE	FALSE	FALSE	F
15	Margine di errore	79	9	61	20	50	30	40
16								
17								
18	La distanza di due colonne sulla base delle colleseis							
19								
20	Largezza della colonna più intercolonnio					90		
21	Largezza media di un collema					171		
22	Distanza della prima collesis dal punto d'attacco dell colonna precedente					60		
23	Distanza della seconda collesis dal punto d'attacco dell colonna precedente					33		
24								
25	Margine di errore					20		

Ausgabe

Figure 14. Example of the use of Holger Essler's spread-sheet based on modular arithmetic (photo R. Janko)

mathematical formula $\delta \geq 2\pi t$, where δ denotes the decline and t denotes the thickness of the material (normally 0.15 mm).[73] Experiments with models and verified actual examples show that the decline remains fairly constant except for a few wildly greater declines, where a single spiral was wound much more loosely.

Exact measurement of the circumference is also vital for placing *(frammenti) sottoposti* ('pieces placed under') and *sovrapposti* ('pieces placed over'), which range in size from part of a single letter (Figure 3) to a large piece of text (Figure 15).[74] These occur both in the originals and (sometimes) in the *disegni*, and also appear in the Derveni papyrus, albeit rarely. They are pieces of a layer other than the main one that is visible: *sottoposti* are displaced pieces of a previous circumference, which may be seen to run under the main layer; *sovrapposti* are pieces of a later circumference, which sometimes visibly overlie the main layer. These are terribly hard to detect. Some claim that they can always see them even in the multispectral images, which of course are two-dimensional. In my experience, however, they are best seen only in the original three dimensions, and even there one often has trouble deciding whether they lie under or over the main layer. I always test both possibilities for placing them, and often find that apparent *sovrapposti* are in fact *sottoposti* and *vice versa*.

Knowing the circumference of the roll at any given point, a difficult task, is vital for placing such fragments, especially those that are tiny,

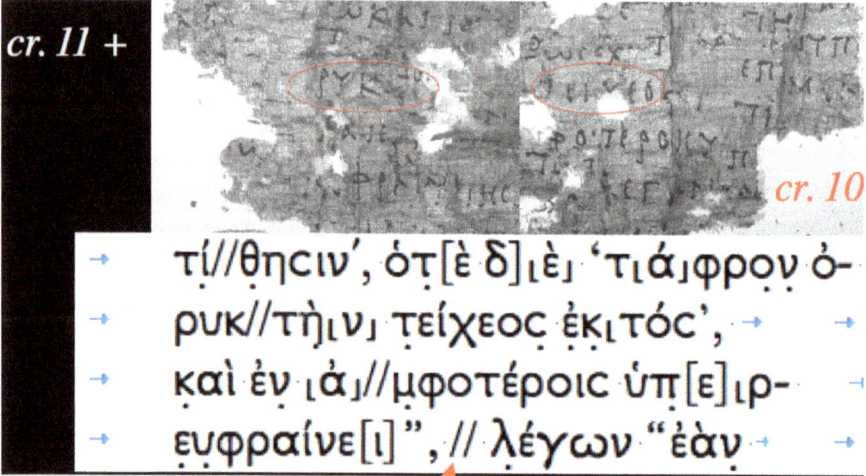

Figure 15. Join between *sottoposto* and *sovrapposto* in P. Herc. 994 crr. 10 and 11 (photos Brigham Young University/B.N.N., copyright, all rights reserved)

as is most often the case. Conversely, finding and placing them can determine the circumference. Extraneous letters should always be checked against the text roughly one circumference earlier and one circumference later. If they fit, they provide the most exact measurement of the circumference imaginable. Extraneous letters are not always from the previous or succeeding circumference, but may have originated several circumferences away. However, it is very difficult to find the location of such letters at a distance of more than one circumference, since the measurements are rarely exact enough. Also, I have hardly ever managed to place them across a break between *cornici*, because the cut makes it hard to be sure of the exact height on the other side, even though the letters must belong at almost exactly the same height in the adjacent circumference; rolls were never wound diagonally.

Sovrapposti and *sottoposti* were sometimes transcribed from the original papyrus into the *disegni*, and these can be very helpful for reconstruction; if extraneous letters appear in *disegni* that are not now in the original, they are normally *sovrapposti* which have since fallen away and perished. If the circumference is known, the letters may be found to belong one or two circumferences later. Conversely, if a *disegno* offers a coherent text that is now interrupted in the original by extraneous letters, the latter are probably preserved on a *sottoposto* which has only become visible since the *disegno* was made. These phenomena also appear in old photographs of the papyri. They lie at the origin of the myth, or rather the suspicion propagated by scoffers and sceptics, that letters appear and disappear in the Herculaneum papyri according to papyrologists' wishes; in reality letters only disappear, as the papyri slowly disintegrate, and the 'new' ones replace only in appearance those that have actually vanished for ever.

The presence of a *kollesis* can prove or refute the placing of upper or lower fragments that are broken horizontally; the line of the *kollesis* should run vertically through both fragments. The same test may apply to the crack that precedes the *kollesis* (see Part I). Once successive *kolleseis* have been found, the distance between each one and the next needs to be determined as exactly as possible. These widths can be used to calculate the average width of all the *kollemata* observed in the roll (Figure 16).[75] The widths of *kollemata* vary considerably, even within a single roll, but they are nonetheless a useful indication as to whether the reconstruction is correct. Like column-to-column widths, *kollemata* vary in their incidence with regard to the successive circumferences. Hence modular arithmetic can be used to calculate the probability that

994 cr. 15	49A	start	col. 23 litt. 12	2.8 to right	2.8 + 12.4 = 15.0
994 cr. 16	49B	end	col. 25 litt. 16	12.4 from left	2.8 + 12.4 = 15.0
994 cr. 16	50	whole	col. 25 litt. 16– col. 27 litt. 16	**14.5**	**14.5**
994 cr. 16	51A	start	col. 27 litt. 16	1.0–1.5 to right	1.5 + 14.9 = 16.4
994 cr. 17	51B	end	col. 30 litt. 4	14.9 from left	1.5 + 14.9 = 16.4
994 cr. 17	52	whole	col. 30 litt. 4– col. 31 litt. 7	**15.7** (with lost layer)	**15.7**
994 cr. 17	53A	start	col. 31 litt. 7	3.8 to right	3.8 + 12.0 = 15.8
994 cr. 18	53B	end	col. 33 litt. 14	12.0 from left	3.8 + 12.0 = 15.8
994 cr. 18	54	whole	col. 33 litt. 14– col. 35 litt. 19+2	**16.0**	**16.0**
994 cr. 18	55A	start	col. 35 litt. 19+2	0.2 to right	0.2 + ⟨0.5⟩ + 15.0 ≈ 15.7
994 cr. 19	55B	end	col. 38 litt. 3	15.0 from left	0.2 + ⟨0.5⟩ + 15.0 ≈ 15.7
994 cr. 19	56A	start	col. 38 litt. 3	13.4 to right	13.4 + 2.3 = 15.7
994 cr. 2	56B	end	in *agraphon*	2.3 from left	13.4 + 2.3 = 15.7
994 cr. 2	57	start	in *agraphon*	10.5 to right	10.5+ (**incomplete**)
					average = 274.4 + 17 = 16.1
					maximum = 17.8
					minimum = 14.5

Figure 16. Extract from table of measurements of *kollemata* in Philodemus' *On Poems* 2 (R. Janko)

a particular *kollesis* falls within the next circumference, again using Essler's spread-sheet, which has a setting for this calculation. However, the probabilities provide less precision than in the case of column-to-column widths.

Stichometry, i.e. the numerals that the scribes employed to verify the number of lines or columns that they had copied, is, where it exists, a valuable check on the reconstruction of the roll.[76] Not all rolls have stichometry, and it can take different forms. Column-numbers may appear in the upper margins, perhaps with the total of the number of columns (σελίδες) at the end of the manuscript; these are easy to interpret.[77] It is more usual to find stichometric signs in the left margins, together with a stichometric total at the end of the roll, introduced by the abbreviation ἀριθ(μός) and written in the Attic system of acrophonic numerals. The signs comprise the Greek alphabet of twenty-four letters (or twenty-five, if, as occasionally seems to happen, the digamma is included). If more signs are needed, the series of letters is repeated, starting again with alpha. They often have horizontal bars over them, under them, or in both positions. There may also be stichometric points, i.e. dots in the left margins at regular intervals: each interval corresponds to ten *stichoi*. Since a *stichos* was originally the length of a hexameter, and prose texts at Herculaneum are written in shorter lines about half as long as that, one cannot simply convert the number of lines in the papyrus into *stichoi* or *vice versa*: the conversion factor must be determined.

The first step towards using stichometry for reconstruction is to find it. Margins must be scanned closely for signs, though often all they yield is marks where the scribe tested his pen. Sometimes, despite one's best efforts, only a couple of signs can be found. But even these can suffice for the reconstruction of an entire roll.

The next step is to determine the interval between signs. The usual interval in prose texts written in narrow columns of 18–20 letters is 180 or 200; this number was deemed to equal 100 *stichoi* or hexameter verses. If the full height of the roll is preserved, the interval can be discovered without difficulty. If stichometric points are used, they will appear every ten stichoi; so the interval will be the number of lines which separates two successive points multiplied by ten. Even if the bottom or top of the roll has perished, so that the number of lines per column is unknown, all is not lost, since even a few signs provide more fixed points on which to base calculation than one would expect. The start of the roll, even if lost, remains of course line 1, and the end of the roll, if reasonably intact, provides another fixed point. Simultaneous algebraic equations can be created to solve the problem.[78] Different solutions to the equations can be tested in a spread-sheet into which one can insert varying intervals between signs and different average numbers of lines per column. Even though the number of lines per column will fluctuate slightly, most of these tests will predict that stichometric signs will occur at places where one is certain that they do not; by elimination, the correct number of lines per column can be found.[79] Philodemus' *On Poems* 4 was an especially illuminating case, since for a long time the stichometry made no sense. Eventually David Blank proved to me that an irregularity in the column-to-column width, where there seemed to be an exceptionally wide intercolumnium, was in fact no such thing, but rather a place where a whole column was lost under the next one; because the overlap occurred in successive intercolumnia, where there were no letters running under the next circumference, the transition between layers was almost completely invisible. Once the lost column was posited, the stichometry was quickly solved with algebra.[80]

Stichometry can readily be used to calculate the original number of columns in the complete roll and its original length, and to check and solidify the entire reconstruction. The stichometry can be compared with the number of observed columns (which can be multiplied by the column-to-column width), the number of *kollemata* (multiplied by their average or total width), the cumulative sum of the circumferences as they have been measured or posited, and the physical widths of extant pieces of papyrus to determine whether, and where, any lost columns and missing circumferences may lie. When the unrollers of Herculaneum papyri lost the leading edge, they sometimes had to cut away layers of papyrus that could contain quite a number of columns. Earlier editors were often unaware of such losses, which can now be determined quite exactly. Careful attention to all these aspects of the material support of our texts permits them to be reconstructed with hitherto unimagined exactitude. The work is laborious in many respects, but does pay off. To determine the length of the entire roll, one must make allowance for the titles and unwritten portions at the end, and allow the same amount for those at the beginning, which is almost always lost.[81]

Lastly, other features internal to the texts themselves can contribute to their reconstruction, such as gradual changes in the number of letters per line or in the number of lines per column, the presence of a second scribal hand for a certain portion of the papyrus, the presence for a stretch of a few columns of notes or accents added by a reader (this appears in *On Poems* 1), or the series of textual parallels between summaries and rebuttals of opponents such as Philodemus often employs: for example, the summary and rebuttal on *On Music* 4 or the summary in *On Poems* 1 that is rebutted at the end of the book, continuing throughout *On Poems* 2.[82] Which features are present will vary according to the idiosyncrasies of the particular text, but one needs to watch out for them.

My own system for reconstruction, which I learned from Daniel Delattre,[83] is to build a paper model of the entire roll at its actual size, using print-outs of the digital images where available, and otherwise print-outs of images of the *disegni*, both adjusted to the correct scale (Figure 17). These materials are fastened with small pieces of plastic tape to a long roll of paper, put together from separate sheets by using the same plastic tape. The tape must be of the kind that can be torn off or removed without damaging the surface to which it lightly adheres; never use glue. The backing has drawn on it in pencil column-to-column widths to serve as a guide and a first indication of errors in placement. If necessary, the roll can readily be shortened or lengthened at any given point by inserting more paper backing, in quantities that correspond to the column-to-column width. The model needs to be stretched out on a table at least two metres long in front of a large window (the trailing ends of the scroll can be allowed to fall into cardboard boxes on the floor at either end). Good light is essential; sunlight reflected off

Figure 17. Paper model of Philodemus' *On Poems* 2, length 16 m (photo M. Hannoosh)

snow is best. The model can be rolled, stored and transported in a stiff cardboard tube.

Applying all the principles explained above, one starts with an initial guess, laying out the pieces in what one deems the most likely order. Many problems will at once appear —fragments that cannot join, columns that do not fit into the regular spacing of the column-to-column widths, and so on. By constantly striving to better the text, and by constantly trying different combinations of pieces, one gradually improves the model. The hardest steps are probably two.

The first is to manage the transition between the initial part preserved only in *disegni* and the extant pieces of papyrus. This can be very awkward, since an error of only one column can prevent one from integrating the two segments. Often the mistake lies in a confusion as to which hemicylinder (*sezione*) in the segment preserved only in *disegni* corresponds to the same hemicylinder in the extant portion. One must always test the other possibility, even if it seems to be wrong.

Secondly, the final decision that the model is correct is a source of great procrastination and anguish.[84] One's edition can only be finished once it has final column-numbers, but during the reconstruction these continue to change; in draft texts, I mark column-numbers with footnote-numbers that adjust automatically, until the reconstruction is stable. But how can one ever be sure that the reconstruction is right, and apply these final column-numbers? One is never entirely sure, and our work in this challenging field must always be deemed probable rather than certain; but when repeated rearrangements yield impossibilities of the same kind, when work on the text itself seems subject to the law of diminishing returns, when all the calculations outlined above (or as many of them as can be applied) have been done and yield consistent results, and when the imposition of this particular arrangement keeps yielding good textual continuity, it is time to... work on a different project for a while, and to pause before accepting the column-numbers as final. For once these numbers are in the text, everything else, including cross-references, the discussion of the papyrus and its language and content in the introduction, and the *index verborum*, will depend on them and will be fixed. Thereafter the numbers can no longer be changed without immense and ungrateful labour. Thus it is always with a heavy heart and deep foreboding, and not with any feeling of triumph or even satisfaction, that I conclude that the numeration of the columns is stable enough to be adopted for my edition, and at last insert the final column-numbers into the *index verborum*.

As Vergil feelingly put it, *labor omnia vincit | improbus*. Only when clad in an armament of unremitting effort and the magic of numbers, harnessing fire-breathing bulls and facing down armed skeletons left and right, can one plough the field of these papyri and reap their harvest of new texts.

Notes

1. The closest analogues are M. Capasso, *Manuale di papirologia ercolanese* (Galatina, 1991), pp. 229–236, and D. Delattre, *La Villa des Papyrus et les rouleaux d'Herculanum. La Bibliothèque de Philodème* (Liège, 2006), neither in English. D. Sider, 'The Special Case of Herculaneum', in *The Oxford Handbook of Papyrology*, ed. by R.S. Bagnall (Oxford and New York, 2009), pp. 303–319, admits some inaccuracies (pp. 306–310). I. Gallo, 'The Herculaneum Papyri', in *Greek and Latin Papyrology*, transl. M.R. Falivene and J.R. March, Institute of Classical Studies (London, 1986), pp. 36–45, has a very basic account. W.A. Johnson, *Bookrolls and Scribes in Oxyrhynchus* (Toronto, 2004), does not treat Herculaneum papyri, but provides much invaluable comparative material from Oxyrhynchus. E.G. Turner, *Greek Papyri: an Introduction* (2nd edn, Oxford, 1980) did not

even list *P. Herc.* among abbreviations for papyri, and his first edition (1973) ignores carbonized papyri.

2. On these see Delattre, *La Villa des Papyrus*, pp. 26–27.

3. The Johannowsky papyrus from Thmouis in the Nile delta, also kept in the Officina dei Papiri, is likewise mounted on a *cornice* without glass: see G. Del Mastro, 'Il papiro Johannowsky: un papiro di Thmouis?', *Aegyptus*, 90 (2010), 23–36. Like the other tax-rolls from Thmouis, it is preserved flat; this fact renders these papyri more readily legible than other carbonized ones, and it will be reconstructed like non-carbonized tax-rolls.

4. E.g. the tax-roll in Strasbourg from Hermoupolis that has been cut into sections: see R.-L. Chang, *Un dossier fiscal hermopolitain d'époque romaine (P. Stras. inv. gr. 897–8, 903–5, 939–68, 982–1000, 1010–13, 1918–29): édition et commentaire* (IFAO, Cairo, forthcoming).

5. See also Delattre, *La Villa des Papyrus*, pp. 102–105.

6. On the role of the CISPE see Delattre, *La Villa des Papyrus*, pp. 109, 133–134.

7. V. Litta, *I papiri ercolanesi* II. *Indice topografico e sistematico*, Quaderni della Biblioteca Nazionale di Napoli IV. 6 (Naples, 1977), has been replaced by A. Travaglione, *Catalogo descrittivo dei Papiri Ercolanesi* (Naples, 2008); both are held in the Officina.

8. M. Gigante, *Catalogo dei Papiri Ercolanesi* (Naples, 1979).

9. M. Capasso, 'Primo supplemento al *Catalogo dei Papiri Ercolanesi*', *Cronache Ercolanesi*, 19 (1989), 193–264; G. Del Mastro, 'Secondo supplemento al *Catalogo dei Papiri Ercolanesi*', *Cronache Ercolanesi*, 30 (2000), 157–241.

10. For a description of the Officina see Delattre, *La Villa des Papyrus*, pp. 106–109.

11. On the unrolling see Capasso, *Manuale*, pp. 88–118; A. Angeli, 'Lo svolgimento dei papiri carbonizzati', *Papyrologia Lupiensia*, 3 (1994), 37–104; Delattre, *La Villa des Papyrus*, pp. 29–39.

12. On their conservation see Delattre, *La Villa des Papyrus*, pp. 25–27.

13. H. Essler, 'Bilder von Papyri und Papyri als Bilder', *Cronache Ercolanesi*, 36 (2006), 103–143 (pp. 103–127).

14. Even the new *cartoncini* have been replaced in cases where Fackelmann or Kleve remounted the pieces, but these have been preserved.

15. A. Fackelmann, 'The Restoration of the Herculaneum Papyri and Other Recent Finds', *BICS*, 17 (1970), 144–145; Capasso, *Manuale*, pp. 110–112. The earlier backings are kept in the Officina.

16. His report on his restoration of that papyrus is published in T. Kouremenos, G.M. Parássoglou and K. Tsantsanoglou, *The Derveni Papyrus* (Florence, 2006), pp. 4–5.

17. Its operative end must be prevented from scratching the glass by a ring of soft plastic foam. Similar microscopes in the near-infrared spectrum are also invaluable (see R. Janko, 'Parmenides in the Derveni Papyrus: New Images for a New Edition', *ZPE*, 200 (2016), 1–21.

18. B. Fosse, K. Kleve and F.C. Störmer, 'Unrolling the Herculaneum Papyri', *Cronache Ercolanesi*, 14 (1984), 9–15; Capasso, *Manuale*, pp. 112–116; Delattre, *La Villa des Papyrus*, pp. 110–112. As the method is invasive, it has been abandoned.

19. On the drawings see Capasso, *Manuale*, pp. 119–128.

20. The shelf-mark is Ms. Gr. class. c. 2. They were catalogued by W. Scott, *Fragmenta Herculanensia* (Oxford, 1885).

21. For the characteristics of these see M. Capasso, 'Per la storia della papirologia ercolanese III: il Piaggio a lavoro', in *Bicentenario della morte di Antonio Piaggio*, ed. by M. Capasso (Galatina, 1997), pp. 61–76, showing that Piaggio's drawings contained multiple columns; R. Janko, 'New Fragments of Epicurus, Metrodorus, Demetrius Laco, Philodemus, the "Carmen De Bello Actiaco" and Other Texts in Oxonian *Disegni* of 1788–1792', *Cronache Ercolanesi*, 38 (2008), 5–95.

22. There is a set of good images of them on the internet at the website of the Herculaneum Society.

23. Ms. Clar. Press d. 44. On Davy's activities see F. Longo Auricchio, 'L'esperienza napoletana del Davy', in *Proceedings of the XIXth International Congress of Papyrology*, ed. by A.H.S. El-Mosallamy (Cairo, 1992), pp. 189–202.

24. Royal Collections Inventory No. 1076170.

25. Study of these unpublished *disegni* has begun (Guay and Janko in progress). They depict parts of *P. Herc.* 59, 97, 177, 241, 371, 373, 396, 494, 495, 502, 811, 1138, 1484, 1620, and 1671. Of these, 396, 502, 1484 and 1620 are in Latin, and the rest are in Greek.

26. This procedure was introduced when the Accademia Ercolanese was refounded in 1787.

27. R. Janko, with D.L. Blank, 'Two New Manuscript Sources for the Texts of the Herculaneum Papyri', *Cronache Ercolanesi*, 28 (1998), 173–184; R. Farese, 'Catalogo degli "illustrazioni" e degli interpreti', *Cronache Ercolanesi*, 29 (1999), 83–94.

28. Ms. Gr. class. c. 2, vol. 8.

29. Images of *HV* are available on the website of the Herculaneum Society.

30. Shelf-mark III 411.501; cf. R. Janko, *Philodemus: On Poems Book One* (Oxford, 2000), p. 40.

31. J. Hammerstaedt, 'Christian Jensen's and Wolfgang Schmid's Unpublished Herculanean Papers', in *Proceedings of the XXVth International Congress of Papyrology*, ed. by T. Gagos (Ann Arbor, 2010), pp. 291–298; R. Janko, ed., *Philodemus* On Poems *Books Three and Four, with the Fragments of Aristotle* On Poets (Oxford, 2011), pp. 155–157.

32. On photography of the papyri see Capasso, *Manuale*, pp. 142–148.

33. Janko, 'Parmenides in the Derveni Papyrus'.

34. S.W. Booras and D.R. Seely, 'Multi-Spectral Imaging of the Herculaneum Papyri', *Cronache Ercolanesi*, 29 (1999), 95–100; Delattre, *La Villa des Papyrus*, pp. 113–116.

35. For similar cautions see Delattre, *La Villa des Papyrus*, p. 115.

36. Cf. Johnson, *Bookrolls*, pp. 91–98.

37. Cf. *ibid.*, pp. 100–118.

38. The principle of *sezioni* was discovered by M.L. Nardelli, 'Ripristino topografico di *sovrapposti* e *sottoposti* in alcuni papiri ercolanesi', *Cronache Ercolanesi*, 3 (1973), 104–111.

39. M. Capasso, *Volumen: aspetti della tipologia del rotolo librario antico* (Naples, 1995), pp. 73–98; Delattre, *La Villa des Papyrus*, pp. 41–42. The Derveni papyrus too must already have had such a rod, which was *c.* 1.2 cm in diameter (Janko, 'Parmenides in the Derveni Papyrus').

40. Cf. Johnson, *Bookrolls*, pp. 88–91.

41. For these rules see Janko, *Philodemus: On Poems Book One*, pp. 75–76.

42. I owe this technique to Jim Porter. Now, however, bold type is beginning to be used for letters transposed from a different layer. These are best left in the old convention, i.e. //α//, at least until the text is ready for publication.

43. Usener's *Glossarium Epicureum* and Vooys' *Lexicon Philodemeum*, rare works available only in exceptional libraries, are invaluable resources for Herculaneum papyri in particular. The references are keyed, respectively, to *HV* and to old Teubner editions of Philodemus, which also need to be to hand. The index to Sudhaus' edition of Philodemus' *Rhetoric* is useful too, not to mention the *indices verborum* of more recent editions.

44. Philodemus' works are still so inchoate that most are not included in the *TLG*. A draft of a digital version of his texts created for the *TLG* was made available to the Philodemus Translation Project. A version of it without

diacritics, dots and brackets has proved extraordinarily useful for finding supplements, along with a version with even the spaces removed.

45. M. McOsker, 'The Number of Papyrus Rolls Excavated from the Villa dei Papiri: Some Overlooked Evidence', *Cronache Ercolanesi*, 46 (2016).

46. Janko, 'New Fragments of Epicurus', showing that the worst confusion among the numbers occurred in *c.* 1790.

47. See Delattre, *La Villa des Papyrus*, pp. 130–131.

48. D.L. Blank, 'Reflections on Rereading Piaggio and the Early History of the Herculaneum Papyri', *Cronache Ercolanesi*, 29 (1999), 55–82; Delattre, *La Villa des Papyrus*, p. 32.

49. See D.L. Blank and F. Longo Auricchio, 'An Inventory of the Herculaneum Papyri from Piaggio's Time', *Cronache Ercolanesi*, 30 (2000), 131–147, and for the exact date Janko, *Philodemus:* On Poems *Book One*, p. 8 n. 1.

50. Their dimensions are given in old Neapolitan *palme* and *oncie*, where one *palma* = 26.37 cm and one *oncia* = 2.1976 cm. The first part of the catalogue is still undiscovered.

51. The introduction to my edition of Philodemus' *On Poems* 2 (Janko, in preparation) will contain an analytical table of all the papyri that were opened down to 1796.

52. Blank and Longo Auricchio, 'An Inventory'. Those which do not follow numerical order list the papyri in relative order of unrolling. The 'Nota di tutti i disegni de' papiri d'Ercolano svolti, e questi col numero secondo si trovano segnati nell'inventario' (*ibid.*, pp. 133–136), a draft which is in the Bodleian Library (Ms. Gr. class. c. 10, f. 36), was written on 2 Sept. 1807, as is known from the fair copy in the Archivio di Stato di Palermo (Reale Segreteria fasc. 5512). Its only notable variants are that entry 908 records 'frammenti Latini' instead of 'frammenti Greci', and 994 lists 'Disegni diecisette' rather than 'Disegni trentasette'.

53. Archivio dell'Officina dei Papiri (A.O.P.) XVII 11, listing 1756 items.

54. A.O.P. XVII 12; for its authorship see Janko, *Philodemus:* On Poems *Book One*, p. 14 n. 1.

55. A.O.P. XVIII 13.

56. H. Essler, 'ΧΩΡΙΖΕΙΝ ΑΧΩΡΙΣΤΑ. Über die Anfänge getrennte Aufbewahrung der Herkulanischen Papyri', *Cronache Ercolanesi*, 40 (2010), 173–189; he publishes all the relevant data down to March 1802, but only some thereafter.

57. See Capasso, *Manuale*, pp. 245–252; A. Travaglione, 'Incisori e curatori della *Collectio Altera*. Il contributo delle prove di stampa alla storia dei

papiri ercolanesi', in *Contributi alla Storia della Officina dei Papiri*, iii, ed. by M. Capasso (Naples, 2003), pp. 87–178. There is no convenient database of the personnel, published or unpublished. Editions by myself and others provide information piecemeal on those people whom we have encountered, e.g. that Pessetti was dismissed as *interprete* in 1811, Caterino was appointed in 1812, Genovesi in 1822, Ottaviano and Quaranta in 1826, and Lucignano in 1832. Since posts at the Officina were treated more or less as hereditary or as a family business, many employees share surnames, which can complicate matters.

58. See further G. Houston, *Inside Roman Libraries: Book Collections and Their Management in Antiquity* (Chapel Hill, 2014), pp. 87–129, 280–286.

59. G. Del Mastro, *Chartes. Catalogo Multimediale dei Papiri Ercolanesi* (Naples, 2005).

60. R. Janko, 'Reconstructing (again) the Opening of the Derveni Papyrus', *ZPE*, 166 (2008), 37–51.

61. On the method see Delattre, *La Villa des Papyrus*, pp. 116–119.

62. A. Schober, 'Philodemi *De pietate* pars prior', diss. Königsberg, 1923, pr. in *Cronache Ercolanesi*, 18 (1988), 65–125.

63. D. Delattre, 'Philodème, *De la musique*: livre IV, colonnes 40* à 109*', *Cronache Ercolanesi*, 19 (1989), 49–143.

64. D. Obbink, *Philodemus:* On Piety *Part I: Critical Text with Commentary* (Oxford, 1996).

65. A.O.P. XVII 10. There is also the 'Notamento de' rami incisi' of 1840 (A.O.P. XVII 15). Neither is published.

66. Janko, *Philodemus:* On Poems *Book One*, pp. 19–20; Delattre, *La Villa des Papyrus*, pp. 32–33.

67. Janko, 'Reconstructing'.

68. Cf. Delattre, *La Villa des Papyrus*, pp. 120–121.

69. *Ibid.*, pp. 121–130.

70. Essler, 'Bilder', 103–127.

71. H. Essler, 'Rekonstruktion von Papyrusrollen auf mathematischer Grundlage', *Cronache Ercolanesi*, 38 (2008), 273–307.

72. This is available upon application to Prof. Essler.

73. See Janko, *Philodemus:* On Poems *Book One*, pp. 108–109; Janko, *Philodemus* On Poems *Books Three and Four*, pp. 43–46, with a formula for calculating the length of the scroll based on its diameter. On the length of rolls

see Janko, *Philodemus: On Poems Book One*, pp. 118–119; Delattre, *La Villa des Papyrus*, pp. 50–51.

74. On their importance see Delattre, *La Villa des Papyrus*, pp. 119–121.

75. Capasso, *Volumen*, pp. 55–72; Delattre, *La Villa des Papyrus*, pp. 48–49.

76. For stichometry see K. Ohly, 'Die Stichometrie der Herkulanischen Rollen', *Archiv für Papyrusforschung*, 7 (1924), 190–220 and *Stichometrische Untersuchungen* (Leipzig, 1928); Obbink, *Philodemus: On Piety*, pp. 62–63; Delattre, *La Villa des Papyrus*, pp. 44–48.

77. Delattre, *La Villa des Papyrus*, pp. 49–50.

78. For examples of such calculations see Janko, *Philodemus: On Poems Book One*, pp. 114–18; Janko, *Philodemus On Poems Books Three and Four*, pp. 198–207.

79. Janko, 'Parmenides in the Derveni Papyrus', on the stichometry of the Derveni papyrus.

80. Janko, *Philodemus On Poems Books Three and Four*, pp. 198–207.

81. On initial and final titles at Herculaneum see G. Del Mastro, *Titoli e annotazione bibliologiche nei papiri greci di Ercolano*, Cronache Ercolanesi Suppl., 5 (Naples, 2014).

82. Janko, *Philodemus: On Poems Book One*, pp. 121–189; Delattre, *La Villa des Papyrus*, pp. 128–130.

83. See Delattre, *La Villa des Papyrus*, pp. 116, 121, on the importance of this step. He advocates digital models too, but they are hard to manipulate.

84. Delattre relates how he twice thought his reconstruction was finished before it actually was: see *La Villa des Papyrus*, pp. 125–127.

Bibliography

Angeli, A., 'Lo svolgimento dei papiri carbonizzati', *Papyrologia Lupiensia*, 3 (1994), 37–104

Blank, D.L., 'Reflections on Rereading Piaggio and the Early History of the Herculaneum Papyri', *Cronache Ercolanesi*, 29 (1999), 55–82

Blank, D.L., and Longo Auricchio, F., 'An Inventory of the Herculaneum Papyri from Piaggio's Time', *Cronache Ercolanesi*, 30 (2000), 131–147

Booras, S. W., and Seely, D. R., 'Multi-Spectral Imaging of the Herculaneum Papyri', *Cronache Ercolanesi*, 29 (1999), 95–100

Capasso, M., 'Primo supplemento al *Catalogo dei Papiri Ercolanesi*', *Cronache Ercolanesi*, 19 (1989), 193–264

Capasso, M., *Manuale di papirologia ercolanese* (Galatina, 1991)

Capasso, M., *Volumen: aspetti della tipologia del rotolo librario antico* (Naples, 1995)

Capasso, M., 'Per la storia della papirologia ercolanese III: il Piaggio a lavoro', in *Bicentenario della morte di Antonio Piaggio*, ed. by M. Capasso (Galatina, 1997), pp. 61–76

Chang, R.-L., *Un dossier fiscal hermopolitain d'époque romaine* (P. Stras. inv. gr. 897–8, 903–5, 939–68, 982–1000, 1010–13, 1918–29): édition et commentaire (IFAO, Cairo, forthcoming)

Del Mastro, G., 'Secondo supplemento al *Catalogo dei Papiri Ercolanesi*', *Cronache Ercolanesi*, 30 (2000), 157–241

Del Mastro, G., *Chartes. Catalogo Multimediale dei Papiri Ercolanesi* (Naples, 2005)

Del Mastro, G., 'Il papiro Johannowsky: un papiro di Thmouis?', *Aegyptus*, 90 (2010), 23–36

Del Mastro, G., *Titoli e annotazione bibliologiche nei papiri greci di Ercolano*, Cronache Ercolanesi Suppl., 5 (Naples, 2014)

Delattre, D., 'Philodème, *De la musique*: livre IV, colonnes 40* à 109*', *Cronache Ercolanesi*, 19 (1989), 49–143

Delattre, D., *La Villa des Papyrus et les rouleaux d'Herculanum. La Bibliothèque de Philodème* (Liège, 2006)

Essler, H., 'Bilder von Papyri und Papyri als Bilder', *Cronache Ercolanesi*, 36 (2006), 103–143

Essler, H., 'Rekonstruktion von Papyrusrollen auf mathematischer Grundlage', *Cronache Ercolanesi*, 38 (2008), 273–307

Essler, H., 'ΧΩΡΙΖΕΙΝ ΑΧΩΡΙΣΤΑ. Über die Anfänge getrennte Aufbewahrung der Herkulanischen Papyri', *Cronache Ercolanesi*, 40 (2010), 173–189

Fackelmann, A., 'The Restoration of the Herculaneum Papyri and Other Recent Finds', *BICS*, 17 (1970), 144–145

Farese, R., 'Catalogo degli "illustrazioni" e degli interpreti', *Cronache Ercolanesi*, 29 (1999), 83–94

Fosse, B., Kleve, K., and Störmer, F.C., 'Unrolling the Herculaneum Papyri', *Cronache Ercolanesi*, 14 (1984), 9–15

Gigante, M., ed., *Catalogo dei Papiri Ercolanesi* (Naples, 1979)

Hammerstaedt, J., 'Christian Jensen's and Wolfgang Schmid's Unpublished Herculanean Papers', in *Proceedings of the XXVth International Congress of Papyrology*, ed. by T. Gagos (Ann Arbor, 2010), pp. 291–298

Houston, G., *Inside Roman Libraries* (Chapel Hill, 2014)

Janko, R., *Philodemus:* On Poems *Book One* (Oxford, 2000; ²2003)

Janko, R., 'New Fragments of Epicurus, Metrodorus, Demetrius Laco, Philodemus, the "*Carmen De Bello Actiaco*" and Other Texts in Oxonian *Disegni* of 1788–1792', *Cronache Ercolanesi*, 38 (2008), 5–95

Janko, R., 'Reconstructing (again) the Opening of the Derveni Papyrus', *ZPE*, 166 (2008), 37–51

Janko, R., *Philodemus* On Poems *Books Three and Four, with the Fragments of Aristotle* On Poets (Oxford, 2011)

Janko, R., 'Parmenides in the Derveni Papyrus: New Images for a New Edition', *ZPE*, 200 (2016), 1–21

Janko, R., *Philodemus* On Poems *Book Two* (Oxford). In preparation

Janko, R., with Blank, D.L., 'Two New Manuscript Sources for the Texts of the Herculaneum Papyri', *Cronache Ercolanesi*, 28 (1998), 173–184

Johnson, W. A., *Bookrolls and Scribes in Oxyrhynchus* (Toronto, 2004)

Kouremenos, T., Parássoglou, G. M., and Tsantsanoglou, K., *The Derveni Papyrus* (Florence, 2006)

Litta, V., *I papiri ercolanesi* II. *Indice topografico e sistematico*, Quaderni della Biblioteca Nazionale di Napoli IV. 6 (Naples, 1977)

McOsker, M., 'The Number of Papyrus Rolls Excavated from the Villa dei Papiri: Some Overlooked Evidence', *Cronache Ercolanesi* 46 (2016)

Longo Auricchio, F., 'L'esperienza napoletana del Davy', in *Proceedings of the XIXth International Congress of Papyrology*, ed. by A.H.S. El-Mosallamy (Cairo, 1992), pp. 189–202

Nardelli, M. L., 'Ripristino topografico di *sovrapposti* e *sottoposti* in alcuni papiri ercolanesi', *Cronache Ercolanesi*, 3 (1973), 104–111

Obbink, D., *Philodemus:* On Piety *Part I: Critical Text with Commentary* (Oxford, 1996)

Ohly, K., 'Die Stichometrie der Herkulanischen Rollen', *Archiv für Papyrusforschung*, 7 (1924), 190–220

Ohly, K., *Stichometrische Untersuchungen* (Leipzig, 1928)

Piquette, Kathryn E. forthcoming. 'Illuminating the Herculaneum Papyri: testing new imaging techniques on unrolled carbonised manuscript fragments', *Digital Classics Online 3(2)*.

Schober, A., 'Philodemi *De pietate* pars prior', *Cronache Ercolanesi*, 18 (1988), 65–125 (diss. Königsberg, 1923)

Scott, W., *Fragmenta Herculanensia* (Oxford, 1885)

Sider, D., 'The Special Case of Herculaneum', in *The Oxford Handbook of Papyrology*, ed. by R.S. Bagnall (Oxford and New York, 2009), pp. 303–319

Travaglione, A., 'Incisori e curatori della *Collectio Altera*. Il contributo delle prove di stampa alla storia dei papiri ercolanesi', in *Contributi alla Storia della Officina dei Papiri*, iii, ed. by M. Capasso (Naples, 2003), pp. 87–178

Travaglione, A., *Catalogo descrittivo dei Papiri Ercolanesi* (Naples, 2008)

Usener, H., *Glossarium Epicureum*, ed. by M. Gigante and W. Schmid (Rome, 1977)

Vooys [Vooijs], C. J., *Lexicon Philodemeum*, i (Purmerend, 1934)

Vooys [Vooijs], C. J., and D. A. van Krevelen, *Lexicon Philodemeum*, ii (Amsterdam, 1941)

NOTE: This chapter was originally published with errors. A corrected version of the chapter was released on 30 October 2017. The original errors are described below and have now been corrected:

- The omission of attribution to Kathryn Piquette of Reflectance Transformation Imaging (RTI)
- The incorrect Figure 9
- Missing figure captions

What is a Critical Edition?*

Glenn W. Most
University of Chicago/Scuola Normale Superiore di Pisa, USA/Italy

Collating texts in ancient China

An old Chinese figurine represents a scriptural activity being performed in a way that may come as a surprise to some readers.[1] The object in question is made of celadon, a kind of Chinese pottery produced with a gray-green glaze, and it is very small, only 17.2 cm (less than 7 inches) in height. It is a funerary figurine unearthed from a tomb at Jinpenling, Changsha, Hunan province, in 1958; the date is inscribed on a brick, and the tomb dates to the second year of the Yongning reign, Western Jin Dynasty (ca. 302 CE). It is now preserved in the Hunan Provincial Museum in the city of Changsha.

The object represents two clerks collating and checking the accuracy of manuscripts. Many of us are likely to think of the collation of texts

---

This lecture was given on 22 September 2014 at Stockholm University.

* Parts of this article overlap or coincide, with certain modifications in expression but also some improvements in substance, with various earlier publications of mine: 'Preface', in *Editing Texts – Texte edieren. Aporemata 2,* ed. by Glenn W. Most (Göttingen: Vandenhoeck und Ruprecht, 1998); 'Introduction', in Sebastiano Timpanaro, *The Genesis of Lachmann's Method,* edited and translated by Glenn W. Most (Chicago: University of Chicago Press, 2005); Lorraine J. Daston and Glenn W. Most, 'History of Science and History of Philologies', *Isis,* 106:2 (2015), 378–390; 'Introduction', in *Canonical Texts and Scholarly Practices: A Global Comparative Approach,* ed. by Anthony Grafton and Glenn W. Most (Cambridge: Cambridge University Press, 2016). I have chosen to retain in this published article some traces of the oral character of the original lecture, and not to burden it with a full apparatus of references to the vast scholarship on all the issues discussed here.

How to cite this book chapter:
Most, G. W. 2016. What is a Critical Edition? In: Crostini, B., Iversen, G. and Jensen, B. M. (eds.) *Ars Edendi Lecture Series, vol. IV.* Pp. 162–180. Stockholm: Stockholm University Press. DOI: http://dx.doi.org/10.16993/baj.g. License: CC-BY 4.0

as a solitary activity, undertaken in silence and performed by the eye. We imagine a modern scholar sitting in a library with a printed text and a manuscript in front of him, or a pre-modern scholar with two manuscripts on his desk; in either case he is looking alternately at the one and then at the other, blocking out all distractions so that he can focus on one of the texts in front of him and can compare it, letter for letter, word for word, with the other one.

Here, by contrast, it is not one person who is involved but two, and they are engaged in an intense joint activity that is at least as much interpersonal as it is intertextual. They kneel or squat facing each other across a small wooden table on which a pen, an ink stone, and books made of bamboo have been placed; the table separates them but at the same time links them as a physical object and as the embodiment of the ancient tradition in which they have their place. The figure on the left holds a book in his right hand and is ready to write something onto it with a pen held in his left hand. The one on the right is holding a pile of books. The figure on the right stares fixedly at the face of the other one, perhaps most precisely at his right ear. He is saying something of great importance to the other man, and he wants to be quite certain that his oral communication reaches its goal unimpeded. The man on the left seems to be staring out into empty space beyond the man on the right, so that no sensory impressions will distract him from that urgent communication. Each one leans toward the other as an expression of the intensity of their collaboration. The two blocks out of which they are sculpted are correlated with one another and connected by an intimate complementarity in a kind of elegant inter-scriptural tango. And as in any good tango, the partners are asymmetrical: the man on the right has been placed a little bit lower and is leaning slightly more toward his colleague in a gesture of respect, indeed of deference. For their interdependent collaboration is articulated unmistakably as a strict hierarchy. Both men are wearing distinctively ornate headgear; but the hat on the left man's head has an additional ornament on its back that affirms his higher status. The one on the right has to do only one job: he has to pronounce out loud as precisely and clearly as possible what he reads on his text. But the one on the left has a number of jobs to do: he must listen to his colleague, understand what he says, compare what he hears to what he sees on the page in front of him, and then if necessary write something onto that page. The one on the right is using his brain, his eyes, and his mouth; the one on the left is using those three organs as well, but also his ear and his hand.

These two men are engaged in correcting manuscripts, and they are doing so in a collaborative, oral and aural, way. The man on the left is checking, word for word, what he hears from the man on the right against what he can see in the manuscript he is holding. Pen poised to make a correction at any moment, he is waiting to hear one reading and to see a different one before he strikes to emend where he finds a discrepancy. We might have expected the sculptor to show these two men actually looking at their manuscripts, to which their labors are in fact directed; but instead he has chosen to show the one man looking at the other and the second man looking into space. A moment's reflection is enough to explain his choice. For what else could he have done? He could have shown both scribes looking down at their respective manuscripts; but if he had, he would have shown something that a viewer could not have interpreted otherwise than as two independent scholars, each one reading his own manuscript next to but not in collaboration with the other. Or he could have shown one looking down at a manuscript and the other looking at his colleague; but this would have conveyed a one-way act of dictation, which represented one person speaking and the other simply copying down what he heard.

Instead, the sculptor has shown us both men engaged primarily with one another and only secondarily with the texts that are their true raison d'être. What is more, he has focused all of our attention on the left scholar's right ear, into which his colleague pours his words and toward which he and we direct our concentrated gaze. At the beginning of their collaboration stand various written exemplars of the same text that differ in various points from one another; at the end stand once again the same written exemplars, now corrected and standardized with one another. But the collaboration itself is not visual but oral, not written but spoken. A scriptural tradition involving canonical texts —for what other kind would these clerks be paid to control?— is represented here as an act of oral transmission and constant reciprocal checking. Yet it is not only a rational scholastic procedure that we witness. Collation is figured here simultaneously as the transmission of certain values —attention, obedience, precision, collegiality— that are important not only for their embodiment in canonical texts but also for their instantiation in the acts by which those texts are copied and checked (as well as in all other activities). And at the same time it seems to suggest a ritual procedure, one following, with scrupulous seriousness, an ancient code of conduct in which success is a form of piety and in which failure would entail dire theological consequences. Are we reading too much into this tiny sculpture to see the man on the right as expressing not only deference toward his superior but also a certain degree of anxiety —as though the only guarantee for the accuracy and transparence of this act of textual transmission and of all the values and institutions that depended upon its success were their unremitting attention to their ancient, tedious, and indispensable labor? After all, the man on the right is younger, and he is still a reader; perhaps, if he does his job very well and is otherwise ordered in his life, he might someday himself become a corrector —and if he does not, he certainly will not. So what is at stake for the man on the right in his scholarly collation is not only the world, the nation, and the future of mankind —but also his own career.

Writing and Canons

In fact, the practice of collation was oral, and aural, for many centuries, and not only in Confucian China but also in the West. Evidently our prejudices about the nature of collation rest on very limited experience. They reflect practices that came into being in the modern scholarly library, with its rules imposing silence and separation upon its users, and they give a false idea of the way textual work has been carried out in the past, in the Greek and Roman traditions and in others as well. The similarity in the practice of manuscript collation in various cultures separated from one another in space and time is the result of an inherent tension between two widely attested facts: on the one hand, the privilege given by some traditions to certain canonical texts; and on the other, the vicissitudes of the transmission of texts by means of handwriting. Those cultural traditions that have assigned a preeminent importance to a small body of canonical texts —religious, philosophical, literary, legal, observational, and other kinds— have historically faced a perplexing set of problems. For the central role that these texts have played in their institutions has meant that they usually had to be reproduced over and over again —not only because any material bearer was liable to damage over time, but also because empires expanded, institutions proliferated, and users multiplied. And, inevitably, the more often they were reproduced by hand, the more they were altered.

A written record has this advantage over an oral utterance, that it lasts in time beyond the moment of expression, in a physical form independent of the speaker's and listeners' memories. Of course, even an oral utterance can be repeated and propagated (consider rumors); but most often it is subjected to constant modification during the process of its transmission (the Vedas provide an exception of a remarkably stable oral tradition that proves the general validity of this rule). But writing too has its limitations, for it is restricted to a single spatial location and must be entrusted to an ultimately perishable medium to bear it. For one reason or another —either because the existing copy no longer suffices for the new, spatially dispersed uses to which it is now to be put (usually, new readers), or because it has become damaged over time (by overuse, inadequate materials, or simple old age)— it may become desirable to produce new copies of written texts. Before the age of photographs, photocopies, and scanners, which copy texts by purely mechanical processes simply on the basis of the contrast between lighter areas and darker ones, the only way to produce new copies was to transcribe them by hand from old copies, element for element, most often semantic unit for semantic unit. If greater accuracy of transmission was required, this could be done visually, by a scribe copying onto one new medium the text he saw before his eyes (but the disadvantage was the smaller number of copies that could thereby be produced at the same time from a single exemplar); if on the other hand a large number of copies was sought after, an acoustic procedure could be preferred, whereby the exemplar was read out before a group of scribes who listened to it and copied down, each onto his own medium, what they thought they had heard (at the cost of greater inaccuracy, due to homonyms, distraction, noise, the differences between spelling and pronunciation, and other forms of interference). It is only a guess, but probably a good one, that for most of the history of human culture the normal situation was one which began with a single exemplar to be copied (the source text) and ended up, as result and usually as purpose, with more than one copy of the text (the source text plus the target text, or multiple target texts): transmission normally entailed multiplication. And given that the procedure was performed neither by machines nor by gods but by humans, and that humans err, transmission always entailed variation, and multiplication of copies usually entailed proliferation of variants. And above all, these variants —which, depending on one's point of view and cultural goals, could be regarded either as innovations or as errors— became exponentially more numerous with every further act of copying. So the cultures involved —Mesopotamian, Egyptian, Hebrew, Greek, Latin, Arabic, Vedic, Chinese, Tibetan, Japanese, and some others— had to deal with a fundamental and potentially deeply unsettling paradox: the texts that were central to many of their most important activities were available to them only in copies that diverged from one another in at least some passages; and the older the originals were, and the more often they had been copied, the more discrepancies were likely to exist between them.

Comparison reveals that all or almost all cultures of which we have records have developed some of the same techniques and institutions for minimizing the probability of this problem or for dealing with its deleterious consequences when they have come about. Royal libraries and official copies of important texts are found invariably in such cultures; so too are scribal schools, with rigorous professional procedures for training and testing scribes. The restriction of literacy to a small caste of highly trained professionals (and sometimes to their masters) entrusted with access to the canonical texts was one way to limit textual variance in Mesopotamia, Egypt, and elsewhere; what happens when a more widespread and less highly professionalized portion of the populace achieved literacy is demonstrated by the astonishing errors of all sorts that festoon Greek and Latin papyri, graffiti, curse tablets, amulets, magical texts, and other forms of popular culture. So too, various philological techniques for dealing with textual variance once it occurs seem to be very widespread. Methods of copying manuscripts, orally and visually, one by one or in groups, practices of collating manuscripts, usually orally and in pairs (as we have seen), and modes of emendation of manuscripts (erasure, interlinear correction, marginal annotation) have tended to be surprisingly invariant throughout the world and over centuries, at least until recently.

Yet cultures can also differ from one another in their attitude and approach to the problems posed by manuscript variance. The Vedic tradition puts a unique premium upon the ability to memorize exactly extraordinarily extensive classical texts in Sanskrit, thereby in effect reducing the likelihood of textual variation arising and proliferating because of the copying of written exemplars. The Chinese, by contrast, are reported to display a high degree of sangfroid about the differences that obtain among copies of classical texts (which they are said to regard not as errors or as variants but as versions), and yet archaeological, anecdotal, and pictorial evidence suggests that collation of manuscripts did indeed take place, and if so textual variance may well have caused at least some Chinese scholars to feel misgivings. But in any case it is the ancient Greek tradition that seems to have felt the strongest anxiety about divergent copies of texts and to have developed methods earliest and most systematically for dealing with these. Over and over again during the course of antiquity, Greek political leaders established standard collections of important texts —perhaps already in the late 6th century

BCE the Athenian tyrant Pisistratus for the epics of Homer, certainly in the latter 4th century BCE the Athenian statesman Lycurgus for the texts of the three great Athenian tragedians, and certainly too starting in the early 3rd century BCE the Ptolemaic kings in Hellenistic Alexandria for all the preceding works of Greek literature thought worth preserving. Such Ptolemaic institutions as the library (the "Mouseion", a temple of the Muses), the head librarian, the library catalogue, the edition, the commentary, and the monograph went on to become models first for later Greek culture, then for ancient Rome, and then, through the mediation of Rome and Latin, for post-Classical Europe. In the present article I focus first on the edition in general, and then on the critical edition.

What is an edition?

What is an edition? The words for 'edition' in various languages — ἔκ-δοσις (*ek-dosis*), *e-ditio, Aus-gabe, ut-gåva*— can provide a helpful hint. For they have in common the suggestion of giving something out to people, of bringing it for them from an inside to an outside, from a place where few can see it, and perhaps not without some difficulty, to another place where many can see it, and with at least somewhat greater convenience.

To put the point drastically, we might say that an edition can be thought of as a mechanism intended to bring people texts from out of an archive in to a market. An archive is like a wine-cellar for words: since what is produced far exceeds the possibilities of immediate consumption, prudence can suggest that the excess (or at least that portion of the excess that is not immediately discarded) should be stored someplace out of the way, where it will not interfere with present needs but can wait patiently until it can be brought out someday to serve future ones. An archive always has rules that restrict access to what is stored in it, to make sure that the texts (the bottles) are not used by the wrong people, at the wrong time, in the wrong way; even public archives are not unconditionally public, to say nothing of private ones. And even if access to the archive can be gained, the texts (the wines) it preserves are not easy to enjoy without special knowledge: often the manuscripts (the vintages) are old and delicate, and for reasons of language, script, or circumstances they can be extremely difficult to read (the wine must be decanted with the greatest care, the taste may require skill and training to be enjoyed). A market, on the other hand, is characterized by the principle (not necessarily the fact) that anyone who has the necessary money can have unrestricted access to it, can purchase the wares put on display and sale there, and can use them thereafter in whatever way he sees fit.

Why should anyone be willing to go to the trouble of editing a text? Some contingent reasons are evident, no doubt compelling in many cases, and not particularly interesting: editing texts is one way to advance one's career, to make money, to attach one's own small name to someone else's big one, to irritate one's colleagues, to have fun, to learn. In terms of the marketplace, the edition of an author always intervenes into a determinate literary situation and pursues particular intentions with regard to the other books available at any one time and also achieves particular effects that are often quite different from those intentions. But the fundamental purpose in making an edition, what is specific to this activity and characterizes it as such, is to make available texts to which people would not otherwise have access, to put more people into a position to do with these texts things which they could not have done otherwise —above all, to do things that the editor himself could not have possibly envisioned. The editor of a text is like a man who plants a fruit tree that he hopes will continue to bear fruit long after his own death: he is making available a resource, in which he has an interest himself, so that people whom he does not know and who have interests different from (and perhaps even violently opposed to) his own will be able to make use of it for their own ends.

If there exists only one copy of the document in question, it must be published if it is to be used at all by anyone who does not go into the archive himself; if there exist more than one copy of it, then the editor has the separate problem of deciding just which one or ones, in what combination, to publish. The latter situation in particular poses challenging problems, which have much exercised Classical philologists over the last twenty-five centuries. To have only a single source greatly simplified the editor's task: he (it was of course usually a he) could attempt to transcribe it as faithfully as he wished, intervening into the text as he saw fit, so as to correct obvious errors or to effect what he considered to be improvements of various sorts. But what was he to do when he had available two source texts? Given the proliferation of variants, these were bound to differ from one another in their readings, at least occasionally, if they were of any considerable length: on what basis was he to choose which reading to put into the target text? However rarely such a situation occurred —and presumably for many centuries it did not occur frequently except in the largest scriptoria, monasteries, and libraries— it must have happened regularly enough for a certain set of rule-of-thumb criteria of choice to develop: whichever seemed to be the grammatically or semantically or logically better reading would be preferred from case to case, or both readings could be imported into the target text with or without an expression of greater authorization for one of them. The next step methodologically will have been to give a general preference to the one source text over the other available one whenever possible, either suppressing apparently equipollent readings in the latter or indicating them as inferior alternatives: this will have simplified the editor's task, freeing him from the obligation to apply thought to the choice among variants from case to case and, in effect, reducing once again the number of source texts. But at this point a new question arose: on what basis was the editor to choose which one of the available sources he was to prefer? Over the centuries, various contradictory criteria were developed, each with its own partial and specious justification: the oldest manuscript; the most legible manuscript; the one which appeared to have the most good readings; the one that had the fewest corrections; the one that had the most corrections; the one which derived from an authoritative provenance; the one that was closest to hand; and so forth. And of course even then the editor was still free as he saw fit to make whatever he thought were corrections and other improvements. And the complexities entailed by having two manuscripts were multiplied enormously with every new manuscript that was added to the pile.

As far as we can tell, this was already the situation that obtained in the 4th and 3rd centuries BCE among the Alexandrian philologists who worked on Homer. Given that Homer was by far the most important and central text of ancient Greek culture and that many traces of learned commentary on him from the 4th century BCE until the 14th century AD have been transmitted, we are in a fairly good position to make informed guesses about what the ancient philologists did with his text —though in fact there has always been much disagreement among modern scholars not only about many details but also about some larger issues, and some of what I present here as being likely is in fact hotly contested.[2]

The centrality of Homer to classical Greek literature and education meant that the philologists who worked on him at the Library in Alexandria had available many manuscripts of his poems, gathered from cities and individuals throughout the Greek world. What did they do with them? From the fragmentary, ambiguous, and sometimes contradictory ancient sources it is possible to reconstruct, in admittedly a rather schematic (and surely in certain regards greatly oversimplified) form, the following sequence of the names of three literary scholars and to connect them with a set of specific technical terms that designate the distinguishable products of their activities: (1) Antimachus of Colophon (fl. ca. 400 BCE), credited with the first ἔκδοσις (*ekdosis*) of Homer; (2) Zenodotus (fl. ca. 280 BCE), credited with an ἔκδοσις and the first διόρθωσις (*diorthôsis*) of Homer; and (3) Aristarchus (ca. 220–143 BCE), credited with at least one ἔκδοσις and διόρθωσις and with the first ὑπομνήματα (*hypomnêmata*) on Homer.[3]

Let us consider this sequence of scholars and scholarly text genres in a bit more detail.

(1) Antimachus was a learned epic poet who was writing a century or more before the foundation of the Library in Alexandria. A number of ancient scholia refer to an ἔκδοσις under his name, hence one associated with him in some way, either prepared by him or belonging to him or both;[4] but what precisely this ἔκδοσις was is entirely obscure. If we do decide to assign an ἔκδοσις to Antimachus (as the evidence suggests we should), we should nonetheless be very cautious about understanding the term as referring in this case to a scholarly edition based upon standardized philological techniques and conceived with the intention of publishing it; it is likeliest that the references made by ancient scholars to Antimachus' ἔκδοσις are in fact the result of their projecting anachronistically back onto him a terminology that was suitable to their own, later times, but not to his. All that we can be sure of is that there was extant in Alexandria a copy of a version of Homer's poetry that was considered to have been Antimachus'; but we do not know just what the source and nature of that version was. Given that Antimachus was a celebrated poet, and was renowned for his historical knowledge, it is perhaps likeliest that this manuscript was simply the personal copy of Homer's poetry that he himself had owned, and that was regarded as prestigious because of the owner's celebrity and poetic taste. But whether he had purchased it, or had it made for himself, or had made it himself, and if so by what procedures and according to what criteria, we cannot know.

(2) In the case of Zenodotus, we are on somewhat firmer ground.[5] There are scores of references to his edition of Homer in the scholia to that poet, and the Byzantine encyclopedia *Suda* reports that he was the first man to have been a corrector (διορθωτής) of the poems of Homer. With regard to his edition (ἔκδοσις), we are surely dealing with the

product of a set of standardized scholarly practices designed to make available and intelligible a copy of a certain version of Homer's poetry; after all Zenodotus was the first head of the Library at Alexandria, and there is good reason to think that it was considered to be part of his duties not only to collect books, organize them, and ensure their preservation, but also to make available an authoritative edition of the most important of them, those of Homer. As for his correction of it (διόρθωσις), the term used usually designates the process of marking up a finished manuscript, going through it after it has been written and checking it for mistakes of any kind, which are then signaled and corrected by various more or less standardized markings made either on the words involved, between the lines, or in the margins; a proof-reader was called in Greek a διορθωτής (*diorthôtês*), and we can imagine the activity of διόρθωσις as being something along the lines of what proof-readers or copy-editors do (or used to do) in modern printing houses. Thus we may suppose that the absence of any reference to a διόρθωσις by Antimachus means that the edition associated with his name did not bear corrections or marginalia of particular interest, whereas the ἔκδοσις prepared by Zenodotus did. But if this is the case, then the relation between Zenodotus' ἔκδοσις and his διόρθωσις becomes problematic. For how did he prepare his ἔκδοσις? Did he do so himself, by preparing a new copy on the basis of existing ones? That is hardly likely: for if he had made his own copy, why would he have had to correct it? To be sure, one might imagine that he had had a copy prepared by a scribe who copied some existing text, and then went through it himself and corrected its mistakes; but if this was what he had done, we would expect his corrections to be minor rectifications of simple scribal errors and not the very different variants that are reported under his name. So the likeliest explanation is that, out of the very many manuscripts of Homer that Zenodotus acquired for his Library, he selected that already existing one that he thought was the best, or at least the least bad, and then went through it line by line correcting it, in the sense of marking passages he thought were problematic, adding textual variants, marking lines that he thought ought to be deleted, and so forth. On what basis did he perform these activities? Did he work on the basis of comparison with other manuscripts (i.e. did he find the variants in other manuscripts?), and if so was this comparison systematic or inconsistent, or did he work on the basis of his own intuitions, conjectures, and literary taste (i.e. did he propose his own conjectural emendations?)? We do not know the answers to these questions for sure, and the reason is that the ancient Greeks did not know the answers to them either. For evidently Zenodotus simply marked his changes but did not explicitly explain them anywhere in writing (though presumably he did explain them orally in his teaching for his pupils) —it cannot be accidental that there is no evidence that Zenodotus prepared any commentaries or treatises (ὑπομνήματα/ *hypomnêmata*) to which later Greek scholars could have had recourse in order to understand his editorial choices. It seems to me most likely that what Zenodotus did in his edition was some mixture of unsystematic consultation of some other manuscripts on the one hand and divinatory emendation on the other; but even if this should happen to be true, the exact proportion of each ingredient is quite unknown, and some modern scholars have argued vigorously that in fact what he did was all the one or all the other.

(3) It was Aristarchus who seems to have taken the further step of not only preparing an edition (or editions) and correcting it (or them), but also adding to these products of his scholarship various written commentaries or treatises, ὑπομνήματα/*hypomnêmata*, in which he explained in some detail the grounds on which he had made his textual choices.[6] Here too he seems to have selected one manuscript and marked it up, rather than having a new one made on the basis of compilation and comparison of existing manuscripts; but whether this in fact was the case, and if so on what basis he made his choice, is quite uncertain. Some of the evidence seems to suggest, and indeed it is possible, that he performed this procedure twice, choosing at two different times two different manuscripts (or the same one twice?), marking them up, and preparing two sets of commentaries on them; but this too is uncertain, and controversial.

If this schematic reconstruction is correct, then it means that it took at least a century, from the time of Zenodotus in the early 3rd century BCE to that of Aristarchus in the early 2nd century, for the scholarly genres of edition, commentary, and monograph that seem so familiar and natural to us today to become differentiated and to develop into something like the forms we know. It was in any case the Alexandrian philologists who bequeathed to later generations of scholars the model of the traditional, pre-critical editions that dominated European culture until the end of the eighteenth century. During this whole period, anyone who wanted to edit an author would take some one manuscript and use that as a guide. Whenever something struck him as odd or mistaken, in any way at all, he could change it if he wished to do so, either by comparing it with one or more other manuscripts that he had access to (*ope codicum*) or on the basis of his own erudition, intelligence, native wit, or literary taste (*ope ingenii*). Where the manuscript's readings did not bother him, he left them as they were —as they say in America, "If it ain't broke, don't fix it".

This pre-critical editorial method may sound innocuous, but in fact it never was. Its fundamental defect was not only that it inevitably produced many false positives —that is, passages where some editor thought the transmitted text was mistaken and emended it when in fact it was perfectly acceptable. Far more insidious than this was the fact that this method inevitably produced very many more false negatives — passages that bothered no one but in which in fact the text was unsound. For there is no rational reason to suppose that manuscripts produce nonsense wherever they happen to be mistaken and are correct wherever they happen to agree in a plausible reading. Nonetheless, this remained the only way of editing texts throughout antiquity, the Middle Ages, and the Early Modern period.

What is a critical edition?

It was only starting at the end of the eighteenth century, when German scholars were eager to found a new, national science of *Altertumswissenschaft*, one that could lay claim to a much higher degree of scientificity (*Wissenschaftlichkeit*) than earlier or foreign scholars had managed to achieve, that this traditional way of editing texts came to seem unsatisfactory. And it is not accidental that the first and most influential formulation of the new conception of how to edit texts was promulgated in Friedrich August Wolf's *Prolegomena ad Homerum* of 1795, the foundational text of modern Classical philology and *Altertumswissenschaft*. Wolf's treatise, which was intended as a preface to his own edition of Homer, provides in its opening pages a lucid analysis of the differences between pre-critical and critical editions that has gone on to shape all modern theories of text editing.[7] Wolf distinguishes here between two kinds of ways of editing texts: the one is fun and easy, but the other is hard work; the one is useful, but the other is more useful; the one operates by *ope ingenii* and *ope codicum* and is what scholars used to do, but the other laboriously collects all the transmitted readings, compares them with one another, and applies emendation in a consistent manner; the one corrects texts only where the scholar perceives a problem and is ultimately frivolous and desultory, but the other aims at a true, continuous, and systematic examination and evaluation of the evidence;

the one corrects only obvious errors, but the other seeks to determine the author's own text by checking every reading, and not only suspicious ones, and is willing (like a doctor) to substitute less attractive but more genuine readings for attractive but specious ones, examines sources, classifies manuscripts, and (like a judge) assigns them their relative values, and is loath to suggest conjectural emendations without manuscript support. While Wolf does not actually use the term 'critical edition', there can be no doubt that what he meant is what this phrase designates. The difference he establishes between pre-critical and critical editorial practice is sharp and evident: pre-critical editions are top-down, they start with a received authority and gradually change it bit by bit; whereas critical editions are bottom-up, they start with all the surviving witnesses and work their way up until they have reached the witnesses' proximate, and eventually ultimate, sources. This is not only a difference of methodology, it is also one of social standing and ethos: for the pre-critical edition is described in terms of aristocratic ideals, of graceful wit and irresponsible dexterity, while the critical one has all of the bourgeois virtues of hard work and the tedious collection and scrutiny of evidence —it is worth recalling that the years of the preparation and publication of Wolf's *Prolegomena* coincided with the French Revolution. Finally, the goals of the two kinds of edition are widely disparate: the pre-critical edition aims to produce an impeccable text, i.e. one that conforms to the tastes and knowledge of the age of its editor; but the critical edition aims to provide an authentic text, i.e. one that conforms to the tastes and knowledge of the age of its author.

As for the term 'critical edition', I do not in fact know who the first person was who used it. My suspicion is that the term '*editio critica*' was in use for some time before Wolf described the practice in his *Prolegomena* without applying this terminology. But during the years at the end of the eighteenth and the beginning of the nineteenth century, it must have become quite popular, in part because it answered the needs of this post-revolutionary period, in part because it was thereby enabled to acquire some of the prestige of Kant's Critical philosophy. The formula is itself a hybrid typical of its age of transition: for 'critical' suggests the stern and unsparing rational critique of transmitted authority, the characteristic mode of thought of the Enlightenment; but here that 'critical' aspect is directed as a means towards the goal of an 'edition', in a typically Romantic hope of returning somehow to a lost origin, to the classical author's very own text. In any case, this ideal of a critical edition is critical in at least two senses: first in that it considers the textual tradition critically rather than simply trusting it; and second in that it provides its competent readers with all the materials they need in order to put its own authority into question critically and to improve it by using the means it provides them.

As it happened, Wolf himself never went on to prepare the kind of critical edition of Homer that he had called for in his *Prolegomena*. But over the subsequent decades, his German followers worked out the implications of the theory he had expressed so clearly. The first attempt to provide a thoroughly mechanical and systematic procedure for rationalizing and standardizing the choice among manuscripts, and hence among readings, was developed during the nineteenth century and since the beginning of the twentieth century has been known as 'Lachmann's method' because of its association with Karl Lachmann, a German Classicist who produced celebrated editions of texts in Latin, Greek, and medieval and modern German. 'Lachmann's method' is genealogical and largely mechanical in nature, and aims at providing a standardized, rational procedure for editing texts on the basis of multiple manuscripts, thereby minimizing the editor's need to rely upon his personal judgment in order to choose among variant readings. Its goal is to determine the filiation of manuscripts, i.e. to ascertain which ones have been copied from which other ones: given that every act of transcription is likely to introduce new errors (for this is how this model understands variants), a manuscript B, if it has been copied mechanically from a manuscript A, will have all the errors that A had (if it does not have all of them, then it has probably corrected some of them during the transcription and hence is likely not to have been copied mechanically after all), and it is also likely to have at least one new error of its own; if this can be shown to be the case, then B can be discarded for the purposes of the constitution of the text it shares with A, since B, compared with A, brings no new information that is not erroneous. Thus, if the manuscripts and groups of manuscripts of a given text can be shown to be related to one another as depicted in the accompanying diagram (Figure 1).

'Lachmann's method' aims to establish a genealogical stemma of transmission by excluding direct copies and determining family relations, and thereby to permit, as far as possible, a purely mechanical choice among variants. The procedure is mechanical, both in the sense that it must presuppose the unthinking transcription of manuscripts if it is to be applied to them and in the sense that the determination of relations of filiation is achieved on the basis of simple rules and calculations of probability. Ideally, choices of manuscripts and of readings based

1. if a reading in group β is identical to the corresponding reading in manuscript C, then this gives us with certainty the reading in group α.

2. if a reading in manuscript A is identical to the corresponding reading in group α, then this gives us with certainty the reading in the archetype ω.

3. if a reading in group β is different from the corresponding reading in manuscript C but is identical to the reading in manuscript A, then the reading in group β and manuscript A gives us with high probability the corresponding reading in the archetype ω.

4. if a reading in group β is different from the corresponding reading in manuscript C but the reading in manuscript C is identical to the reading in manuscript A, then the reading in manuscript C and manuscript A gives us with high probability the corresponding reading in the archetype ω.

5. It is only if the corresponding readings in manuscript A, group β, and manuscript C are different from one another that we cannot know with any certainty or even probability what the corresponding reading in the archetype ω was.

Figure 1.

upon this method will be rational, in that they will depend not upon the taste of the individual scholar, but upon objective evidence that can be mathematized and evaluated; and hence they will be capable of becoming standardized, for any scholar, young or old, inexperienced or expert, should in principle come up with exactly the same results if s/he is given the same information. We may interpret 'Lachmann's method' as a defensive reaction to the proliferation of possible source texts, intended to reduce them to a more manageable number, and can identify it as one important element in the professionalization of Classics during the nineteenth century, since it established rules that all who wished to be recognized as full members of the discipline could be expected to follow so as to produce uniform and hence generally acceptable results.

Within the millennial Western tradition, there seems to be little decisive change in methods and techniques of textual editing until the nineteenth century —even printing, which has attracted so much attention, did not transform the activity of textual editors as profoundly as some scholars have suggested. It is only in the nineteenth century that the situation in Europe was altered decisively by a series of innovations, such as ease of travel and communications, the pacification and reclamation of parts of Italy and the Eastern Mediterranean, the expansion of the scholarly community, the reorganization of the university and of scientific research, the establishment of the Big Science model for the organization of large-scale industrialized research into antiquity, and the invention of processes for copying texts mechanically without human intervention. 'Lachmann's method' was one particularly notable sign of this transformation; another, closely connected one, was the development of the historical-critical edition, which since the latter part of the nineteenth century has become one of the identifying markers for Western textual philology. Both procedures, and others, can be interpreted as ways in which, within Classical philology, fundamental features of nineteenth-century science become expressed: mechanization, standardization, quantification, historicization, industrialization. Over the course of the past several generations, we have certainly acquired some distance to nineteenth-century science: but we are no less certainly its heirs, and we have not yet learned to understand fully the transformations it produced, let alone to emancipate ourselves from them.

To be sure, 'Lachmann's method' was only one, very extreme and mechanistic version of critical editions. And Lachmann is no longer revered as uncritically as he was during his lifetime and in the following generation. But the concept of a critical edition in this very specific sense — reconstructing a text not on the basis of a single manuscript corrected sporadically, but on that of the systematic collection, examination, classification, and evaluation of all the extant witnesses, including manuscripts, citations, scholia, and other evidence— this concept has remained a pillar of Classical philology (and not only of Classical philology) ever since. It is only from the point of view of this theory of the critical edition that, by contrast, the two Chinese clerks with whom we began can indeed come to seem non-critical or pre-critical. We will be in a better position to understand what they were really up to when we do not simply measure them with the standard of the modern European critical edition but come instead to recognize that Lachmann too, with all his extraordinary legacy, is best understood not as the inevitable culmination of the development of editorial techniques, but as a particularly interesting modern European instantiation of a long-drawn-out and still ongoing process of grappling with texts.

Notes

1. http://www.hnmuseum.com/hnmuseum/eng/collection/collectionContent1. jsp?infoid=01 1198a6ecba4028848311 8d94210484#
See also cover picture *Canonical Texts and Scholarly Practices: A Global Comparative Approach*, ed. by Anthony Grafton and Glenn W. Most (Cambridge: Cambridge University Press, 2016).

2. The basic study remains Rudolf Pfeiffer, *History of Classical Scholarship from the Beginnings to the End of the Hellenistic Age* (Oxford: Clarendon, 1968); for an up-to-date survey of all the issues, with rich bibliography, see *Brill's Companion to Ancient Greek Scholarship*, ed. by Franco Montanari, Stefanos Matthaios, and Antonios Rengakos, 2 vols (Leiden: Brill, 2015), especially Fausto Montana, 'Hellenistic Scholarship', pp. 60–183; Markus Dubischar, 'Typology of Philological Writings', pp. 545–599; and Franco Montanari, 'Ekdosis. A Product of the Ancient Scholarship', pp. 637–672.

3. On the difficulties of understanding precisely what is meant by the terms ἔκδοσις and διόρθωσις, see Pfeiffer, *History of Classical Scholarship*, pp. 71–72, 94, 110, 122, 215–16, 277. I omit from this list of Alexandrian scholars Aristophanes of Byzantium (ca. 257–180 BCE), who was extremely important for the history of ancient Greek philology in other regards but not for innovations with regard to the typology of editions and other scholarly writings on Homer (see on him Pfeiffer, *History of Classical Scholarship*, pp. 172–209, especially 172–181).

4. Cf. Pfeiffer, *History of Classical Scholarship*, pp. 93–94.

5. *Ibid.*, pp. 105–119, especially 105–117.

6. *Ibid.*, pp. 210–233, especially 214–218.

7. See Friedrich August Wolf, *Prolegomena to Homer (1795)*, trans. and ed. Anthony T. Grafton, Glenn W. Most, and James E.G. Zetzel (Princeton: Princeton University Press, 1985), pp. 43–45.

Bibliography

Daston, Lorraine J. and Glenn W. Most, 'History of Science and History of Philologies', *Isis*, 106:2 (2015), 378–390

Dubischar, Markus, 'Typology of Philological Writings', in *Brill's Companion to Ancient Greek Scholarship*, ed. by Franco Montanari, Stefanos Matthaios, and Antonios Rengakos, 2 vols (Leiden: Brill, 2015), pp. 545–599

Montana, Fausto, 'Hellenistic Scholarship', in *Brill's Companion to Ancient Greek Scholarship*, ed. by Franco Montanari, Stefanos Matthaios, and Antonios Rengakos, 2 vols (Leiden: Brill, 2015), pp. 60–183

Montanari, Franco, 'Ekdosis. A Product of the Ancient Scholarship', in *Brill's Companion to Ancient Greek Scholarship*, ed. by Franco Montanari, Stefanos Matthaios, and Antonios Rengakos, 2 vols (Leiden: Brill, 2015), pp. 637–672

Most, G., 'Preface', in *Editing Texts – Texte edieren. Aporemata 2*, ed. by Glenn W. Most (Göttingen: Vandenhoeck und Ruprecht, 1998)

Most, G., 'Introduction', in Sebastiano Timpanaro, *The Genesis of Lachmann's Method*, edited and translated by Glenn W. Most (Chicago: University of Chicago Press, 2005)

Most, G., 'Introduction', in *Canonical Texts and Scholarly Practices: A Global Comparative Approach*, ed. by Anthony Grafton and Glenn W. Most (Cambridge: Cambridge University Press, 2016)

Pfeiffer, Rudolf, *History of Classical Scholarship from the Beginnings to the End of the Hellenistic Age* (Oxford: Clarendon, 1968)

Wolf, Friedrich August, *Prolegomena to Homer (1795)*, trans. and ed. Anthony T. Grafton, Glenn W. Most, and James E.G. Zetzel (Princeton: Princeton University Press, 1985)

The Digital Revolution in Scholarly Editing

Peter Robinson
University of Saskatchewan, Canada

It is now a standard topic (even, a meme) in the discourse of textual scholarship to speak of the revolution in our profession occasioned by digital methods. The technology that brought us those methods also brought us Google. A search on "Digital revolution in textual scholarship" brings us over four million results, dispersed across multiple scholarly areas: the Greek New Testament, medieval vernacular poetry, nineteenth-century English poetry, Sanskrit epics, modernist literature.[1] Of course, as academics, we do not all agree. Just to use the word "revolution" is to cast provocations upon the waters —some will say: of course it is a revolution; others will say, no it is not. In this article I argue that the changes we may see in scholarly editing may amount to a revolution. However, the reasons I think it may be a revolution differ from those usually given. Further, I think the effects of this revolution may reach far further than is usually supposed. Indeed, this revolution may be "revolutionary".

Is access to manuscript images a "fast" revolution?

De Toqueville, the founder of modern discussions of revolution, distinguished between "fast" revolutions —political and sudden— and "slow" revolutions, which might take generations, but achieve a complete transformation of society.[2] One could argue that the sudden and astonishing availability of millions of images of manuscripts and books online is a "fast" revolution. Before this, if you wanted to know what the Beowulf Manuscript or a Shakespeare First Folio looked like you had to find a book with an image. Usually, the book offered one

This lecture was given on 9 December 2014 at Stockholm University.

How to cite this book chapter:
Robinson, P. 2016. The Digital Revolution in Scholarly Editing. In: Crostini, B., Iversen, G. and Jensen, B. M. (eds.) *Ars Edendi Lecture Series, vol. IV.* Pp. 181–207. Stockholm: Stockholm University Press. DOI: http://dx.doi.org/10.16993/baj.h. License: CC-BY 4.0

and only one image, and that in shades of grey.[3] Now, the whole of the Beowulf manuscript is online, freely available and just a few clicks away, and in full colour too.[4] One can find not just one first folio online, but many more, and few weeks go by without an announcement, that library A is putting a new collection of manuscripts online. It used to be that you needed special permission to see a whole manuscript online, or deep pockets to pay for a facsimile or commission a set of photographs. In twenty-five years up to 8 July 2009 the British Library allowed only four scholars to inspect the 347 leaves of the great 4th-century Codex Sinaiticus in their possession.[5] On that day, images of the whole manuscript went online and were seen by over a million people in the next few months. Surely, this is a revolution, and a very fast one.

Fast: but not a revolution. A few years ago, my successor as Professor of Textual Scholarship at De Montfort University, Leicester, Tony Edwards, declared to an audience of textual scholars and digital humanists that the digital revolution had really changed nothing in textual scholarship.[6] All it meant, he argued, was that we could now look at digital images online, rather than having to go to the British Library. It made matters more convenient, like travelling on a faster train or bus. But it did not amount to a revolution. Nothing fundamental was changed. I agree with Professor Edwards. There are numerous scholars and others who declare that to have all the manuscripts, all the books of the world online, is revolutionary. We are giving access to everyone, for just the cost of an internet connection, to materials which used to be available only to the most privileged of scholars. Everyone can now wake up in the British Library.[7]

However, providing access changes nothing, of itself. If people actually use that access to make new editions, new scholarship, of a kind never seen before, which readers may use in ways never known before, then that would indeed be a revolution. But this has not happened. We now have thousands of manuscripts and millions of books online. And what are people doing with all this? The language used to describe these collections is revealing: in almost no case, are these abundances of materials described as "editions". They are "archives", "thematic research collections", perhaps "arsenals", but not editions.[8] Indeed, looking over many of these collections, such as the manuscript image collections in Manuscriptorium, in e-Codices, in Bavarian State Library initiatives, not to mention the millions of books in Google Books, the Hathi Trust, in Europeana —none of these could in any way be called editions. One presumes in editions at least a minimum level of scholarly intervention, in selection of material, in the provision of transcriptions, annotations and commentary. These are almost entirely absent from these collections. These look like nothing so much as the vast microfilming endeavours of the last century: updated to glossy digital, usually packaged in manners which put the creating and funding institutions in the best possible light, but still nothing more than the raw material of scholarship. As Edwards argued, the digital world only makes these more accessible. No revolution in that.

However, digital methods are being used to create many objects which are indeed editions. Perhaps, these might qualify as the components of a fast revolution. Consider the many editions made with Stefan Hagel's "Classical Text Editor" software, or with Wilhelm Ott's TUSTEP system. A glance shows these are remarkably familiar. There is a base text which appears at the top of the page. Below are layers of apparatus: reporting variants in many witnesses, references to sources, editorial notes. Scholarly introductions and appendices top and tail the edition. Further: these editions are commonly published in book form by exactly the same publishers who have, for centuries in some cases, been publishing scholarly editions.[9] They are made by the same community, of tenured academics, of doctoral students and postdoctoral researchers within the academy, which has produced books looking just like this, published (often with handsome government subventions) by the same presses, and destined for the same shelves in the same university libraries where they wait for years to be discovered by an avid reader who will treasure what they offer. We could celebrate that such editions can now be made with a facility never before possible, and celebrate too that the highest standards of meticulous textual scholarship are being maintained into the digital era. We could also take comfort of the reassuring persistence of the authority of the academy in the structures underlying these editions. They are made only by those qualified to make them, published only by presses which understand the value of what they are publishing. We could congratulate ourselves, that we can make more such editions, more conveniently. But this would not be a revolution.

Arguments such as these have led commentators as diverse as Thomas Tanselle and Barbara Bordalejo to assert that indeed, the digital revolution has not changed the fundamental model of scholarly editing.[10] An edition is an edition, an editor is an editor, and that is that. If in the digital world, we do not change what we do, we do not change what we make, we do not change who we are: there is no revolution. I agree with Tanselle, Bordalejo and Edwards: there is no revolution in digital editing. Not now. Not yet. But there could be such a revolution. I contend that in the next years what we do as editors may change. The editions we make may change. And most radically of all, who we are may change. Indeed, I think this is already happening. Let us consider each of these in turn: what we do; the editions we make; and who we are.

Elements of a revolution: changing what we do

In approximate order of difficulty, we may deal first with the first: what we do. I have already said, that the provision of masses of digital images online does not constitute any kind of revolution. If we do nothing with those images, nothing happens. But some of us are doing things with these digital images. We might transcribe the text of those manuscript images. Transcription of original materials is in itself hardly novel or revolutionary. But the digital medium is leading us into areas where we are having to think about what we do, as editors, in ways we have never had to think about before. Consider the simple noun, transcription. It sounds simple enough: you look at the manuscript and you record what you see. As two decades now of scholars making digital transcripts of original textual materials have discovered, it is not so simple at all.[11] A single manuscript page contains an almost limitless number of signs. Consider the first page of the Hengwrt manuscript of Geoffrey Chaucer's *Canterbury Tales*, now in the National Library of Wales, and probably the oldest surviving manuscript of the *Canterbury Tales*.[12] We see ornamentation in the left margin and a decorative capital, part of the page torn or eaten away (perhaps by rats) at the top, text in different inks and possibly written by different scribes at different times, text in margins, erasures or holes or other gaps, heavy staining on the right hand bottom corner. This even before we start on transcription of the page: whereupon we discover that a letter in the fourth line of the page (on Figure 1, left), which we confidently transcribe as the letter "s", is actually very different from this letter "s" in the seventh line (Figure 1, right).

Should we not record this difference? And indeed, the differences among all the forms of all the letters? And of course: all the marks upon the page, the staining, the marginalia. Should we not record all these, too? In the world of print, there was no need for these decisions. An "s" was an "s"; the editor might offer a note here and there about staining,

Figure 1. Two forms of the letter "s" from the first page of the *Canterbury Tales* in the Hengwrt manuscript

rats and wormholes. But now: one can contemplate the possibility of recording all the forms of every letter; the precise point on every page where the text lies; the exact sequence of writing of the text, letter by letter, as painstakingly constructed by the editor.

One might question the intellectual justification for such minute analysis: that we can now perform such prodigies does not mean that we should. Perhaps so. But even to consider these matters shows that how we see text in primary sources in the digital age has changed. Consider Figure 2:

From the context we know this should be the word "down". It appears that we have here an excellent instance of the use of macron over the letter u to indicate abbreviation of a nasal. Accordingly, we might transcribe the word straightforwardly as dou[n], and encode the macron as an

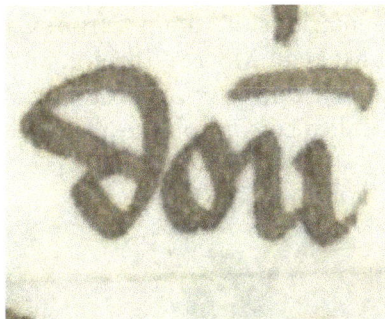

Figure 2. "doun" (modern "down") from Corpus Christi College Oxford MS 198 (Cp) (Cp) fol. 54r, Miller's Tale 633

abbreviation of n. This is in perfect accord with the textbook account of a macron over final u as an abbreviation of final n. If all we were doing was looking at this single word in this manuscript we would see no problem here at all. But in the transcriptions we are making, we are not looking just at this word in this manuscript —as we might do, if all we were doing was looking for variants from a base text, and quarrying occasional readings from the manuscript. Instead, we find ourselves looking at every word: at every case where we see a macron over something which might be a u. And what we see undermines our certainty.

While in the third, fourth and fifth examples of Figure 3 it might be possible to interpret the macron as an abbreviation of a final /n/ (which requires that we interpret the final two minims as /u/), in the first and second examples the /un/ is written out in full and the macron cannot represent an abbreviation. Indeed, this is the usual case. Thousands of times, as Figure 4 shows for spellings of "whan" and "when", we find "when", "in", "upon", "slepen", "been", where there is a macron over the final two minims, which must represent /n/ and hence the macron must be simply decorative.

Indeed, we discover that scribes, over and over, don't seem to care whether the two minims are joined at the top (as in a modern printed n; the second example in Figure 4) or joined at the bottom (as in a modern printed u; the third example in Figure 4), or not joined at all (the first example in Figure 4). And then, what we call a macron takes a bewildering variety of forms. Sometimes it is indeed a single straight

Figure 3. other representations of "doun": from Cambridge, Fitzwilliam Museum McLean MS 181 (Fi) fol. 8r, General Prologue 395; Cp fol. 37v, Knight's Tale 1797; Cp fol. 29v, Knight's Tale 1196; Cp fol. 20r, Knight's Tale 519; Cp fol. 29v, Knight's Tale 1196

Figure 4. Three forms of "whan/wben" from the Fitzwilliam manuscript: folios 2r, General Prologue ; 16r, Knight's Tale 36; 17v, Knight's Tale 143.

stroke over the letter. Sometimes it extends over several letters. Often it is curved. And very often it appears as a loop, beginning at the base of the last minim and arching back over the two minims of the u/n character and preceding letters. Attempting to devise transcription protocols in these circumstances is a complex dance with a collection of hydra. The intentions of the scribes appear increasingly opaque and distant, and we are left searching our own intentions. Exactly what are we trying to record; for who; and why?[13] Our answer is that our transcripts are our best guess at how the manuscripts might most usefully be read. This is a far less confident assertion than to say (for example) that our transcription aims "to record the appearance of the text in the manuscript" (Digital Scriptorium guide, see fn. 10) or "to give a truthful representation of what the writer actually wrote" (*Low Country Digital Library Transcription Manual*, 2013, p.2 at http://lcdl. library.cofc.edu/sites/default/files/lcdldocumentation/Transcription-Manual-LCDL-2013.pdf). Nonetheless, it is the furthest we feel we can go. We have considered the uses we might make of the transcriptions, and tried to imagine how others might use them, and transcribed the documents accordingly.

The complexity of our task is a direct result of our decision to transcribe the whole text of each manuscript into digital form. If we were simply picking a few readings here and there from the manuscripts, we would not have these problems. Why go to all this effort? For us, the difficulty is the reason. It is difficult because we find we are struggling to understand the writing practices of the scribes and the conventions which govern the presentation of the manuscripts. It is from this close engagement with difficult problems that new knowledge arises. It is easy to look at the manuscripts from a distance and think you understand all you see. However, transcription in the digital medium has forced us to look very closely at the manuscripts and we are puzzled by what we see. Already, we understand more than we did about what scribes do. We see the extent to which convention governs much of their practice; we see too how conventions change from scribe to scribe. As more and more manuscripts are transcribed, new questions and new knowledge will arise. Most certainly, we do not transcribe manuscripts in the digital era as we might have done a century ago, and we do not look at manuscripts the same way.[14]

There is a very concrete way in which our full transcription of manuscripts into digital form has changed what we do. Traditionally, manuscripts have been foliated —had their pages numbered— in a very simple way. The cataloguer numbers the first surviving folio as "1" (usually writing "1" in the top right of the recto), numbers the next one "2", and carries on to the last surviving folio. This has advantages. It provides an unambiguous way of referring to each folio and it can be done without having to spend any time looking at the contents or structure of the manuscript. If the task is to foliate a large number of manuscripts, and if there is only a limited time to do this work, this is the clearly the best way to proceed: hence the very large number of manuscripts foliated by this method. But in projects such as ours, where we are transcribing the full text of the manuscripts, this leads to odd results. Consider two manuscripts of the *Canterbury Tales*, the Hengwrt manuscript, Peniarth 392D at the National Library of Wales (Hg) and British Library Sloane MS 1686 (Sl2). Earlier, I referred to the first page of the text of the Hengwrt manuscript (Hg). This page is traditionally numbered "2" because at some point in the history of the manuscript, someone decided to bind a quite unrelated single leaf from a musical manuscript in front of this first page. So this single leaf became "1", and the first page of the *Tales*, which was also the first page of the first regular quire of 8, became "2". In contrast, the Sl2 manuscript of the *Tales* has lost its first page (as analysis of the quire shows), and hence the text of the *Tales* commences at line 63. However, in this case traditional foliation awards this page the number "1", although this was not the original first page of the manuscript. The result is puzzling. It appears from the foliation as if something is missing from the beginning of Hengwrt, while nothing is missing from Sl2. In fact the reverse is the case.

Nor are these isolated cases. Of the eighty-four manuscripts holding the *Tales*, just seven are exactly now as they were five or six hundred years ago, with no pages lost, no pages added, no pages moved. For these seven, the traditional foliation is perfectly satisfactory. For the other 77, it is misleading, sometimes profoundly so. Accordingly, we have long wanted to change how we foliated the manuscripts. Our aim is to show how pages have been lost, added, and reshuffled. You can see the results of this in our foliation of the Hengwrt manuscript. First, we start our foliation at 1, not 2, ignoring the unrelated singleton added later at the beginning of the manuscript. Second, three whole quires, beginning with folio 199, have been moved from late in the manuscript so they now come between folios 86 and 87. Third, a single sheet which we label 127a has been placed between folios 127 and 128. Fourth, a whole ten folio quire has been inserted between folios 137 and 138: we label these

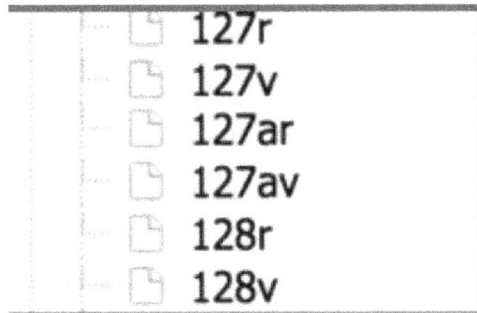

Figure 5. Foliation of folios 127 through 128, showing the added singleton leaf (127a).

folios as 137a1 through 137a10. Finally, the foliation goes from 198 to 223 because, as we have seen earlier, the three quires holding folios 199 to 222 have been moved to between folios 86 and 87. Figure 5 shows how, according to these principles, we foliate the sequence 127v, 127a (the singleton inserted after 127) and 128:

   There are several benefits in this refoliation. First, it immediately informs the reader that the manuscripts as we now have them are commonly incomplete, disordered, with material added and lost. Second, it focuses the reader's attention on the consequences of these changes to the original manuscript: in the case of Hengwrt, the shift of three quires, the addition of a single sheet and the addition of a whole quire. These consequences may turn out to be significant for our understanding of the text. Consider the case of the added folio after 127. The Merchant's Tale finishes on folio 127v and folio 128r starts with line 13 of the Franklin's Tale, written in the same ink as the end of the Merchant's Tale. Notably, there is exactly enough space on 127v at the end of the Merchant's Tale to contain the first twelve missing lines of the Franklin. One may reason that the scribe did not write these twelve missing lines immediately because they were not available. The scribe knew that he needed to leave space for exactly twelve lines, and did so, continuing with the thirteenth line on the next folio (128r).

   And then, something very odd happens. It appears that at some later point, those twelve lines did become available to the scribe. But not only those twelve lines: a linking passage clearly intended to follow the Merchant also became available to the scribe. There was not sufficient space to include both the twelve lines and the linking passage at the base of 127v, and so the scribe wrote both on a single sheet and inserted it in the manuscript after folio 127. We label this sheet as 127a, because it appears after the original 127. The ink in which this page is written is markedly paler in color than the ink on the surrounding folios. We see this paler ink elsewhere in the manuscript, in sections which appear written late in the manuscript's construction. What one does not see immediately, but which closer analysis shows, is that it appears that the original text of the link suggested that the next tale following the Merchant's Tale should be the Squire's Tale, not the Franklin's Tale, as is the case in most other manuscripts.[15]

Here, our new foliation indicates immediately to the reader that there is a problem. The reader is motivated to investigate: and finds evidence of what was available to the scribe at various times and what the scribe did with it. The traditional foliation, which numbers these three folios in simple numeric sequence, shows none of this. Of course, refoliation as we have done it can only be carried out when you have very full evidence of the manuscript. You need to know the quiring of the manuscript: that is how we are able to say that the ten folios which we label as 137a1 through 10 form a complete quire, and how we are able to say that this additional quire is placed at the centre of an existing quire of six, thereby making an irregular quire of 16. You also need to know exactly what text is on each page. This allows us to correlate missing text with missing pages— or the reverse, indeed. In several cases, we are able to identify a manuscript that has disordered text but no apparent disorder in the foliation. In these cases it appears that the manuscript's exemplar had its folios jumbled, so disordering the text, and the scribe simply copied what was in the exemplar even though it made no sense.[16]

One could have carried out such a refoliation in days before the digital revolution. Indeed, the great Chaucer scholar Henry Bradshaw refoliated the much-damaged Canterbury Tales manuscript Cambridge Gg.4.27 in this way in the nineteenth century. However, in the time when few people looked at the manuscripts themselves, and when those few were likely to be scholars with a good understanding of what they were looking at, one might argue that there was little benefit in a refoliation such as that executed by Bradshaw. But now, manuscripts are appearing all over the web, and many of the people who are looking at them are new to their study. We know far more about the manuscripts, partly because of the improved access to digital images, and partly because we are now transcribing more and more manuscripts. A huge help for us in our refoliation was the decades of work done by Dan Mosser towards his

Catalogue of the Manuscripts and Incunables of the Canterbury Tales.[17] Here again: the digital world is leading us to change what we do.

Elements of a revolution: changing what we make

Because of digital methods more of us now transcribe manuscripts than ever before, we look at manuscripts in ways we never did before, we may enumerate their pages and construction in new ways. You may argue, and I would agree, that desirable and useful as these changes may be, this falls someway short of a revolution. A great number of editions are still being made without transcription of manuscripts, and certainly requiring no refoliation of the manuscripts. Even if many more people were transcribing and refoliating manuscripts, still this may not amount to a revolution. I remarked earlier that we could count something as a revolution if it changed what we do, what we make, and how we are. Changing what people do, how people work, would be no revolution if it meant that people are still making the same things.

However, some have argued that the digital world is bringing us a new kind of edition. The ease and excellence of digital imaging, and the accompanying interest in manuscript transcription, has given rise to what Elena Pierazzo calls "documentary digital editions", or Keirnan "image-based scholarly edition".[18] In the last decades, a small cottage industry has sprung up around the transcription of manuscripts into digital form. We may see this with the list of digital editions maintained by Patrick Sahle at http://www.digitale-edition.de/. Many of these editions are what one might call digital facsimile transcripts, focussing on a single manuscript and recording its text in precise form, page by page, line by line and character by character. These editions —and they most certainly are editions, in the basic sense that an editor is scrutinizing every mark on the page— characteristically focus on two elements: the exact disposition of the text on each page and on the writing process. The first of these corresponds to "diplomatic" or "facsimile print" editions, the second to "genetic editions". Both kinds of edition are, of course, well established in the print world. We can date the first to the mid-nineteenth century, with such exemplars as Tischendorf's facsimile print transcript of Codex Sinaiticus.[19] We could go back even earlier, to the handwritten facsimile copies of Ari hin Frodi's Islendinga bok, made by Jon Erlendsson around 1651.[20] We can date the second to the initiatives of Louis Hay, which sparked the "critique genetique" movement which in turn found an institutional home in ITEM, with parallel streams of activity showing themselves in the transcription of the authorial manuscripts of Joyce, Beckett, Melville and Nietsche, among others.[21] This catalogue of historical precedents suggests that, in itself, this move to "digital documentary editing" is not as revolutionary as some of its proponents claim. One might argue, that all these editions do is present familiar objects in digital form. Even if it were revolutionary, one might argue that the revolution is potential, as yet unrealized, and liable to fizzle to nothing after all: yet another utopian dream wrecked on cold reality. The editions listed by Sahle are impressive. But when we consider the number of editions produced by TUSTEP and Classical Text Editor (see above), and recall that the major scholarly publishers among them have published many times this number of scholarly editions over the years (459 listed at http://www.oxfordscholarlyeditions.com/. Over 1500 at http://www.brepols.net/, searching for "edition") this number looks less impressive. Further, a number of the editions listed by Sahle appear as effectively self-published, appearing on a university website and so hostages to the shifting policies of that university. Browsing through these editions reveals broken links, browsers which do not display as one might expect, or editions which are no more than electronic equivalents of a print publication. There are imaginative and remarkable projects here; and there are many which are not. In the context of the wide world of scholarly editions, the editions listed by Sahle appear as an insurgency. As with all revolutions, the insurgents display various levels of intensity, commitment and achievement. But these insurgents have not seized power.

I noted above that Elena Pierazzo argues that these are a new kind of edition: she calls them "a new type of editorial object", which she labels as a "documentary digital edition" (elsewhere, she calls them "digital documentary editions") and which she says record "as many features of the original document as are considered meaningful by the editors, displayed in all the ways the editors consider useful for the readers including all the tools necessary to achieve such a purpose".[22] First, the core transcripts at the centre of these editions appear like nothing so much as diplomatic editions, well-known to textual scholars for centuries. Gregory Pass defines a diplomatic edition as "an edition (in print or online) of an historic manuscript text that seeks to reproduce as accurately as possible in typography all significant features of the manuscript original, including spelling and punctuation, abbreviations, deletions, insertions, and other alterations".[23] This describes rather well the digital transcripts listed by Sahle and described by Pierazzo.

The difference is that Pass is describing print books while Pierazzo is describing digital materials, and Pierazzo also includes tools and variant views in her description. Thus, typically, a digital transcript might offer alternative ways of seeing the text, toggling abbreviation on or off. However, there are rather few other tools offered by the actual digital editions listed by Sahle. They usually offer a search tool, they sometimes offer the facility to see the text and image side by side (a surprising number do not): that seems to be all. You can navigate from page to page; there might be indices of various kinds. But you can do these things with print editions too.

Indeed, these digital editions as described by Pierazzo, including the Jane Austen manuscript edition for which she had considerable responsibility, are surprisingly inert. You can view the transcription and image page by page, you can move from page to page, exactly as you can for a print edition. As in a print edition, there is one interface, that provided by the production team, and only one. We are offered a diplomatic view only of the text, and that is all. In a comparison of this edition with a print edition, this edition does not come off very well. It is in its favour, that it is free on the internet. But some of the things one might expect of a print edition —particularly, a table of contents detailing exactly what is in each manuscript volume— are absent from this digital edition. Nor do we find compensation in other areas. One might expect to be able to read either of the two chapters of Persuasion given here as a continuous text, without having to flick from page to page. Or one might want to load the text of a chapter into another system, a PDF viewer for instance, to read, annotate or print. You cannot do that either. In all, this looks like an uneasy compromise: it has some things a print edition might not have and some things a digital might have, while missing other things print and digital editions might have.

Not much revolution here, one might say. Indeed, one would expect a diplomatic edition in digital form is not going to be very different from one in print form. However, there are other kinds of edition: particularly, editions of texts in many manuscripts. Unsurprisingly, these are very rare among the editions listed by Sahle, which are almost all editions based on single witnesses. However, some have been made. My own editions of the Canterbury Tales, Prue Shaw's editions of the Dante, the transcripts of the Piers Plowman Electronic Archive and the Birmingham/Münster editions of the Greek New Testament are editions of texts which exist in multiple witnesses. Let us look at Prue Shaw's edition of Dante's *Commedia*, which may reasonably be seen as

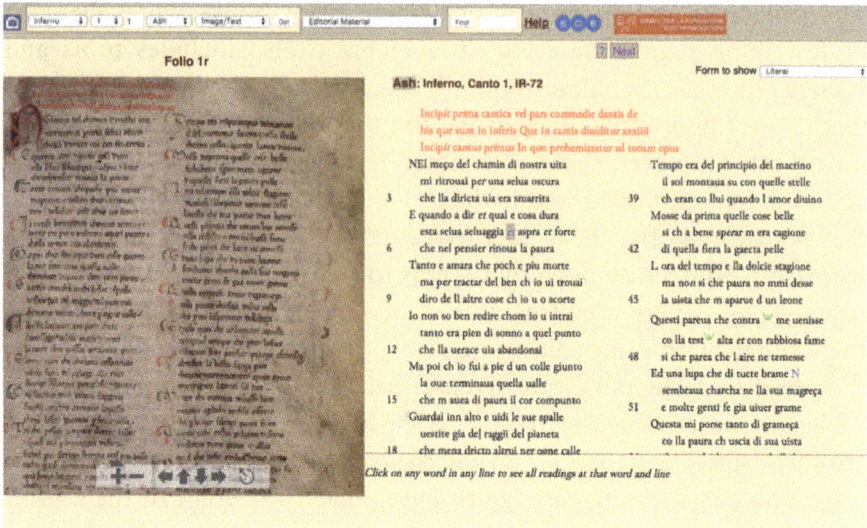

Figure 6. The Shaw edition of Dante's *Commedia*, showing the first page of the Ashburnham manuscript

the most fully conceived and realized digital edition of a text in many versions.[24]

At first, this looks like another of the many single witness image plus transcription we have discussed. We open with an image of the manuscript on the left and a transcription of the manuscript page on the right. We see that the transcript offers multiple views: we can look at a transcription of the text as it literally appears, or as first written by the scribe, or after any of multiple layers of correction. Further, this is not just one witness: there are seven manuscripts, and the full text of two editions. However, this edition is considerably more than a set of transcripts of the seven manuscripts. Probe further: we find a word-by-word collation of the seven manuscripts and two editions, thus.

We see among other things that this collation includes information about the various layers of copying in the manuscripts. This collation is given for all 95,000 words in the 14,223 lines of the Commedia, and allows us, at every word, to see how the seven manuscripts and two editions agree. Note too that this collation is fully regularized: that is, variation in spelling has been filtered out so that the collation presents only variants with likely stemmatic significance.

This edition does not only include a collation. Clicking on the 'VMAP' symbol beside lines the collation brings up what we call a variant map.

Figure 7. The word-by-word collation of two lines of Dante's *Commedia*, from Shaw's edition

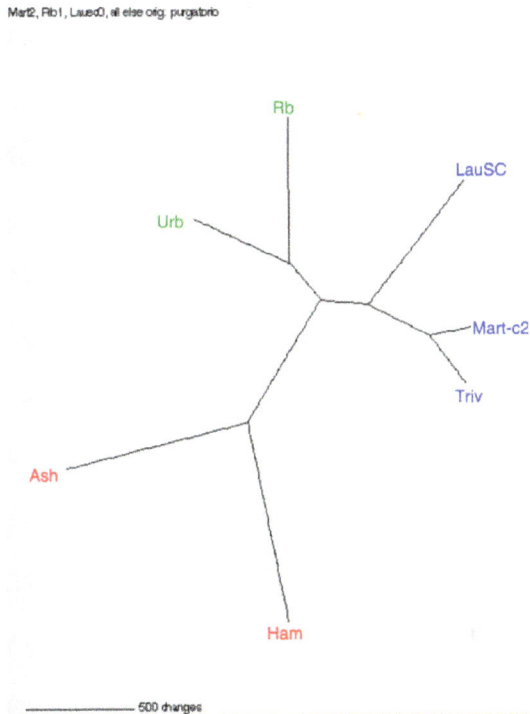

Figure 8. The variant map for Purgatorio 18, 57: "e de primi appetibili"

This resembles a stemma, in that it appears to group manuscripts and texts in some kind of tree-like relationship: thus Mart/Triv, Urb/Rb and Ash/Ham appear to form three distinct pairs.[25] Where does this diagram come from? The extensive introductions provided by Shaw and others explain that this diagram was made by phylogenetic software, developed for evolutionary biology, which creates a hypothesis of the family relations among the manuscripts based on the readings they share and do not share in the collation. Throughout the introduction, Shaw examines the evidence provided both by phylogenetic and traditional philological methods. In 1964, the great Dante scholar Giorgio Petrocchi produced a stemma of the relations among the early manuscripts of the Commedia.[26] In 2000, Federico Sanguineti challenged Petrocchi's stemma, alleging that the single manuscript at the top left of Figure 8, Urb, was independent of all other mss of the Commedia and therefore equivalent in authority to all the other 800 manuscripts of the Commedia.[27] One can read in the editorial material Shaw's careful demolition of Sanguineti's arguments. Further, the reader can test in the collation, in the variant maps, and in the variant database tool provided by Shaw, whether Shaw is right. Here is the core evidence of the common descent of Urb and another manuscript, Rb, which validates Petrocchi against Sanguineti, in the form of some 300 variants identified by the VBase search tool as likely to have been present in the shared ancestor of Urb/Rb.

Yet, there is one thing missing from Shaw's edition. She does not provide her own edited text. This absence strikes me as the single most remarkable element of the edition. It shifts the focus away from the editor, as maker of a text, to the documents themselves and what we might learn from them. The centre of the edition is not the product: the edited text, with all else seen as ancillary, preparatory, and explanatory. The centre of the edition is process: the search for understanding of all these documents and how they relate to each other. Nor is Shaw alone in this view of an edition in the digital age, as not requiring an edited text. Our editions of sections of the Canterbury Tales also lack an edited text. While the Nestle-Aland Greek New Testament text can be found within the Greek New Testament edition websites at Münster and Birmingham, it is almost invisible, indeed irrelevant. The absence of an edited text from both the Shaw edition and the Greek New Testament sites declares clearly: the aim of these editions is something other than the establishment of a text.

If an edition no longer needs an edited text, one might ask: why do we need an edition?

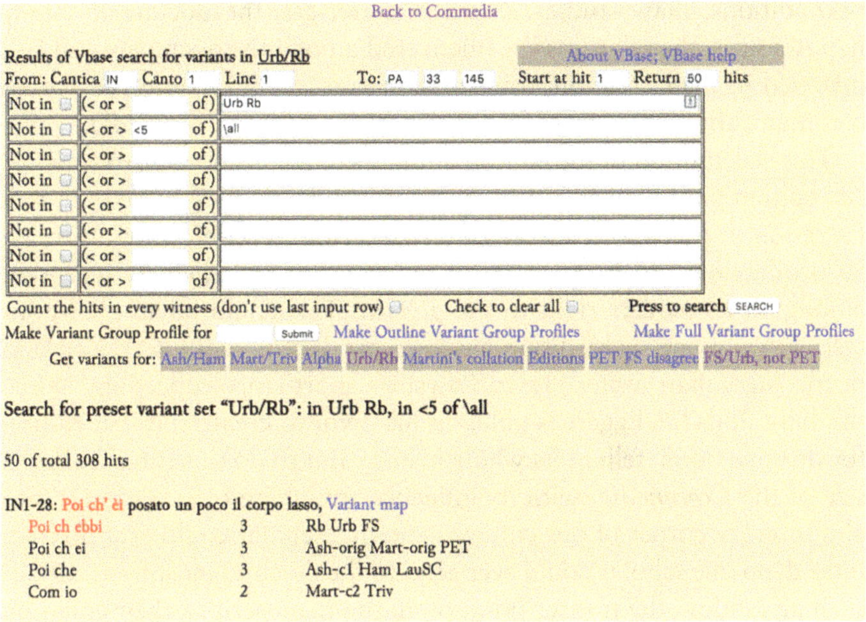

Figure 9. VBase search for Urb/Rb variants

In the midst of this confusion of documents, one might also ask: where is Dante, and the work we know as the Commedia? F.W. Bateson asked: if the Mona Lisa is in the Louvre, where is *Hamlet*?[28] The best answer for this that I know (and it is not Bateson's answer) is that Hamlet is in all the documents, all the versions, all the performances of *Hamlet*, and in the minds of all who have ever encountered *Hamlet*. There is no one *Hamlet*, no one *Commedia*, no one definitive text we can point at and say, this is what Dante wrote. Yet: we still think of something we call the *Commedia*. This has led several scholars to ask, from different directions, what do we mean by the term "work" in the digital age, for example in the essays in a recent number of Ecdotica edited by Barbara Bordalejo, with articles by her, Paul Eggert, Peter Shillingsburg, Hans Gabler and myself.[29] Here is the definition I offer of a "work" in that collection: the work is the set of texts which is hypothesized as organically related, in terms of the communicative acts which they present. In this definition, the task of an editor of the *Commedia* is to identify the documents which witness the communicative act we call the *Commedia*, and then to define how all the documents are related to each other and what each tells us of the *Commedia*, as Shaw does. In this definition, the *Commedia* is grounded in the seven manuscripts and two editions Shaw studies. These manuscripts, the documents Shaw hypothesizes, the relations she uncovered among the documents and all involved in their creation, transmission and reception, and the acts of communication we extract from them: these are the *Commedia*.

This redefinition of the edition amounts to a considerable expansion. An edition, it follows, is not just the production of a text. It is a narration of the whole history of a work, from its conception, through its production and first and later publication, and then its reception among all its readers right to the present. This could be an enormous task. Exactly one such edition has been produced: Paul Eggert's edition of the Australian writer Henry Lawson's short story collection "While the Billy Boils".[30] Eggert is able, on his own, to create such an edition for this one book, telling its whole history. But to do this for a work the size of the *Commedia*, with its influence stretching over centuries into almost every corner of our culture —no one scholar could ever do that. Indeed, no one scholar could ever achieve the first and most basic task of such an edition, the transcription of all the manuscripts, their collation and analysis. With considerable funding and help, and huge individual effort, Shaw was able to do this for just seven manuscripts, and it took fifteen years. How long would the full 800 manuscripts take?

Elements of a revolution: changing who we are

Now finally, we arrive at what I believe may be truly revolutionary about the impact of the digital age on scholarly editing. Every edition I have discussed so far has been made according to what we might call the Alexandrian consensus. The librarians gathered the many texts of Homer together; the scholars studied them and created a text; a grateful world took that text and read it.[31] This model rests on two pillars. The first pillar is that only qualified scholars may examine the primary documents. The second pillar is that only qualified scholars have the authority to make a text the rest of us may read. Both pillars are now fallen. We are moving to a world where every manuscript and every book from the past is online, free for anyone to look at. You no longer need to be tenured and well-connected to see a manuscript: increasingly, all you need is an internet connection. As for academic authority: peer-review and tenure committees are fine things but no-one is going to assert that only approved scholars can read manuscripts. If anyone doubted this, the Transcribe Bentham and similar projects has shown that transcriptions of even very demanding material can be made by people without formal training.[32]

Here is what we have: we want to make editions based on all the manuscripts, possibly hundreds, even thousands of them. We want to trace the history of a work through all its manifestations: every publication, every version. The materials are available free online to everyone. We do not have enough students and scholars to do this work within the academy. We know there are interested and committed people who can help us. So let us thrown open the doors, and invite others to join us. "Crowdsourcing" is the word of the moment: writing encyclopedias, correcting newspaper transcripts, and now scholarly editing. These are tasks for the wisdom of crowds.

Indeed, we need people to help us. Several major projects, including our own, are experimenting with opening up our work to others. We could do this in two ways. We could say to people: give us your work, and we will use it as we wish. Or we could say: we will work together and anyone can use what we make. The difference is small, it seems: but critical. Traditionally, we scholars like to own and control what we make. This is my edition. I want to control how it is used. You may contribute, but I will control what you contribute. In the world of print, where the target was a fixed printed object distributed by a publisher who was happy to hold the exclusive license for your edition, this was a fortunate coalescence of interests.

But in the digital world, that attitude cripples. I make my digital edition, I create a beautiful interface for it, then I wrap it up in copyright and other licensing restrictions so that it can only be used in the ways, and even by the people, whom I approve. There are numerous problems with this. First: who is going to maintain that interface, that edition, when you are no longer there, or you have run out of funding? What happens to all those carefully made transcripts, all that work? Second: why would people want to contribute to your edition, when you are going to control their work— so that they might even lose access to their own work? There are other arguments too: one might question the morality of work done with public support, as is the case for virtually all editions, becoming effectively the private property of the editors.

It is for these reasons that we, and several others, argue that we should publish the base materials of our editions —particularly the transcripts and the images— under the Creative Commons Attribution licence. Indeed we should go further than that. We should make it as easy as we can for others to take what we have made, to adapt it and augment it in any way they wish, and then republish it. And that includes commercial publishers. If they can take what we have made and publish it and make money from it, excellent. In this world, our transcripts of Canterbury Tales manuscripts would appear in many places across the web. Some scholars might add annotations to them, links to other materials, commentaries, glossaries. Others might alter them for their own purposes. Instead of our own, single, monolithic edition, there would be a flourishing ecoculture of overlapping sites, using our material in multiple ways, each finding their own readership. I have to say that persuading scholars to relinquish control of what they have made is not easy. We have been trained, since our first undergraduate days, to regard our research as dragons value their gold: of more value if we hoard it than if we spend it. But in the digital world, giving and taking is all that matters.

And, there are people, many, many of them, who want to take what we make. I have mentioned the Codex Sinaiticus website: within the first four months of the sites launch, over 1.25 million people visited it. Less spectacular perhaps, but equally impressive, are the figures for Barbara Bordalejo's online Variorium edition of Darwin's *Origin of Species*: over the last two years, this has averaged a steady 500 users a month, with around thirty of those each month spending more than half an hour looking at the site.[33] And here, too, is our view of how we might bring the Canterbury Tales, its text, manuscripts, and performance, to the born-digital generation. We call this the CantApp:

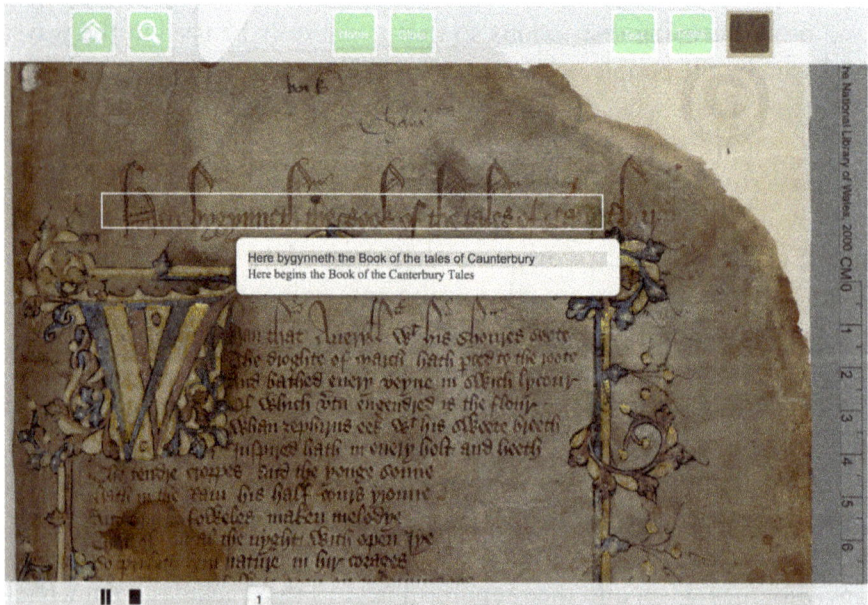

Figure 10. The CantApp, opening page

Bordalejo's Darwin *Variorum* could not have been made without the work of others before her; we should like our CantApp to inspire others to take our work and do better. We all know the topos that we are standing on the shoulders of the scholars who have preceded us. The digital age offers a variant on this. As well as stand on the shoulders of others, we should help others to stand on our shoulders. This will change who we are. Now, that would be revolutionary.

Notes

1. Among many essays and books incorporating (while sometimes criticizing) this meme, see Jerome McGann, *Radiant Textuality* (New York: Palgrave, 2001); pages 53–74 reprint his essay 'The Rationale of Hypertext', originally published online in 1995 and available at www2.iath.virginia.edu/public/jjm2f/rationale.html and in print in *Electronic Text: Investigations in Method and Theory*, ed. by Kathryn Sutherland (Oxford: Oxford University Press, 1997); *Digital Critical Editions*, ed. by Daniel Apollon, Claire Bélisle and Philippe Régnier (Urbana, Chicago and Springfield: University of Illinois Press, 2014): Tara Andrews, 'The Third Way: Philology and Critical Edition in the Digital Age', in *Variants 10*, ed. by Wim Van Mierlo (Amsterdam and New York: Rodopi, 2013).

2. Roger Boesche, *Tocqueville's Road Map: Methodology, Liberalism, Revolution, and Despotism* (Lanham, MD: Lexington, 2006), pp. 86–87.

3. There is a full print facsimile of the Beowulf manuscript edited by Julius Zupitza, *Beowulf. Autotypes of the unique Cotton ms. Vitellius A XV in the British Museum, with a transliteration and notes* (London: N. Trübner, for the Early English Text Society, 1882; reprinted in 1959 and 1969). A single page of the manuscript, fol. 160v, is reproduced as Figure 1 of the most widely used edition of *Beowulf: Klaeber's Beowulf and the Fight at Finnsburgh. Fourth Edition*, ed. by R. D. Fulk, Robert Bjork and John D. Niles (Toronto, Buffalo, London: University of Toronto Press, 2008).

4. *Electronic Beowulf 4.0*, ed. by Kevin Kiernan (University of Kentucky, 2015), at http://ebeowulf.uky.edu/ebeo4.o/start.html [accessed 31 October 2015].

5. Personal communication, Scott McKendrick, British Library. The digital edition is http://www.codexsinaiticus.org/ [accessed 31 October 2015].

6. A.S.G. Edwards paper, delivered in a Master Class at the Centre for Textual Scholarship at De Montfort University on 1 June 2006; reported by Peter Shillingsburg, 'How Literary Works Exist: Convenient Scholarly Editions', *Digital Humanities Quarterly*, 3:3 (2009) #18, at http://www.digitalhumanities.org/dhq/vol/3/3/000054/000054.html [accessed 31 October

2015]. See too Edwards' critique of digitization in 'Back to the Real?', *Times Literary Supplement* 7 June 2013, where he argues (inter alia) that success of digitization in reaching many readers (e.g. the 10,000 hits a month on the Codex Sinaiticus website) is not scholarship but "a new branch of the entertainment industry."

7. Emma Beer, 'Waking up in the British Library', *Ariadne*, 43 (2005), at http://www.ariadne.ac.uk/issue43/wakingupinbl-rpt.

8. Kenneth M. Price, 'Edition, Project, Database, Archive, Thematic Research Collection: What's in a Name?', *Digital Humanities Quarterly*, 3:3 (1009), at http://www.digitalhumanities.org/dhq/vol/3/3/000053/000053.html.

9. For TUStep: see the list at http://www.tustep.uni-tuebingen.de/ed3.html, numbering over 900 volumes; for Classical Text Editor, see the list at http://cte.oeaw.ac.at//?ido=pub, for some 150 volumes.

10. Thomas Tanselle, 'Foreword', in *Electronic Textual Editing*, ed. by Lou Burnard, Katharine O'Brien O'Keefe and John Unsworth (New York: Modern Language Association, 2006), pp. 1–6 (p. 6); Barbara Bordalejo, 'The Texts We See and the Works We Imagine', *Ecdotica*, 13 (2013), pp. 64–75 (p. 75).

11. One can index the difficulty of manuscript transcription from the proliferation of articles, manuals and guides over the last decades. A few examples: my own attempt, with Elizabeth Solopova, to define protocols for manuscript transcription for the manuscripts of the Canterbury Tales, in "Guidelines for Transcription of the Manuscripts of the Wife of Bath's Prologue"; see too Alois Pichler's argument that "Texts are not objectively existing entities which just need to be discovered and presented, but entities which have to be constructed in "Advantages of a Machine-Readable Version of Wittgenstein's Nachlass", p. 774. Pichler's view (which is effectively identical to mine and Solopova's) is attacked by Renear as "anti-realist": see the account of the discussion in my "What Text Really is Not, and Why Editors have to Learn to Swim". The distinction between levels of transcription is also discussed by Barbara Bordalejo in "The Commedia Project Encoding System". See also, among many others: the "Basic Conventions for Transcription" for the Scriptorium project at http://scriptorium.english.cam.ac.uk/handwriting/materials/conventions/; the CENDARI project guide at http://www.cendari.eu/sites/default/files/ARGTranscriptions.pdf; and many more.

12. The whole manuscript is online at https://www.llgc.org.uk/?id=257; the first page is there numbered as "folio 2r".

13. You can read about our efforts to answer these questions in the Canterbury Tales Project blog and wiki, at www.textualcommunities.usask.ca, a discussion informed by the conflicting perspectives presented by the studies referred to in footnote 11.

14. Recording of these lower-level "graphetic" features of scribal writing (the different forms of each letter, indeed of each stroke) might be useful for the making of "scribal profiles" as advocated by Angus McIntosh, 'Scribal Profiles from Middle English Texts', *Neuphilologische Mitteilungen*, 76 (1975), 218–235.

15. This explanation follows that given by John Manly and Edith Rickert, *The Text of the Canterbury Tales: Studied on the Basis of All Known Manuscripts*, 8 vols (Chicago: Univ. of Chicago Press, 1940), I, 271–272. Compare the discussion of these folios by Estelle Stubbs, 'Observations: Section IV', in *The Hengwrt Chaucer Digital Facsimile* (Leicester: Scholarly Digital Editions, 2001).

16. For example: in Oxford New College MS 314 (Ne) the text of the Parson's Tale appears in the following order: segments 1–98, 532–580, 162–273, 687–735, 320–532, 99–161, 582–687, 273–320, 735–end. The shifts from sequence to sequence occur mid-page and mid-segment. Sense can be made of this if one presumes that in the ancestor copy of this tale the text of the seven segments 99–735 occupied three quires of eight. The first and last two leaves of the first quire (containing 99–161 and 273–320) were swapped with the first and last two leaves of the third quire (containing 532–580 and 687–735) to give the order in which the Parson's Tale now appears in Ne.

17. Daniel W. Mosser, *A Digital Catalogue of the Pre-1500 Manuscripts and Incunables of the Canterbury Tales* (Blacksburg VA: 2nd edn, Virginia Tech, 2013).

18. Kevin Kiernan, 'Digital Facsimiles in Editing', in *Electronic Textual Editing*, ed. by Lou Burnard, Katherine O'Brien O'Keeffe and John Unsworth (New York: Modern Language Association of America, 2006), pp. 262–268; Elena Pierazzo, 'A Rationale of Digital Documentary editions', *Literary and Linguistic Computing*, 26 (2011), 463–477.

19. Constantin von Tischendorf, *Bibliorum Codex Sinaiticus Petropolitanus*, 4 volumes (Leipzig, 1862).

20. Vésteinn Ólason, *Íslendingabækur – The Books of The Icelanders*, Richard and Margaret Beck Trust Lecture, University of Victoria (20 March 2003). At http://web.uvic.ca/~becktrus/assets/text/vesteinn_01.php.

21. Jedd Deppman, Daniel Ferrer and Michael Groden, *Genetic Criticism: Texts and Avant-textes* (Philadelphia: University of Pennsylvania, 2004).

22. Pierazzo, 'Rationale', p. 475.

23. Gregory A. Pass, *Descriptive Cataloging of Ancient, Medieval, Renaissance, and Early Modern Manuscripts* (Chicago: Association of College and Research Libraries, 2003), p. 144.

24. Prue Shaw, *Dante Alighieri. Commedia. A Digital Edition*. (Leicester and Florence: Scholarly Digital Editions and SISMEL, 2010).

25. Mart: Milan, Biblioteca Nazionale Braidense, Aldina AP XVI 25; Triv: Milan, Biblioteca dell'Archivio Storico Civico e Trivulziana, Ms. Trivulziano 1080; Rb: Florence, Biblioteca Riccardiana, Ms. Riccardiano 1005 and Milan, Biblioteca Nazionale Braidense, Ms. AG XII 2; Urb: Città del Vaticano, Biblioteca Apostolica Vaticana, Ms. Urbinate latino 366; Ash: Florence, Biblioteca Medicea Laurenziana, Ms. Ashburnham 828; Ham: Berlin, Staatsbibliothek zu Berlin Preußischer Kulturbesitz, Ms. Hamilton 203.

26. Dante Alighieri, *La Commedia secondo l'antica vulgata a cura di Giorgio Petrocchi*, Edizione Nazionale a cura della Società Dantesca Italiana, 4 vols (Milano: Arnoldo Mondadori Editore, 1966–1967).

27. Dantis Alagherii, *Comedìa. Edizione critica per cura di Federico Sanguineti* (Firenze: Edizioni del Galluzzo, 2001).

28. F.W. Bateson, 'Modern Bibliography and the Literary Artifact', in *English Studies Today*, ed. by Georges A. Bonnard (Bern: 2nd edn, Francke Verlag, 1961), pp. 67–77 (p. 70).

29. Peter M. Robinson, 'The Concept of the Work in the Digital Age', in *Work, Text and Document in the Digital Age*, ed. by Barbara Bordalejo, *Ecdotica*, 10 (2013), pp. 13–41.

30. Paul Eggert, *The Biography of a Book: Henry Lawson's While the Billy Boils* (Philadelphia and Sydney: Penn State University Press and University of Sydney Press, 2013).

31. L.D. Reynolds and N.G. Wilson, *Scribes and Scholars: A Guide to the Transmission of Greek and Latin Literature* (Oxford: 4th edn, Oxford University Press, 2013), pp. 6–16.

32. Tim Causer and Valerie Wallace, 'Building a Volunteer Community: Results and Findings from Transcribe Bentham', *Digital Humanities Quarterly*, 6:2 (2012), online at http://www.digitalhumanities.org/dhq/vol/6/2/000125/000125.html.

33. Barbara Bordalejo, ed., *Online Variorum of Darwin's Origin of Species* (Darwin Online, 2009), at http://darwin-online.org.uk/Variorium/index.html.

Bibliography

Andrews, Tara, 'The Third Way: Philology and Critical Edition in the Digital Age', in *Variants 10*, ed. by Wim Van Mierlo (Amsterdam and New York: Rodopi, 2013), pp. 61–76

Bateson, F.W., 'Modern Bibliography and the Literary Artifact', *English Studies Today*, ed. by Georges A. Bonnard (Bern: 2nd edn, Francke Verlag, 1961), pp. 67–77

Beer, Emma, 'Waking up in the British Library', *Ariadne*, 43 (2005), at http://www.ariadne.ac.uk/issue43/wakingupinbl-rpt

Beowulf: Klaeber's Beowulf and the Fight at Finnsburgh. Fourth Edition, ed. by R.D. Fulk, Robert Bjork and John D. Niles (Toronto, Buffalo, London: University of Toronto Press, 2008)

Boesche, Roger, *Tocqueville's Road Map: Methodology, Liberalism, Revolution, and Despotism* (Lanham, MD: Lexington, 2006)

Bordalejo, Barbara, ed., *Online Variorum of Darwin's Origin of Species* (Darwin Online, 2009), at http://darwin-online.org.uk/Variorium/index.html

Bordalejo, Barbara, "The Commedia Project Encoding System", in Prue Shaw (ed.) *Dante Alighieri: The Commedia. A Digital Edition.* Birmingham: Scholarly Digital Editions and Florence: Sismel, 2010.

Bordalejo, Barbara, 'The Texts We See and the Works We Imagine', *Ecdotica*, 13 (2013), 64–75

Causer, Tim and Valerie Wallace, 'Building a Volunteer Community: Results and Findings from Transcribe Bentham', *Digital Humanities Quarterly*, 6:2 (2012), online at http://www.digitalhumanities.org/dhq/vol/6/2/000125/000125.html

Dante Alighieri, *La Commedia secondo l'antica vulgata a cura di Giorgio Petrocchi*, Edizione Nazionale a cura della Società Dantesca Italiana, 4 vols (Milano: Arnoldo Mondadori Editore, 1966–1967).

Dantis Alagherii, *Comedìa. Edizione critica per cura di Federico Sanguineti* (Firenze, Edizioni del Galluzzo, 2001).

Deppman, Jedd, Daniel Ferrer and Michael Groden, *Genetic Criticism: Texts and Avant-textes* (Philadelphia: University of Pennsylvania, 2004)

Digital Critical Editions, ed. by Daniel Apollon, Claire Bélisle and Philippe Régnier (Urbana, Chicago and Springfield: University of Illinois Press, 2014)

Edwards, A.S.G., 'Back to the Real?', *Times Literary Supplement*, 7 June 2013

Eggert, Paul, *The Biography of a Book: Henry Lawson's While the Billy Boils* (Philadelphia and Sydney: Penn State University Press and University of Sydney Press, 2013)

Electronic Beowulf 4.0, ed. by Kevin Kiernan (University of Kentucky, 2015), at http://ebeowulf.uky.edu/ebeo4.0/start.html

Electronic Text: Investigations in Method and Theory, ed. by Kathryn Sutherland (Oxford: Oxford University Press, 1997)

Kiernan, Kevin, 'Digital Facsimiles in Editing', *Electronic Textual Editing*, ed. by Lou Burnard, Katherine O'Brien O'Keeffe and John Unsworth (New York: Modern Language Association of America, 2006), pp. 262–268

McGann, Jerome, 'The Rationale of Hypertext', *Electronic Text: Investigations in Method and Theory*, ed. by Kathryn Sutherland (Oxford: Oxford University Press, 1997), pp. 19–46

McGann, Jerome, *Radiant Textuality* (New York: Palgrave, 2001)

McIntosh, Angus, 'Scribal Profiles from Middle English Texts', *Neuphilologische Mitteilungen*, 76 (1975), 218–235

Manly, John and Edith Rickert, *The Text of the Canterbury Tales: Studied on the Basis of All Known Manuscripts,* 8 vols (Chicago: Univ. of Chicago Press, 1940)

Mosser, Daniel W., *A Digital Catalogue of the Pre-1500 Manuscripts and Incunables of the Canterbury Tales* (Blacksburg VA: 2nd edn, Virginia Tech, 2013)

Ólason, Vésteinn, *Íslendingabækur – The Books of The Icelanders*, Richard and Margaret Beck Trust Lecture, University of Victoria (20 March 2003), available at http://web.uvic.ca/~becktrus/assets/text/vesteinn_01.php

Pass, Gregory A., *Descriptive Cataloguing of Ancient, Medieval, Renaissance, and Early Modern Manuscripts* (Chicago: Association of College and Research Libraries, 2003)

Pierazzo, Elena, 'A Rationale of Digital Documentary Editions', *Literary and Linguistic Computing*, 26 (2011), pp. 463–477

Price, Kenneth M., 'Edition, Project, Database, Archive, Thematic Research Collection: What's in a Name?', *Digital Humanities Quarterly*, 3:3 (2009), at http://www.digitalhumanities.org/dhq/vol/3/3/000053/000053.html

Reynolds, Leighton D. and Nigel G. Wilson, *Scribes and Scholars: A Guide to the Transmission of Greek and Latin Literature* (Oxford: 4th edn, Oxford University Press, 2013)

Robinson, Peter and Elizabeth Solopova, "Guidelines for Transcription of the Manuscripts of the Wife of Bath's Prologue", in *The Canterbury Tales Project Occasional Papers*, ed. by Norman F. Blake and Peter M.W. Robinson (Oxford: Office for Humanities Communication, 1993), pp. 19–52

Robinson, Peter M., 'The Concept of the Work in the Digital Age', in *Work, Text and Document in the Digital Age*, ed. by Barbara Bordalejo [=*Ecdotica*, 10 (2013)], pp. 13–41

Shaw, Prue *Dante Alighieri. Commedia. A Digital Edition.* (Leicester and Florence: Scholarly Digital Editions and SISMEL, 2010)

Shillingsburg, Peter, 'How Literary Works Exist: Convenient Scholarly Editions', *Digital Humanities Quarterly* 3:3 (2009) #18, at http://www.digitalhumanities.org/dhq/vol/3/3/000054/000054.html   [accessed   31 October 2015]

Stubbs, Estelle, 'Observations: Section IV', *The Hengwrt Chaucer Digital Facsimile* (Leicester: Scholarly Digital Editions, 2001).

Tanselle, Thomas 'Foreword', in *Electronic Textual Editing*, ed. by Lou Burnard, Katharine O'Brien O'Keefe and John Unsworth (New York: Modern Language Association, 2006), pp. 1-6

von Tischendorf, Constantin, *Bibliorum Codex Sinaiticus Petropolitanus*, 4 volumes (Leipzig, 1862)

Zupitza, Julius *Beowulf. Autotypes of the unique Cotton ms. Vitellius A XV in the British Museum, with a transliteration and notes* (London: N. Trübner, for the Early English Text Society, 1882; reprinted in 1959 and 1969)

CORPUS TROPORUM
Studia Latina Stockholmiensia (SLS)/*Corpus Troporum* (CT)

CORPUS TROPORUM I, Tropes du propre de la messe. 1. Cycle de Noël, éd. Ritva Jonsson. SLS 21. Stockholm 1975.

CORPUS TROPORUM II, Prosules de la messe. 1. Tropes de l'alleluia, éd. Olof Marcusson. SLS 22. Stockholm 1976.

CORPUS TROPORUM III, Tropes du propres de la messe. 2. Cycle de Pâques, éd. Gunilla Björkvall, Gunilla Iversen, Ritva Jonsson. SLS 25. Stockholm 1982.

CORPUS TROPORUM IV, Tropes de l'Agnus Dei. Edition critique suivie d'une étude analytique par Gunilla Iversen. SLS 26. Stockholm 1980.

CORPUS TROPORUM V, Les deux tropaires d'Apt, mss. 17 et 18. Inventaire analytique des mss et édition des textes uniques par Gunilla Björkvall. SLS 32. Stockholm 1986.

CORPUS TROPORUM VI, Prosules de la messe. 2. Les prosules limousines de Wolfenbüttel, Herzog August Bibliothek Cod. Guelf. 79 Gud. lat., par Eva Odelman. SLS 31. Stockholm 1986.

CORPUS TROPORUM VII, Tropes de l'ordinaire de la messe. Tropes du Sanctus. Introduction et édition critique par Gunilla Iversen. SLS 34. Stockholm 1990.

CORPUS TROPORUM IX, Tropes for the Proper of the Mass. 4. The Feasts of the Blessed Virgin Mary. Edited with an Introduction and Commentary by Ann-Katrin Andrews Johansson. CT. Stockholm 1998.

CORPUS TROPORUM X, Tropes du propre de la messe. 5. Fêtes des Saints et de la Croix et de la Transfiguration. A Introduction et commentaires (Pp. 647 + carte + 13 photos). B Édition des textes (Pp. 560). Par Ritva Maria Jacobsson. CT. Stockholm 2011.

CORPUS TROPORUM XI, Prosules de la messe. 3. Prosules de l'offertoire. Édition des textes par Gunilla Björkvall. CT. Stockholm 2009. Pp. X + 254.

CORPUS TROPORUM XII, Tropes du Gloria, vol 1, Introduction et édition des textes, (428pp.), Vol. 2. Aperçu des manuscrits (2438pp.+32 planches), Par Gunilla Iversen, SLS 61, Stockholm 2014.

Pax et Sapientia. Studies in Text and Music of Liturgical Tropes and Sequences, in Memory of Gordon Anderson, ed. Ritva Jacobsson. SLS 29. Stockholm 1986.

Recherches nouvelles sur les tropes liturgiques. Recueil d'études réunies par Wulf Arlt et Gunilla Björkvall. SLS 36. Stockholm 1993.

STUDIA LATINA STOCKHOLMIENSIA
Published by Stockholm University
Nos. 1–22
Editor: Dag Norberg

1. *Nils-Ola Nilsson*. Metrische Stildifferenzen in den Satiren des Horaz. Stockholm 1952. Pp. VIII+220.

2. *Dag Norberg*. La poésie latine rythmique du haut moyen âge. Stockholm 1953. Pp. 120. Out of print.

3. *Ulla Westerbergh*. Chronicon Salernitanum. A Critical Edition with Studies on Literary and Historical Sources and on Language. Stockholm 1956. Pp. XXXII+362. Out of print.

4. *Ulla Westerbergh*. Beneventan Ninth Century Poetry. Stockholm 1957. Pp. 91. Out of print.

5. *Dag Norberg*. Introduction à l'étude de la versiDzcation latine médiévale. Stockholm 1958. Pp. 218. Out of print.

6. *Dag Norberg*. Epistulae S. Desiderii Cadurcensis. Stockholm 1961. Pp. 91.

7. *Lars Elfving*. Étude lexicographique sur les séquences limousines. Stockholm 1962. Pp. 283.

8. *Birgitta Thorsberg*. Études sur l'hymnologie mozarabe. Stockholm 1962. Pp. 184. Out of print.

9. *Ulla Westerbergh*. Anastasius Bibliothecarius. Sermo Theodori Studitae de sancto Bartholomeo apostolo. Stockholm 1963. Pp. XIV+214.

10. *Gudrun Lindholm*. Studien zum mittellateinischen Prosarhythmus. Seine Entwicklung und sein Abklingen in der Briedziteratur Italiens. Stockholm 1963. Pp. 204. Out of print.

11. *Katarina Halvarson*. Bernardi Cluniacensis Carmina De trinitate et de Dzde catholica, De castitate servanda, In libros regum, De octo vitiis. Stockholm 1963. Pp. 161.

12. *Margareta Lokrantz*. L'opera poetica di S. Pier Damiani. Descrizione dei manoscritti, edizione del testo, esame prosodico-metrico, discussione delle questioni d'autenticità. Stockholm 1964. Pp. 258. Out of print.

13. *Tore Janson*. Latin Prose Prefaces. Studies in Literary Conventions. Stockholm 1964. Pp. 180. Out of print.

14. *Jan Öberg*. Serlon de Wilton. Poèmes latins. Texte critique avec une introduction et des tables. Stockholm 1965. Pp. 240. Out of print.

15. *Ritva Jonsson*. Historia. Études sur la genèse des ofDzces versiDzés. Stockholm 1968. Pp. 259.

16. Jan Öberg. *Notice et extraits du Manuscrit Q 19 (XVIᵉ S.) de Strängnäs. Stockholm 1968.* Pp. 91.

17. *Gustaf Holmér*. Le sermon sur Esaü. Discours allégorique sur la chasse de Pierre de Marini. Édition critique. Stockholm 1968. Pp. 133.

18. Herbert Adolfsson. Liber epistularum Guidonis de Basochis. Stockholm 1969. Pp. VIII+317.

19. *Hedda Roll*. Hans Brask. Latinsk korrespondens 1523. Stockholm 1973. Pp. 187.

20. *Tore Janson*. Prose Rhythm in Medieval Latin from the 9th to the 13th Century. Stockholm 1975. Pp. 133.

21. *Ritva Jonsson*. Corpus Troporum I. Tropes du propre de la messe. 1 Cycle de Noël. Stockholm 1975. Pp. 361; 31 pl.

22. *Olof Marcusson*. Corpus Troporum II. Prosules de la messe. 1 Tropes de l'alleluia. Stockholm 1976. Pp. 161; 4 pl.

STUDIA LATINA STOCKHOLMIENSIA
Published by Stockholm University
Nos. 23–46
Editor: Jan Öberg

23. *Tore Janson*. Mechanisms of Language Change in Latin. Stockholm 1979. Pp. 133.

24. *Hans Aili*. The Prose Rhythm of Sallust and Livy. Stockholm 1979. Pp. 151.

25. *Gunilla Björkvall, Gunilla Iversen, Ritva Jonsson.* Corpus Troporum III. Tropes du propre de la messe. 2 Cycle de Pâques. Stockholm 1982. Pp. 377; 32 pl.

26. *Gunilla Iversen.* Corpus Troporum IV. Tropes de l'Agnus Dei. Stockholm 1980. Pp. 349; 32 pl.

27. *Alf Uddholm.* Johannes Ulvichius. De liberalitate urbis Gevaliae oratio et carmen. Kritische Ausgabe mit Kommentar. Stockholm 1980. Pp. 93.

28. *Monika Asztalos.* Petrus de Dacia. De gratia naturam ditante sive De virtutibus Christinae Stumbelensis. Édition critique avec une introduction. Stockholm 1982. Pp. 215.

29. *Ritva Jacobsson,* ed. Pax et Sapientia. Studies in Text and Music of Liturgical Tropes and Sequences, in Memory of Gordon Anderson. Stockholm 1986. Pp. 114.

30. *Monika Asztalos,* ed. The Editing of Theological and Philosophical Texts from the Middle Ages. Stockholm 1986. Pp. 314.

31. *Eva Odelman.* Corpus Troporum VI. Prosules de la messe. 2 Les prosules limousines de Wolfenbüttel. Stockholm 1986. Pp. 181.

32. *Gunilla Björkvall.* Corpus Troporum V. Les deux tropaires d'Apt. Stockholm 1986. Pp. 442.

33. *Claes Gejrot.* Diarium Vadstenense. The Memorial Book of Vadstena Abbey. A Critical Edition with an Introduction. Stockholm 1988. Pp. 395.

34. *Gunilla Iversen.* Corpus Troporum VII. Tropes de l'ordinaire de la messe. Tropes du Sanctus. Introduction et édition critique. Stockholm 1990. Pp. 432; 32 pl.

35. *Ella Heuman, Jan Öberg.* Ericus Olai. Chronica regni Gothorum. Textkritische Ausgabe. Stockholm 1993. Pp. 222.

36. *Wulf Arlt, Gunilla Björkvall,* ed. Recherches nouvelles sur les tropes liturgiques. Recueil d'études. Stockholm 1993. Pp. 480.

37. *Claes Gejrot.* Diplomata Novevallensia. The Nydala Charters 1172–1280. A Critical Edition with an Introduction, a Commentary and Indices. Stockholm 1994. Pp. 237.

38. *Annika Ström.* Lachrymae Catharinae. Five Collections of Funeral Poetry from 1628. Edited with Studies on the Theoretical Background and the Social Context of the Genre. Stockholm 1994. Pp. 307.

39. *Jan Öberg.* Ericus Olai. Chronica regni Gothorum. II. Prolegomena und Indizes. Stockholm 1995. Pp. 85.

40. *Jan Öberg*. Formularia Lincopensia. Zwei spätmittelalterliche Briefsteller aus dem Bistum Linköping (Cod. Upsal. C 204). Textkritische Gesamtausgabe mit Einleitung und Register. Stockholm 1997. Pp. 96.

41. *Peter Ståhl*. Johannes Hildebrandi. Liber epistularis (Cod. Upsal. C 6). I. Lettres nos 1–109. Édition critique avec des analyses et une introduction. Stockholm 1998. Pp. 216.

42. *Jan Öberg*. Petronius. Cena Trimalchionis. A New Critical Edition. Stockholm 1999. Pp. XX+58.

43. *Christina Sandquist Öberg*. Versus Maximiani. Der Elegienzyklus textkritisch herausgegeben, übersetzt und neu interpretiert. Stockholm 1999. Pp. 205.

44. *Claes Gejrot, Annika Ström*. Poems for the Occasion. Three Essays on Neo-Latin Poetry from Seventeenth-Century Sweden. Stockholm 1999. Pp. 199.

45. *Robert Andrews*. Augustinus de Ferraria. Quaestiones super librum Praedicamentorum Aristotelis. Stockholm 2000. Pp. XXXIX+309.

46. *Maria Plaza*. Laughter and Derision in Petronius' Satyrica. A Literary Study. Stockholm 2000. Pp. XII+227.

STUDIA LATINA STOCKHOLMIENSIA
Published by Stockholm University
Nos. 47–48
Editor: Monika Asztalos

47. *Martin Jacobsson*. Aurelius Augustinus. De musica liber VI. A Critical Edition with a Translation and an Introduction. Stockholm 2002. Pp. CXVIII+144.

48. *Gösta Hedegård*. Liber iuratus Honorii. A Critical Edition of the Latin Version of the Sworn Book of Honorius. Stockholm 2002. Pp. 336.

STUDIA LATINA STOCKHOLMIENSIA
Published by Stockholm University
Nos. 49–53
Editor: Hans Aili and Gunilla Iversen

49. *Magnus Karlsson*. Erik XIV. Oratio de iniusto bello regis Daniæ anno 1563 contra regem Sueciæ Ericum 14 gesto. Edited with

introduction, translation and commentary. Stockholm 2003. Pp. 267.

50. *Sara Risberg.* Liber usuum fratrum monasterii Vadstenensis. The Customary of the Vadstena Brothers. A Critical Edition with an Introduction. Stockholm 2003. Pp. 253.

51. *Gunilla Sävborg.* Epistole tardive di Francesco Petrarca. Edizione critica con introduzione e commento. Stockholm 2004. Pp. 262.

52. *Alexander Andrée.* Gilbertus Universalis: Glossa ordinaria in Lamentationes Ieremie prophete. Prothemata et Liber I. A Critical Edition with an Introduction and a Translation. Stockholm 2005. Pp. XIV+323; 3 pl.

53. *Erika Kihlman.* Expositiones Sequentiarum. Medieval Sequence Commentaries and Prologues. Editions with Introductions. Stockholm 2006. Pp. X+356; 12 pl.

STUDIA LATINA STOCKHOLMIENSIA
Published by Stockholm University
Nos. 54–58
Editor: Hans Aili

54. *Alexander Andrée, Erika Kihlman,* ed. Hortus troporum. Florilegium in honorem Gunillae Iversen. A Festschrift in Honour of Professor Gunilla Iversen on the Occasion of her Retirement as Chair of Latin at Stockholm University. Stockholm 2008. Pp. XIX+384; 28 pl.

55. *Elin Andersson.* Responsiones Vadstenenses. Perspectives on the Birgittine Rule in Two Texts from Vadstena and Syon Abbey. A Critical Edition with Translation and Introduction. Stockholm 2011. Pp. VIII + 260.

56. *Erika Kihlman, Denis Searby,* ed. Ars Edendi Lecture Series, vol. I. Stockholm 2011. Pp. 130.

57. *Brian Møller Jensen,* The Story of Justina and Cyprian of Antioch, as told in a Medieval Lectionary from Piacenza. Edition with Introduction and Translation. Stockholm 2012. Pp. 171; 4 pl.

58. *Alessandra Bucossi, Erika Kihlman,* ed. Ars Edendi Lecture Series, vol. II. Stockholm 2012. Pp. 172.

STUDIA LATINA STOCKHOLMIENSIA
Published by Stockholm University
Nos. 59–
Editor: Maria Plaza

59. *Eva Odelman, Denis Searby*, ed. Ars Edendi Lecture Series, vol. III. Stockholm 2014. Pp. 130.

60. *Elin Andersson, Erika Kihlman, Maria Plaza*, red. Latinet i tiden. En festskrift till Hans Aili. Stockholm 2014. Pp. 443; 4pl.

61. *Gunilla Iversen*, Corpus Troporum XII, 1-2, vol 1, Introduction et édition des textes, (428pp.), Vol. 2. Aperçu des manuscrits (438pp.+32 planches). Stockholm 2014.

www.ingramcontent.com/pod-product-compliance
Lightning Source LLC
Chambersburg PA
CBHW051418090426
42737CB00014B/2732